The Wagner Operas

Volume II

VOLUME I INCLUDES:

VOLUME II INCLUDES:

The Wagner Operas

Volume II

BY

ERNEST NEWMAN

HARPER COLOPHON BOOKS

HARPER & ROW, PUBLISHERS

NEW YORK, CAMBRIDGE, PHILADELPHIA, SAN FRANCISCO

LONDON, MEXICO CITY, SAO PAULO, SYDNEY

This work was originally published in one hardcover volume: in Great Britain under the title *Wagner Nights*; and in the United States by Alfred A. Knopf, Inc. It is here reprinted by arrangement with Alfred A. Knopf, Inc.

THE WAGNER OPERAS, Volume II. Copyright © 1949 by Alfred A. Knopf, Inc. All rights reserved. Printed in the United States of America. No part of this book may be used or reproduced in any manner whatsoever without written permission except in the case of brief quotations embodied in critical articles and reviews. For information address Alfred A. Knopf, Inc., 201 East 50th Street, New York, N.Y. 10022. Published simultaneously in Canada by Fitzhenry & Whiteside Limited, Toronto.

First HARPER COLOPHON edition published 1983.

Library of Congress Cataloging in Publication Data

Newman, Ernest, 1868-1959.
  The Wagner operas.

  Reprint. Originally published: New York : A. A. Knopf, 1981.
  Includes index.
  1. Wagner, Richard, 1813-1883. Operas. 2. Operas—Analysis, appreciation. I. Title.
MT100.W2N53 1983   782.1'092'4   83-47569
ISBN 0-06-091073-9 (v. 1)   83 84 85 86 87 10 9 8 7 6 5 4 3 2 1
ISBN 0-06-091074-7 (v. 2)   83 84 85 86 87 10 9 8 7 6 5 4 3 2 1

Contents

The Wagner Operas

Volume II

The Nibelung's Ring

1

ᴛ is only within the last few years that it has become possible to trace the evolution of the stupendous *Ring* drama in complete detail, thanks to the publication of several important documents for the first time. Wagner's scenarios, prose sketches, drafts of the poems and fair copies of them range over a number of years and occupy in all more than 750 pages of closely-written manuscript.

His studies in the 1840's of the Teutonic and Norse mythologies and sagas having supplied him with an immense amount of possible material, his first task was to reduce it to a manageable bulk and give it some sort of dramatic, as distinguished from epic, coherence. This he did in a detailed Prose Sketch which he entitled *The Nibelungen Myth as Scheme for a Drama;* it bears the end-date of the 4th October 1848. The ground plan of this is virtually that of the complete *Ring* as we now know it, from the *Rhinegold* to the *Twilight of the Gods,* though several of the details were modified or completely changed later. A knowledge of all his Sketches, by the way, is essential to our understanding of the tetralogy, as they often reveal something that was at the back of his mind when shaping the drama but could not be transferred to the stage.

The opening sentences of the Sketch of 1848 run thus: "Out of the womb of Night and Death there came into being a race dwelling in Nibelheim (Nebelheim),[1] i.e., in gloomy subterranean clefts and caverns. They are known as the Nibelungs: feverishly, unrestingly they burrow through the bowels of the earth like worms in a dead body: they anneal and smelt and smith hard

[1] "Nebelheim" means literally Home or Place of Mist, Fog, Obscurity, and the like.

metals." One of these Nibelungs, Alberich, the Sketch continues, having possessed himself of the "pure and noble Rhine-gold", and being of an intelligence superior to that of his fellows, fashioned from the Gold a Ring which gave him mastery over them all. They became his slaves, compelled to labour unremittingly to amass for him the immense Nibelung Hoard. His brother Reigin (Mime, Eugel) he forces to make for him a Tarnhelm that enables him to assume any shape or be invisible at will. And so, by means of wealth and might and magic, Alberich sets himself to establish his dominion over the world and all it contains. It will be observed that at this stage there is no mention of the later important motive of Alberich having won the Gold and the power to make the Ring by forswearing love.

In the present *Rhinegold,* as the reader will know, the final cosmic catastrophe has its distant roots in Wotan's desire for world mastery. To secure his power against possible insurgents he needs an impregnable fortress: this he persuades two Giants, Fasolt and Fafner, to build for him, promising them in payment Freia, the goddess of youth — a promise which, as he admits later, he hoped he would not be called upon to make good. When the Giants demand their wage he turns to Loge, the crafty god of fire, for help out of his difficulty. Loge tells him of the Hoard amassed by Alberich, and the Giants agree to accept this in lieu of Freia. Wotan, by superior guile, obtains the Hoard, the Ring and the Tarnhelm from Alberich, who lays the curse of death upon everyone into whose possession the Ring shall come. The two Giants, moved by greed of possessions, accept, in place of Freia, the Hoard and all that goes with it. At once the curse operates: Fafner slays his brother, and then changes himself into a huge Dragon so that he may sleep upon and guard the Hoard.

All this had been conceived in quite another fashion in Wagner's First Sketch. There it is *the whole race* of the Giants, rivals of the Nibelungs, who, troubled at the sight of Alberich's growing power and foreseeing their subjugation by him, yet lacking the intelligence to cope with the menace themselves, turn for help to the Gods, a race already "waxing to supremacy", anxious to govern the world in orderly fashion, but feeling themselves impotent against the dreaded crafty Nibelung. The Gods, *en masse,* contract with the Giants — not simply with two of them but with the whole race — for the building of a fortress from which they can govern the world in security; and when it is finished the Giants demand the Hoard as payment. Thus in the original Sketch both the Gods and the Giants already know of the Hoard, whereas in the present *Rhinegold* neither have the Gods any knowledge of it and of the events that led up to Alberich's acquisition of it until Loge tells them the story,[1] nor do the Giants know anything of it until they too hear the tale and realise the danger they will be in if the Hoard remains in the hands of their terrible Nibelung foe.

2

In the First Sketch of 1848, Wotan, having trapped Alberich by craft and gained possession of the Hoard and the Ring,[2] is willing enough to let the dull-witted Giants have it if only he can keep the Ring, in which, as he knows, is incarnated the power of which Alberich has been stripped: this power Wotan intends shall henceforth be his. But the Giants insist on having the Ring as well as the Hoard, for they too know its immense virtue; and counselled by the three Norns (Fates), who "warn him of the downfall of the Gods themselves", Wotan yields it to them. Alberich, before giving up the Ring, had laid the curse of ruin upon every future possessor of it. But the Giants are too sluggish and stupid to make any use of the power inherent in it: it is sufficient for them that there is an end now to the danger of their falling into servitude to Alberich. They place the whole treasure in a cave in the Gnitaheide (Neidheide),[3] where they leave it in the guard of a monstrous Dragon. (There is no hint, as yet, that this Dragon is one of themselves transformed). Their end — security for themselves — being thus achieved, the Giants relapse into tor-

[1] It is true that in the opera, after Loge's account of the rape of the Gold, Wotan says, "I have heard rumours of the Rhine-gold: runes of riches are hidden in its golden glow: a Ring would confer power and treasure." But the ascription to him of even this much knowledge is superfluous, and, indeed, meaningless: the little speech could be omitted without making any difference to the action. It seems to have occurred to Wagner only at the last moment, when he was writing the poem; there is no suggestion of it in either of his two Sketches for the *Rhinegold*.

[2] Loge does not figure in the Sketch.

[3] The Heath (or Wood) of Envy (or Grudge).

pid impotence, while the race of the Gods rises to a new lustre. They use their now unchallenged power to bestow order on the world; they "bind the elements by wise laws and devote themselves to the careful nurture of the human race."

Yet their power, with all the moral benefit to the world that may flow from that power, is morally flawed at the very core. The peace they had given the world had been achieved not by persuasion and reconciliation but by force and guile. "The purpose of their higher world-order," says the Sketch, "is moral consciousness; but the wrong against which they fight attaches to themselves. From the depths of Nibelheim [where the Nibelungs still groan in bondage, labouring not for themselves but for others] the sense of their own guilt surges up in complaint against them. For the bondage of the Nibelungs is not annulled: merely the lordship has been wrenched from Alberich, and that not for any higher end — the soul, the freedom of the Nibelungs lies buried uselessly under the belly of a sluggish Dragon. Consequently there is justice in Alberich's grievance against the Gods." Yet the latter cannot seize the Hoard and the Ring a second time, in order to render them harmless to the world, without committing yet another wrong. The beneficent deed of liberation can be wrought only by a free Will independent of them. They see in Man a faculty for such a Will; so they strive to implant their own divinity in him and raise him to such a moral height that by his free Will he may win strength enough, independently of the Gods, to cancel out their own prime guilt, even if this means, in the end, their own annulment, in that they will no longer work directly upon the world, being supplanted by the free human consciousness. So they set themselves to bring into being, in the process of time, the human hero who shall redeem them from their primal guilt and fulfil the high moral purpose upon which they have been bent from the beginning.

3

In the present *Ring* it is Wotan who, in pursuit of this aim, takes on human form, contracts a human marriage, and begets Siegmund and his sister Sieglinde, who in the end find each other, recognise in each other the same father, mate in defiance of law, and produce the redeeming hero desired by the God, Siegfried.

But Wagner's original plan had run on somewhat different lines. According to the Sketch of 1848, "vigorous human races, fruited by the divine seed, already flourish. In strife and battle they steel their strength; Wotan's Wish-Maidens carry those of them who are slain in fight to Walhall, where the heroes re-live a glorious life of jousts in Wotan's company." It is long, however, before the favoured race of Volsungs produces the hero longed for by the Gods. At last "a barren Volsung union is fertilised by Wotan by means of Holda's apples which he gives the spouses to eat; and from this marriage spring the twins Siegmund and Sieglinde (brother and sister). Siegmund takes a wife, Sieglinde weds a man (Hunding). But both unions prove sterile, and to beget a genuine Volsung the brother and sister wed each other. Hunding, Sieglinde's husband, learns of this misdeed, casts off his wife, and assails Siegmund. The Valkyrie Brynhilde shields Siegmund, defying the command of Wotan, who has decreed that he shall fall in expiation of his offence", etc. In this first draft, then, Wotan is not, as in the opera, himself the parent of the two fated Volsungs.

From this point onward the Sketch proceeds, in the main, along the lines of the present *Valkyrie, Siegfried* and *Twilight of the Gods.* The final solution of the central moral problem, however, was not the same in 1848 as the one we now know. In the closing scene of the present tetralogy Brynhilde, before hurling the burning brand into Siegfried's funeral pyre, bids the ravens command Loge to "hasten to Walhall, *for the Gods' end dawneth at last."* But in the First Sketch what Brynhilde says is this: "Hear then, ye mighty Gods; your wrong-doing is annulled; thank him, the hero who took your guilt upon him. Into my hands he entrusted the completion of his work: loosed be the thraldom of the Nibelungs, the Ring shall bind them no more. But not Alberich shall receive it; no longer shall he enslave you [i.e., the Nibelungs], but he himself shall be free as you. For to you, wise sisters of the water-deeps, I deliver this Ring. The fire that consumes me, let it cleanse the evil trinket; do ye melt and keep harmless the Rhine-gold that once was ravished from you, for the forging of servitude and ill-hap. One only shall rule, All-Father, Glorious One, Thou [Wotan]. This man [Siegfried] I bring to you as pledge of thy eternal might: good welcome give him, as is his desert!"

As will be seen, Wagner had rounded off his first plan for the drama in logical accordance with its opening premises. Both Alberich and the Nibelungs whom he had enslaved are to be set free, for the Ring by which so much evil was wrought has been restored to the primal innocence of the pure waters. The Gods too are free henceforth to rule the world and lead it upward in growth of moral consciousness — which had been their desire and their purpose from the beginning. Wagner's thought was to go through many metamorphoses before the ending of his drama took the form familiar to us today.

4

One or two other differences between the earliest and the final scheme may be noted here. In the former, Siegfried's first act after he has forged the sword is to avenge on Hunding the death of his father. The Rhinedaughters who accost him during the Gibichung hunt are in the First Sketch mermaids with swans' wings. Nothing is said in the Sketch about Alberich having forsworn love in order to possess himself of the Gold. In the final episode the light from the burning pyre shows Brynhilde, once more the armed Valkyrie on her horse, leading Siegfried by the hand to Wotan, to join the other heroes who guard the Gods; whereas in the *Twilight of the Gods* we see no more of Siegfried and Brynhilde after the blazing up of the fire, which gradually engulfs not only the hall of the Gibichungs but Walhall itself and the Gods and heroes in it.

This, then, was the vast dramatic scheme as it first formed itself in the imagination of the thirty-five-years-old Wagner. Obviously in its huge entirety it could not be condensed into an opera for a single evening, which was all he contemplated at that time. But considerably more than half of the Sketch is taken up by the events that followed the introduction of the race of the Gibichungs into the story; and it is evident from the close detail in which Wagner has worked out this section that even while he was outlining the cosmic story as a whole the final part of it was taking definite shape in his mind as a self-sufficing dramatic action. The ground covered by this section is, indeed, that of the present *Twilight of the Gods* from the moment when the curtain rises on the scene between Gunther, Hagen and Gutrune to the end of the opera. For some reason or other Wagner made a fair copy of his First Sketch between the 4th and the 8th October 1848, and then addressed himself to drafting in prose a scenario, which he completed on the 20th, of the opera he now had it definitely in his mind to write. It was to be in three acts and to bear the title of *Siegfried's Death*. This scenario, which runs to seventeen large pages of print, was published for the first time in 1930.

5

As the spectator of the projected opera would necessarily have to be made acquainted with a great deal that had happened before the action opened in the hall of the Gibichungs, this would have to be conveyed to him at one point or another by means of narrative. Thus in the opening scene of the new Sketch Alberich's son Hagen, very much as in the *Twilight of the Gods*, tells Gunther and Gutrune the story of the Hoard and the power inherent in it, of the slaying of the Dragon by Siegfried, and of the Valkyrie Brynhilde on the fire-girt rock. In the later episode of Hagen's Watch by the Rhine, Alberich tells his son of the Nibelungs and their work in the bowels of the earth, of his own achievement of power by the seizure of the Gold and the forging of the Ring, of his compelling his brother Mime to fashion the Tarnhelm for him, of his amassing of the Hoard, of the fear that then took possession of the Giants, of their compact with the Gods, of his own overthrow by craft, of the God's bestowal of the Ring and the Hoard on the Giants at the bidding and the warning of the Norns, of the guarding of Hoard and Ring by a Dragon, and of Siegfried's slaying of the Dragon and of Mime. Much of this, though not all, has been carried over into the corresponding scenes of the *Twilight of the Gods*. In addition, Siegfried, during the hunting scene, tells the story in the Sketch, as he does more or less in the opera, of his upbringing by Mime, of his own forging of the fragments of his father's shattered sword, of his combat with the Dragon and his slaying of Mime, of his taking the Ring and the Tarnhelm from the cave, leaving the rest of the Hoard there, of his journey to Brynhilde's rock and his conquest of the fire, and of his winning of the Valkyrie maid.

This necessity for elucidating certain parts of the stage drama by means of narrative beset Wagner all through the many phases of the construction of the *Ring*. For the most part the dovetailing of action and narrative is skilfully done: Hagen's tale to Gunther and Gutrune, for instance, not merely instructs the spectator but serves to launch the plan for wedding Gutrune to Siegfried and Gunther to Brynhilde, and so brings the hero within the orbit of Hagen, where his ruin is to be slowly accomplished; and in the same way Siegfried's telling of the tale of his own life to the Gibichungs during the hunt, reaching its climax as it does in the revelation that it was he, not Gunther, who had wakened and wedded Brynhilde, who is now Gunther's bride, not merely enlightens the spectator of *Siegfried's Death* as to all this but furnishes the immediate pretext for Hagen's swift slaying of him. At the same time this procedure on Wagner's part, involving as it did much harking back to earlier aspects of his plan, landed him now and then in trifling difficulties of which he does not seem to have been sufficiently aware at the time. Thus in the Prose Sketch of 1848 for *Siegfried's Death* he had made Hagen tell Gunther and Gutrune, in the opening scene, that Siegfried's seizure of the Hoard has made the Nibelungs subject to him. This was carried over in due course not only into the poem of *Siegfried's Death* but into the much later *Twilight of the Gods,* as thus:

Gunther: This Hoard have I often heard of:
        it holds a treasure most rare?
Hagen: The man who its might can wield,
        the lord of the world will he be.
Gunther: And Siegfried won it in fight?
Hagen: Slaves are the Nibelungs to him;

which naturally moves us to comment that while, in general terms, possession of the Hoard and the Ring may be said to give Siegfried power over the world — as the Wood Bird had told him would be the case after he had slain Fafner — there has never been the smallest hint in the drama of the Nibelungs having become his slaves, or, indeed, of his having any interest in them. As our investigation proceeds we shall come upon other instances in which Wagner has unwittingly carried over into his final plan some earlier motive that now either shows itself as a loose end or is at variance with its context.

6

The Prose Sketch for *Siegfried's Death* still embodies certain features of the original "Sketch for a Nibelungen Drama" that were to disappear from the plan later. Siegfried's sword is still called Balmung instead of Nothung; and other names retain their original spelling. It is once more intended that Siegfried's first deed after making the sword shall be to kill Hunding. Siegfried's colloquy in the forest is with the Wood Birds in the plural, not with a single bird as in the present *Siegfried*. In the scene — corresponding superficially to that in the first act of the *Twilight of the Gods* in which Waltraute comes to Brynhilde's rock to beg her to give up the Ring — it is Brynhilde's eight former fellow-Valkyries who appear. They have come to ask her the meaning of the dying down of the fire that had so long encircled her rock; and Brynhilde seizes the opportunity to tell them — and through them the audience — the story of her punishment for having shielded Siegmund against Wotan's will and of Siegfried's conquest of the flames and his awakening of her. All this narration had become unnecessary by the time Wagner had arrived at the present *Twilight of the Gods*, for it had been fully set forth before the spectator in the *Valkyrie* and *Siegfried*. And in the *Twilight of the Gods*, of course, the meeting with Waltraute has quite another significance than the scene with the eight Valkyries in the Sketch had had. In the latter they are concerned simply with the fate of their erring sister: in the *Twilight of the Gods* Waltraute has come to implore Brynhilde to give back the Ring to the Rhine Daughters and so avert the doom with which the Gods are threatened. In 1848 the present ending of the tetralogy had not occurred to Wagner: *Siegfried's Death* was to end, like the Sketch, with the complete establishment of the Gods' power for good through the redeeming deed of Siegfried.

7

It was on the basis of the scenario of the 20th October 1848 that Wagner went on to write the poem of *Siegfried's Death*. That poem has long been accessible in the Collected Edition of his prose and poetical works, where for some time it confronted researchers with a small puzzle. In his autobiography (published in 1911) Wagner told the world that when he read the poem in 1848 to the actor Eduard Devrient, who was at that time the producer at the Dresden Theatre, the latter pointed out to him a little defect in it from the point of view of practical theatrics. Some knowledge on the spectators' part of the earlier relations of Siegfried and Brynhilde would surely be necessary, he said, if they were to grasp the full tragic significance of the conflict that arises between the pair in the middle of the opera. Wagner recognised the justice of this observation. "I had in fact", he says in *My Life*, "begun the poem of *Siegfried's Death* simply with the scenes that now constitute the first act of the *Twilight of the Gods*, merely explaining to the spectator, in a lyric-epical dialogue between the hero's wife in her solitude and the other Valkyries flying past her rock, all that elucidated the early relationship of Siegfried and Brynhilde. To my joy, Devrient's hint on this point at once turned my thought in the direction of the scenes which I worked out later in the prelude to the drama." [1]

Until lately it was difficult to make sense of this, for every reader of the poem of *Siegfried's Death* knew that it commenced *not* with the scene in the hall of the Gibichungs but with the Norns Scene, which is followed by that between Brynhilde and Siegfried. The mystery was only cleared up when, in 1930, the Prose Sketch for *Siegfried's Death* was published for the first time. It then became evident that Wagner s memory was at fault when he described, in *My Life*, that talk of his with Devrient in October 1848. It was not the *poem* which he had read to Devrient on that occasion; it was the Prose Sketch, which does begin with the scene between Gunther, Hagen and Gutrune. Perceiving that Devrient was right, he at once drew up a supplementary prose plan for a "prelude", as he entitled it — i.e. a Norns Scene and a Siegfried-Brynhilde scene which between them correspond broadly to the present "prelude" to the *Twilight of the Gods*.

[1] The reader should always bear in mind that for Wagner the "first act" of the *Twilight of the Gods* begins with the scene in the hall of the Gibichungs; he invariably referred to the long prologue to this — the Norns scene and the scene between Siegfried and Brynhilde — as the "prelude". Unless he is forewarned the reader will be apt to take this latter term in its usual operatic sense of an orchestral prelude or overture. There is nothing of that kind in the *Twilight of the Gods*.

8

This supplementary Sketch was also published for the first time in 1930. It is based, of course, on the first Sketch for the whole drama as originally projected: the Norns prophesy that when the Gold is returned to the Rhine the Nibelungs, Alberich among them, shall be "free"; it is "the Giants" in general who have built Walhall for Wotan and receive the Ring in payment; these Giants then beget a Dragon to guard the Ring. The scene that follows between Siegfried and Brynhilde runs on the same general lines as the corresponding later one in the *Twilight of the Gods:* the Valkyrie sends the hero out into the world to win glory, and as the curtain falls his horn is heard sounding merrily as he recedes into the distance. The horn melody, the draft concludes, is to be "taken up by the orchestra and developed in a spirited movement", precisely as it is in the now familiar "Siegfried's Rhine Journey".

The next stage in the evolution of the drama was the casting of the scenario and the supplementary Sketch for the "prelude" into verse. This task occupied Wagner from the 12th to the 28th November 1848. He gave his poem the title of *"Siegfried's Death, a grand heroic opera in three acts".* In December he made a fair copy of his manuscript, leaving the text virtually as it was, but making some modifications in the stage directions.

In the following January he worked over the poem once again.[1]

[1] One reason why until recently there were so many gaps in our knowledge of all the stages traversed by the *Ring* is the fact that the various manuscripts are scattered about in private and public possession. That of the first "Sketch for a Drama" is now at Wahnfried. The first manuscript of the poem of *Siegfried's Death* is the property of Siegmund von Hausegger, of Munich; the copy made by Wagner in December 1848 is in the Winterthur (Switzerland) Town Library. This manuscript was drastically revised by Wagner at some later date, and a fair copy of the revision was then made by Nietzsche: it was from Nietzsche's copy (now in Bayreuth) that the poem of *Siegfried's Death* was printed by Wagner in 1871 in the second volume of his Collected Works. All the later editions, of course, follow that imprint; consequently the poem of *Siegfried's Death* which is so well known to all Wagner students represents not the first but a revised version.

Wagner's *third* fair copy of the poem — a model of calligraphy — is in the possession of Herr Eduard Sulzer of Zürich. A *fourth* copy, made in 1850, is at Wahnfried.

He made no changes in the third act, but the first now received the form familiar to us in the *Twilight of the Gods*. In the second act several changes were made: these will be pointed out in our later analysis of the opera. The result of all this recasting was that a third fair copy became necessary. This, which of course represents the *second* actual version of the drama, was made in January or February 1849; and now the "grand heroic" in the title becomes simply "heroic". It is evident that Wagner was now coming up against a difficulty that was to plague him for a long time yet — that of the ending of the work and the summing-up of the moral purport of it in Brynhilde's final words; for on the last page of the beautifully written third copy he made later some significant changes in the text of this episode. The stages by which the close of the vast drama gradually received its present form will be set forth in detail later in our enquiry.

9

In May 1849 Wagner, having become involved in the revolutionary movement in Dresden, had to fly to Switzerland. In the following May he planned to publish the poem of *Siegfried's Death,* and for this purpose he made a fourth fair copy and added a Foreword. At that time he shared the passion of some "reformers" of the period for using the Latin instead of the German script, and for spelling substantives (other than proper names) with a small initial letter instead of the capital customary in Germany. The Leipzig publisher to whom he offered the libretto assured him that if he insisted on these whimsies he would not sell a single copy. The plan for publication therefore came to nothing.

In the late November and early December of 1852 he worked over his latest manuscript afresh, giving it its final form, in which it corresponds in general to the present *Twilight of the Gods.*

Meanwhile, between 1849 and the summer of 1851, he had written a number of prose works, the chief of them being *Art and Revolution, The Art-Work of the Future, Opera and Drama,* and *A Communication to My Friends.* The basic purpose of these was to clarify his own mind with regard to the tremendous new artistic impulses, affecting the whole problem of modern opera, of which he was now inwardly conscious. His artistic intuitions were driving him irresistibly towards a new type of music drama, but he was not yet quite sure how this could be realised in practice. When he had read his Nibelung poem in 1848 to his friends in Dresden some even of the best-disposed among them shook their heads doubtfully over it. While he himself knew well, as he hinted in a letter of November 1850 to Liszt, that *Siegfried's Death* would have to be *musically* something entirely different from *Lo-hengrin,* his friends could as a matter of course conceive the musical structure of the new work only in terms of "opera" past and present; and within the traditional framework of that genre *Siegfried's Death* obviously would not fit. It had no set "forms", no sharply differentiated self-contained numbers — solos, duets, choruses and so forth. The lines were curt, rhymeless, often irregular in length, seemingly unrhythmical and formless because of the total absence of the *carrure* of the ordinary poetic line and stanza. A single illustration will make this clear. The poem of *Lohengrin* had been cast in square-cut rhyming line-lengths of which the opening of "Lohengrin's Narration" may serve as an example:

> *In fernem Land, unnahbar euren Schritten,*
> *liegt eine Burg, die Monsalvat genannt;*
> *ein lichter Tempel stehet dort in Mitten,*
> *so kostbar, wie auf Erden nichts bekannt:*
> *drinn ein Gefäss von wunderthät'gem Segen*
> *wird dort als höchstes Heiligthum bewacht;*
> *es ward, dass sein der Menschen reinste pflegen,*
> *herab von einer Engelschaar gebracht:*

etc. This was poetry in the accepted sense of the term, in lines of regular feet and rhymes. *Siegfried's Death,* however, discarded, in general, the ordinary end-rhymes in favour of the *Stabreim* — answering assonances of the first consonants or vowels of words or syllables, as in the following example, where the assonances are picked out for our present purpose in roman:

> *Was du mir* nahmst,   *nütztest du* nicht, —
> *deinem muthigen* Trotz   *vertrautest du nur!*
> *Nun du, gefriedet,   frei es mir gabst,*
> *kehrt mir mein* Wissen *wieder,*
> *erkenn' ich des Ringes Runen;*

etc. Stabreim was a very ancient device in German and English poetry. It is found in the former as early as the ninth century, and in the latter there is a fine old poem, known as *The Harmonious Blacksmiths,* dating from the fourteenth century, that has quite a Wagnerian ring in its hammering assonances:

> *Swarte smekyd smethes smateryd wyth smoke*
> *Dryve me to deth wyth den of here [their] dyntes,*
>
> . . . .
>
> *Thei spyttyn and spraulyn and spellyn many spelles,*

and so on. Wagner's instinct in 1848 was perfectly sound. His young Siegfried, the symbol of a new and ardent life, could not possibly express himself in regularly shaped verse such as that of *Lohengrin;* a mode of speech would have to be found for him as forthright, as muscular, as himself.

Moreover, Wagner's Dresden friends were puzzled by the curt give-and-take of passages of this type:

Gutrune: Hielt Brünnhild dich für Gunther?
Siegfried: Ihm glich ich auf ein Haar;
         Der Tarnhelm wirkte das,
         wie Hagen mich es wies.
Hagen: Dir gab ich guten Rath.
Gutrune: So zwangst du das kühne Weib?
Siegfried: Sie wich — Gunther's Kraft;

etc. They could imagine no other way of setting such lines as these to music except that of "recitative"; and they had dismal forebodings of what would happen to an opera which, as they saw it, would be largely dry recitative. Wagner, of course, had somewhere at the back of his mind a kind of music entirely different from that of *Tannhäuser* or *Lohengrin,* where, in spite of the unbroken continuity of the texture, the framework of the older forms of solo, duet, ensemble and so forth had still been visible. He must already have seen, though subconsciously rather than consciously, that the solution of his new problem — which was how to let the drama run its unbroken course from the rise of the curtain on each act to the lowering of it, without holding up the action every now and then in order to let a purely musical "form" impose itself on it — lay in a new logic of musical spinning, which would allow music and drama to work hand in hand throughout, instead of first one, then the other breaking the unity by insisting on its own egoistic rights, the result being a continual oscillation between lyrical expansion and explanatory recitative. This complete fusion of drama and music implied two pre-requisites. In the first place the drama itself would have to be conceived *in terms of music;* in the second place the music would have to be of such a kind that no matter how freely it worked itself out according to its own inner laws the drama would be assisted, not constrained, by it.

10

As regards the first of these points, we can see now what was hidden from Wagner's contemporaries — that the *musician* in him was co-operating with and guiding the *dramatist* in every phase of the poem. Here was not the customary procedure of a non-musical playwright putting together a libretto and then handing it over to a composer to be "set to music", the product of their joint labour being afterwards turned over to actors, producers, machinists, designers and all the rest of them to add *their* several little contributions, but of the operation of a complex faculty of which the world had had no experience until then, the operatic creator being at once dramatist, musician, mime, producer, conductor and everything else. It was not even that Wagner, during the creation of an opera, was dramatist *and* composer *and* stage practitioner in successive layers, as it were, the one faculty taking up the job where the other had laid it down. He did not put together the words of *Siegfried's Death* and then "set them to music", and after that "put it on the stage": the three faculties worked simultaneously in him in all the operas of his maturity. This does not mean, of course, that when writing the words he already had in his mind the actual notes that were to accompany them. But the musical *mood* was operative within him all the time, determining or accompanying each of the windings of the drama. We can see the functioning of this double faculty in him in such a seeming trifle as his jotting down in the margin of his *Young Siegfried* [1] the musical rhythms intended to accompany one of Siegfried's speeches to Mime. The words run thus:

[1] This work was the next stage in the evolution of the *Ring*, to which we shall come shortly.

Aus dem Wald fort
in die Welt ziehn!
nimmer kehr' ich zurück!
Wie ich froh bin,
dass ich frei ward,
nichts mich bindet und zwingt!
Mein Vater bist du nicht,
in der Ferne bin ich heim:
dein Herd ist nicht mein Haus,
meine Decke nicht dein Dach!
Wie der Fisch froh
in der Flut schwimmt,
wie der Fink frei
sich davon schwingt:
flieg' ich von hier,
flute davon,

etc.

(From the wood forth
in the world fare,
never more to return!
Gladness floods me
for my freedom,
nothing now binds me here.
My father art thou not,
and afar I know my home;
thy hearth is not my house,
nor thy cave my rightful roof.
As the glad fish
in the flood swims,
as the finch free
on the wind soars:
I fly from here,
fleetly I flow,
like the wind o'er the woods,

etc).

Opposite "Aus dem Wald fort" Wagner has written in the margin of his manuscript:

♪♪♩ | ♩ ♩ ♪♪♩ | ♩ ♩ ♪ ♩ | ♪♪♩ ♪♪♩ | ♩ ♩   (³₄)

opposite "Mein Vater bist du nicht" he has noted this:

♩ | ♩. ♪♪♪ | ♩ ♩ ♪♪ | ♩. ♪♪♪ | ♩ *etc.*

and opposite "Flieg' ich von hier" this:

(²₄) ♩ ♪♪ | ♩ ♩ |

Observe now how he handled the passage later in the score of *Siegfried.*

The boy's impatience at the impotence of the dwarf to forge him the sword he needs has been expressed, from the point denoted by the words

> *Auf! Eile dich, Mime!*
> *Mühe dich rasch;*
> *kannst du 'was Rechts,*
> *nun zeig' deine Kunst! etc.*
>
> (*Up! Quick to it, Mime!*
> *Shape me the sword;*
> *cravest thou praise?*
> *then prove me thy craft!*)

in an impetuous 2/4 accompaniment figure:

When the dwarf asks him "What wouldst thou today with the sword?" the ardent boy breaks into a new rhythm — that of the first of the marginal notes quoted above:

Aus dem Wald fort in die Welt ziehn; nimmer kehr' ich zu - rück!

With the new thought that springs up in him — "My father art thou not" — the rhythm of the lines instantly changes, and with it that of the music, as in the second marginal note:

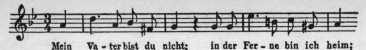

His torrent of similes finished — "Wie der Fisch froh" etc. — he speaks *in propria persona,* as it were, again. The speech-accents now fall on the verbs that hammer out the idea of flight into the world — "*Flieg'* ich von hier, *flute* davon" — and with the change in verbal rhythm comes a change in the musical rhythm. But it will be seen that at this point the present score and the marginal note do not agree. In the latter a change from 3/4 to 2/4 is prescribed; but in the score Wagner continues with the former 3/4:

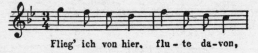

The explanation of this is that on second thoughts he saw that it would be better to make Siegfried sing, instead of the

originally intended — which would have meant holding up the torrent by the crotchet rest — the melodic line shown above to the words "Flieg' ich von hier". But though the metre remains, as before, 3/4, the rhythmical effect is different, because there is no longer an uptake word and an uptake note before the heavy beat of the bar, as there had been, for instance, at "Mein Vater bist du nicht". Here the word ("Vater") that gives its impulse to the line comes second. In "Flieg' ich von hier" the propulsive word comes first, and with the musical stress now falling on "flieg'" and "flute" Wagner gives the lines an energy which they would have lost had he clung to his first idea of phrasing them in 2/4 time with a crotchet rest at the end of each second bar. There is abundant evidence that all the while he was writing his poem he was feeling the drama in terms of music.

11

But his contemporaries necessarily saw the matter in reverse, as it were. He was producing during the years around 1850 a vast amount of argumentative prose and no operas; therefore they began to think of him as a composer with whom theory came first and practice second, whereas, in fact, it was the musician and the poet in him that were driving him towards the creation of so new an inner world that for sheer mind's comfort's sake he had to try to take his bearings in it, and this could be done only by reasoning it all out in prose. It would have been better for him, perhaps, in the long run, if he had never published any of these prose works but waited till he had a new opera to speak for itself to the public. But that was not Wagner's way; he always had an excess of mental energy that had to find other outlets than that of purely creative art. Without these outlets his path as a creator would probably have been cumbered for a while with an immense amount of unassimilable material; by means of his prose speculations he shovelled all this on one side and could then forget it and surrender himself to pure creation. He himself was well aware of this peculiarity of his being. In November 1850, when embarking on the immense treatise *Opera and Drama,* he wrote thus to Liszt: "Between the musical working-out of my *Lohengrin* and that of my *Siegfried* [1] there lies, for me, a turbulent yet, I am confident, prolific world. I had a whole life to clear away behind me, to bring into the forefront of consciousness what was in me only in a sort of twilight, to master my reflection by means of its own self — by getting to the very core of it — in order thereafter to immerse myself again, with clear and joyous consciousness, in the exquisite unconsciousness of artistic creation." After he has finished *Opera and Drama,* he goes on to say, "then, in the spring, joyful and clarified, I will take up my *Siegfried,* and not drop it until I have completed it", i.e., in music.

He was thoroughly aware that works of the type he now had in his mind would mean a break, sooner or later, with the existing German theatre. "I will write no more operas", he told a friend in 1851. "As I do not wish to invent an arbitrary title for my works, I call them dramas, a term which at least will indicate clearly the standpoint from which the thing I am offering should be accepted." Experience soon taught him that whatever else he might do he could not impose a new nomenclature on the world; and so

---

[1] i.e. *Siegfried's Death.*

he had to refer to his works, as everyone else did, as operas. With the existing operatic world and its traditional forms, however, he had finished for good after *Lohengrin*. And as he was living, in the late 1840's and the early 1850's, in a world of political and social upheaval, he easily managed to persuade himself that somehow or other his own new kind of creation was part and parcel of these changes. For the acceptance of his new and regenerating art he looked forward to a new structure of society, and so he became a revolutionist. But he could never make up his mind which of the two, chicken or egg, would have to come first, whether his own creative work would help to build up a new society or such a society would have to come into being before his work could find acceptance. And so, from posterity's point of view, he wasted a vast amount of his time and his intellectual energy on not only artistic but political and social and economic theorising. But we need to remember that his powerful mind was all of a piece; without the gymnastic afforded it by all this ardent and sometimes futile speculation it would have been less athletic; his art would not have had behind it the tremendous driving force that now excites our wonder and compels our admiration.

12

It was his guardian angel that wisely held him back from setting formally to work at the music of *Siegfried's Death* as soon as he had completed the dramatic plan for this, though he must, of course, have been always brooding upon it and doing a certain amount of musical sketching for it. In 1933 there was published for the first time a Sketch,[1] running to some 150 bars, for the music of the Norns Scene with which the opera was to open. It is dated "12 August 1850", and is very interesting in respect both of what was carried over from it into the present *Ring* and what was changed or discarded.

The first thing we observe is that already Wagner's instinct had decided on the key of E flat minor and a 6/4 motion for the opening of his drama. But in this sketch the Norns plunge *in medias res,* without the orchestral preamble that is a feature of the corresponding scene in the *Twilight of the Gods:*

[1] In the possession of M. Louis Barthou.

(The words are: "*1st Norn:* In the east I wove. *2nd N.* In the west I wound. *3rd N.* To the north I cast [the rope]. What woundest thou in the west? *2nd N.* What wov'st thou in the east?" The reader will hardly need to be reminded that for the *Twilight of the Gods* another and more detailed text was written for this scene). It will be seen that the melody foreshadows the one associated in the present *Ring* not with the Norns but with the Valkyries: [1] moreover it loses its vitality in the fourth bar and never regains it, drifting off into an undistinguished quasi-recitative. But it is already evident that even when engaged on his poem Wagner had a *musical* texture and a *musical* form at the back of his mind. If the reader will glance at the poem of *Siegfried's Death* — of which an English version will be found in volume VIII of Ashton Ellis's translation of Wagner's prose works — he will see that in the five lines quoted above — "functional" lines we may perhaps call them, for they define the nature and function of the Norns as the weavers of destiny — the Norns have begun to outline the story of Alberich's theft of the Gold and the events that followed in its train. Three times in the course of their narrative they break off to repeat their "functional" lines. At the conclusion of each section of the story (except, of course, the last), Wagner has written between the staves "3 Takte"; i.e., there are to be three bars of orchestral development at each of these points; and each time the Norns begin their ritual winding of the rope again from east to west and so on they do so to the melody quoted above (or a suggestion of it). The form of the episode is therefore a musical one, a kind of rondo.

At a later stage of this musical sketch we find, at the point where the scene merges into the colloquy between Siegfried and Brynhilde, a descending figure in the orchestra:

[1] See Example No. 74 in our later analysis of the opera.

which has no definable function here, but from which, as we can now see, was subsequently evolved the Treaty motive associated in the present *Ring* with Wotan. (See Example No. 13 below). We first meet with this motive in the *Rhinegold,* the music of which was written between November 1853 and January 1854. The "reminiscence" hunters have for long assured us that this Treaty motive was one of the themes Wagner "borrowed" from Liszt, in whose piano sonata something resembling it appears. The musical sketch we are now considering disposes of that assumption once for all. The first statement of the motive in the *Rhinegold* agrees with the musical Sketch of 1850 in (a) general outline, (b) the change from dotted to non-dotted quavers, (c) the coming to rest on a long note at the end of the descent. But Liszt's sonata was not written until 1852/3, and not published until 1854.

13

We have every reason to be thankful that Wagner did not set to work at the systematic composition of *Siegfried's Death* in 1850. The musician in him was manifestly unripe for it just then; and it may have been because his instinct warned him of this that he did not work out in full whatever musical sketches he may have made at that time. But there was another and a stronger reason for the long delay. On the 3rd May 1851 he had written to a correspondent, "I am now setting to work at the musical working-out of my *Siegfried* [i.e., *Siegfried's Death*]". But only a week later we find him writing to another friend in quite a different vein. "All through last winter I was plagued by an idea which lately has taken possession of me to such an extent that I must bring it to fruition. Did I not once write you with regard to a lively subject? It was that of the youth who sets out to 'learn what fear is' and is so stupid that he never manages to learn. Imagine how startled I was when I realised that this youth is no other than — the young Siegfried, who wins the Hoard and awakes Brynhilde! The plan is now ready. I am gathering my strength together to write next month the poem of *The Young Siegfried.* I will set to work at the music in July", after which, he continues, he will ad-

414

dress himself (in 1852) to the composition of the music of *Siegfried's Death*.

The popular story of the youth too stupid to learn what fear is had long been a favourite with him: already in the Dresden days he had told his friend Kietz that he would write no more "grand operas", but only "fairy tales, such as that of the boy who does not know what fear is." And now in 1851, by one of those tricks of the subconscious so familiar to us in the case of poets, this old folk-tale had become fused in his imagination with that of his hero Siegfried. He was very pleased with his discovery. For one thing, in the new opera (*Young Siegfried*) he could set visibly before the spectator a good many details of the pre-history of the Ring and the struggle for world power which could have been told in *Siegfried's Death* only in narrative form, through the mouth of this character or that. In the second place, a *Young Siegfried*, with its atmosphere of gladsome youth, would serve, he thought, as a welcome foil to the tragic *Siegfried's Death*.

He at once drew up, in some twenty-three lines in pencil, the ground plan of the new three-act opera, to which some supplementary paragraphs were added at some later date. We owe the chance preservation of this precious scrap of material to the fact that the large sheet of paper on which it was written was utilised by him in later years as a wrapper for the first draft of the new poem. The plan now sketched conforms in general to that of the present *Siegfried* — Act I: the scene between Siegfried and Mime, the dwarf's talk with the Wanderer, and the forging of the sword by Siegfried; Act II: the action in the forest (Alberich, Fafner and Wotan), the dialogue between Siegfried and Mime, the death of Fafner, the altercation between Mime and Alberich, the acquisition of the Ring by Siegfried, the birds' [1] warning, the slaying of Mime, and the news brought by the birds of the Valkyrie Brynhilde on the rock; Act III: Wotan and the Wala, Wotan and Siegfried, Siegfried and the awakening of Brynhilde.

14

Broadly speaking, what Wagner was now doing was to elaborate into a three-act opera a single paragraph of the first Prose

---

[1] Here and in a later more extended sketch the birds are still in the plural.

Sketch of October 1848, which had told how, after the slaying of Siegmund by Hunding, Sieglinde had given birth to a son in the forest, how the boy had been brought up and taught smithing by Mime, and so forth along the lines in general of the first act of the present *Siegfried.* There are some small differences, however, between that earlier paragraph and the draft of May 1851, and between both of these and the present opera. For example, Wagner's first idea was to have Mime go on with his labours at the forge during his conversation with the Wanderer! In the Sketch of 1848 Siegfried had forged the sword "under the direction of Mime"; in that of 1851 the boy impatiently smashes up the dwarf's sorry attempt and proceeds to make the weapon himself. In 1851 Siegfried no longer seeks out and slays Hunding as he had done in the first Sketch. In 1848 the wood birds — whose song the boy understands after tasting the Dragon's blood — had warned him to beware of Mime, who plans to do him evil in order to get the Hoard, whereupon Siegfried kills him at once. In the Sketch of 1851 this episode begins to take the more extended shape with which we are familiar today: "the taste of the blood gives also the power to pierce to the true sense of the false words. Mime's dissembling is understood throughout by Siegfried in the sense in which Mime means it. (The birds reveal this also to him)".

At the bottom of the page containing the short swift draft of May 1851 are three jottings which were evidently made later. The first of these, relating to Act I, runs thus: "The Wanderer and Mime. Explanation of the relations between Giants, Dwarfs and Gods. Suggestions of Siegfried's mission, and frustration of Mime's design." Clearly it had occurred to Wagner that here was the opportunity to acquaint the spectator with that primal conflict of Gods, Giants and Dwarfs in which the whole vast dramatic action had had its roots: he now saw his way to do this by means of a series of questions and answers between the Wanderer and Mime. The second jotting is as follows: "Wotan and the Wala. Guilt of the Gods, and their necessary downfall. Siegfried's mission. Self-annihilation of the Gods." Here, it will be perceived, the original ending of the drama had already taken an entirely new turn in Wagner's mind. In the First Sketch of 1848, it will be recalled, Brynhilde, after restoring the Ring to the Rhine and declaring Alberich and the Nibelungs to be free again, had proclaimed that "One only shall rule, All-Father, Glorious One, Thou. This man [Siegfried] I bring to you as pledge of thy eternal might: good welcome give him, as is his desert!" But now, in 1851, the final consummation of the drama is to be not the eternal establishment of the power of the Gods but their annihilation by their own willing of that end.

15

What had brought about this fundamental alteration in Wagner's ethical design? We cannot trace in detail all the mysterious spiritual changes in him that had led to this surprising result; but it has been argued, with a certain plausibility, that by the early 1850's his optimism with regard to the coming of a new and better European social order — one in which the Gods, so to speak, would at last rule the world wisely and well — had given way to a pessimism that saw no way out of the contemporary evil and misery, and that the final blow to his optimism had been dealt by Louis Napoléon's coup d'état of the 2nd December 1851. That unexpected event certainly shook him to his foundations. In 1851 he had been convinced that the trend of opinion in France was towards a new social democracy which would change the face of things for the better; and he shared the general confidence that the French elections in December would be the beginning of an upheaval that would inaugurate an epoch of social and political freedom and happiness not only for France but for Europe. When the news came of Louis Napoléon's seizure of power it was at first, he tells us in *My Life*, something so "absolutely incredible" that he could hardly believe it: "it seemed to me", he says, "that the world was really coming to an end. When the success of the coup d'état was confirmed, and it appeared that what no one had thought possible had actually happened and had all the appearance of enduring, I turned my back on this incomprehensible world as a riddle not worth the attempt to solve. As a joking reminder of our earlier hopes for the year 1852 I suggested, in my correspondence with Uhlig, that we should treat it as non-existent and go on dating our letters December 1851 [1] — in conse-

---

[1] As a matter of fact in only one of his published letters to Uhlig — that of the 22nd January 1852, which he dated "53rd December 1851" — did he

quence of which this month of December seemed to last an inordinate time." And he goes on to speak of the profound depression into which the new state of things had thrown him, its dire effect on his health, and his despair for the future of European culture.

This theory that the change from an optimistic to a pessimistic ending of the *Ring* drama came about through Wagner's political disillusionment at the hands of Louis Napoléon in December 1851 was plausible enough at one time. But the recent publication of his sketches has negated it. We have just seen that the passage in the *Young Siegfried* Prose Sketch of May 1851 running thus, "Wotan and the Wala. Guilt of the Gods, and their necessary downfall. Siegfried's mission. Self-annihilation of the Gods", is a jotting on the lower part of the sheet. Both the ink and the script of this jotting suggest that it was made later than the Sketch itself.[1] How much later, whether days or weeks or months, we do not know. But the actual date is immaterial, for in the main body of the Sketch, in the outline of the third act of *Young Siegfried*, we find this: "Wotan and the Wala: end of the Gods. Wotan's resolution: the Wala sinks into the earth"; and Wagner's letters of that date place it beyond doubt that this plan was committed to paper some time between the 3rd and the 10th May 1851. His decision to change the 1848 ending of his Nibelungen drama had therefore been made long before Louis Napoléon's coup d'état had plunged him into pessimism about the actual world in which his lot as an artist was cast.

16

In the first swift Sketch of the 3rd–10th May 1851 for a *Young Siegfried* there is a sentence which, as it stands, is rather puzzling. In the scene in the second act in which Fafner, Alberich and Mime figure we have this: "Siegfried goes into the cave. — Mime. Alberich. — Siegfried [reappears] with the Ring: all scatter." Why "all"? we cannot help asking, for only Mime and Alberich are

carry out this plan. His account of the matter in the later years when he was writing his autobiography, however, is quite accurate as regards his general state of mind in 1851/2.

[1] A facsimile of the page is given by Otto Strobel in his book *Richard Wagner, Skizzen und Entwürfe zur Ring-Dichtung* (1930).

there besides himself. A glance at the facsimile of the manuscript clears up the mystery. The draft for Act II had originally run thus: "Neidwald. Alberich *comes up out of the earth with Nibelungs: they have to follow him. Reproaches. Appeasement.* — Siegfried and Mime. — S. alone. — Morning. Fafner appears: his dying speech. Bird-song. S. goes into the cave. — Mime. *The Nibelungs seize him: anarchy: promises.* Alberich. *Derision.* Siegfried [emerges] with the Ring: all scatter", etc. It was Wagner's intention, then, in the early days of May 1851, to introduce the Nibelungs — still subject to Alberich — in this scene, and have them seize Mime at their master's bidding: the dwarf makes them promises if they will release him, and Alberich derides his brother. In a further jotting Wagner elaborated the action in this way: Alberich summons the Nibelungs, who reproach him bitterly as the originator of their slavery. He pacifies them, tells them that Mime is bent on getting the Ring, and counsels them to frustrate him, whereupon they all scurry into the earth or into fissures in the rocks and lie in wait. After Siegfried has slain Fafner and gone into the cave, Mime runs in and is seized by the Nibelungs. He promises to liberate them if the Ring falls to him, but Alberich derides him as a deceiver. "Siegfried comes out with the Ring, which he places on his finger. Mime decides to kill him and goes to one side. The Nibelungs declare themselves to be Siegfried's bondsmen: he commands them to go", etc.

A further jotting goes into yet closer detail. Alberich, we learn, is bent on acquiring the Ring again because he knows that if Mime obtains it he, Alberich, will be eternally subject to his brother Nibelung, whereas he himself will know how to deal with the simple boy Siegfried, who is ignorant of the Ring's power. "When Mime enters, the Nibelungs fall upon him: he wants to go into the cave, and makes all kinds of promises in order to get free. Alberich mocks him: the two quarrel. Siegfried comes out with the Ring: all scatter before their new lord. Mime remains concealed. — Bird-song. — Mime comes forward."

From the point of view of a contemporary spectator of *Young Siegfried* — who, we must bear in mind, would have nothing like our present knowledge of the preceding events and psychological and moral motives of the drama, — there was a good deal to be said for Wagner's projected elaboration of this scene. In the end, however, he decided not to introduce the Nibelungs, perhaps because it would have meant employing an ensemble for which he would have no use anywhere else in the opera. It is possible also that already he had a vague suspicion that just as a *Young Siegfried* had become necessary to elucidate some features of *Siegfried's Death*, so it might be necessary for him some day to explain *Young Siegfried* in turn by means of a preliminary opera. But whatever his reasons may have been, he scrapped the episodes in which the Nibelungs were to have taken part, and concentrated the action at this point into the superb scene of mutual recrimination between Alberich and Mime which we have in the present *Siegfried*. When putting his pen through so much of the Sketch of 1851 as he had decided to dispense with, however, he forgot to score out the now meaningless words "all scatter".

17

On the 12th May 1851 he wrote to Bülow, "I have greatly expanded my plan. *Siegfried's Death* is at present unproduceable, and, for the public, ununderstandable; so I am going to preface it with a *Young Siegfried*." Between the 24th May and the 1st June, accordingly, working at fever heat, he drafted a full Prose Sketch for the new opera which runs to twenty-seven pages of print. This Sketch was so detailed, and so much of it was already couched in actual dialogue, that giving it poetic form was fairly easy for him: this task occupied him only from the 3rd to the 24th June. On the 29th he wrote to Liszt apologising for being too exhausted to make him a copy of the poem, as he would have liked to do. Cannot they meet soon, he asks, when he will read the work to his friend? This, he says in a significant passage, will really be the better plan, for he could read it to Liszt in such a way that his intentions would become clearer than the mere written word can make them. He was an incomparable reader of his own dramas; more than one witness has testified that, with his extraordinary range of vocal inflection, the scope and plasticity of his poses and gestures, and the intensity of his feeling, he gave the characters and the action a life which the best of his singers was never able to achieve in the theatre, even with the assistance of the music.

We have arrived, then, at the point when, in May 1851, Wagner felt that he could say all he had to say on the Nibelungen subject in two operas, *Young Siegfried* and *Siegfried's Death.* Had he stopped there, instead of going on to add first a *Valkyrie* and then a *Rhinegold,* would the world have gained or lost? We should have been the poorer, of course, by a large amount of magnificent music. But from the purely dramatic point of view it is possible that we might have gained slightly: for *Young Siegfried* and *Siegfried's Death,* as originally planned, constitute in combination an almost perfect whole.

What had been Wagner's original purpose in 1848? Not a stage packed with so much picturesque incident as we have in the present *Ring,* but a concentrated presentation of one great central dramatic motive, that of the stupendous moral implications and consequences of a single act of well-meant wrong-doing on the part of the Gods. Unless the present-day spectator of the *Ring* has learned to see beyond the actual characters and episodes set before him on the stage he has failed to understand the work at all as it was planned and as it really is. There has been much censure of Wotan for his alleged airy breach of agreement with the Giants; he has been playfully described as the ancient equivalent of a fraudulent building contractor who gets a house built for himself and then tries to bilk the labourers of their wages. That is good enough as a joke, but if it is taken seriously it shows a lamentable failure to grasp the most elementary facts of the matter, as set forth in the First Sketch of 1848 for a Nibelungen drama. We have to rid our minds, in the first place, of all the modern connotations of the word "Gods". For the ancient Teutons, as for the Greeks, the Gods were not all-powerful beings. They were subject to time and change and fate — "necessity" — like ordinary mortals, and like the world itself they were doomed to go down some day. ("Twilight of the Gods" is the most convenient but not the most literal English rendering of this concept: what has been foredoomed to happen is a going-under of the Gods, a passing-away of them in the course of the cycle of ages, just as human and other life on the earth will some day go under or pass away).

Wagner's root-conception was of a world divided between three prime other-than-human forces, each striving for mastery over the others — a race of Giants, incapable of rising above the lowest materialism but too indolent and too stupid to aspire to world-mastery, desirous only of being left to live their own brutish lives in safety; a spirit of acquisition and of domination symbolised by Alberich, whose superior cunning brings him untold wealth, leading to the subjection of the Nibelungs as the first step towards mastery of the world; and a loftier spirit, represented by the Gods, that would fain rescue the world from the two evils that threaten it, on the one hand power incessantly bent on more power for its own base ends (Alberich and Mime), on the other hand a sloth that cares for nothing beyond the lowest satisfaction of the desire to go on living in comfort (the Giants). But these Teutonic Gods lack of themselves not merely the power but a cosmic right to power over the others; they too are subject to law and are prisoners of fate. It is the problem of how to break out of that prison, not for their own sakes but for the world's sake, that constitutes the basic moral problem of the *Ring*.

18

We have seen Wagner's first approach to that problem in 1848; it is a better approach, in some ways, than that of the tetralogy as we now have it. In the latter, Wotan, athirst for world-power, has the Giants build for him a fortress that will give him security; he promises them, in return, Freia, the goddess of youth and gladness and beauty. He has no intention of fulfilling that rash promise, but hopes that when the time comes for payment he will be able to find some means, less disastrous to the race of the Gods, of discharging his debt to the earthy-minded Giants. Loge tells him and the others of the rape of the Rhine-gold and the power it and the Ring have conferred on Alberich, whereupon the brute cupidity of Fafner and Fasolt impels them to ask for this Hoard in lieu of Freia. Wotan deprives Alberich of his Gold, his Ring, his Tarnhelm and his power, by means of guile and force. The Hoard passes into the possession of Fafner and Fasolt; in their base greed they fight for the treasure, Fasolt is slain, and Fafner, changing himself into a Dragon, intends to sleep for endless time upon it. So long as he is alive no one else is strong enough to possess himself of it. But Alberich, though checked, is still dangerous. He lives obsessed by one purpose only, to regain the Hoard and Ring and make himself master of the world. This is the desire also of his brother Mime; and if either of them succeeds there is an end to the human freedom and the growth in moral stature for which Wotan had been striving. To kill the mighty Dragon is a task too great for either of the Nibelungs unaided; but none the less the danger exists for each of them that some day, somehow, the power for world-evil after which they both lust will pass into the hands of the other. The moral grandeur of Wagner's conception of the drama resides in the fact that Wotan, God though he is, is caught in a net of his own weaving: he cannot get power for good into his own hands now without using force, that is to say, by adding another crime against morality to his original one of robbing Alberich by force and craft. This problem he ultimately solves by the creation of a hero, Siegfried, who will win the Hoard unaided and unprompted by the Gods, and, by his death, make it possible for the Gold to be given back to the pure waters from which it was stolen, and the power for evil inherent in it to be broken for ever.

That is the impressive sequence of conceptions underlying the present *Ring*. The first conception of all, however, that of 1848, was in some respects better. There the beginning of the drama had not the quasi-personal form it assumed later by the narrowing down of the opening action to Wotan on the one side and Fasolt and Fafner on the other. This *personalising* of the broad moral conflict was a necessity dictated by the transference of the world-sweep of the action of the saga to the restricted space of the stage. The original cosmic idea was more impressive but less realisable in terms of the theatre: originally it had been not merely Fasolt and Fafner who were concerned in the struggle for world domination but the whole race of Giants. They and Wotan already knew, before the drama opens, of Alberich's seizure of the Gold and the use he had made of it: it was therefore a simple necessity for the Giants to have him deprived of that power, and only by the intervention of the Gods could that be made possible for them. But all this was in essence symbolic rather than personal, which precisely constituted the grandeur of it; and symbols are not easy to realise on the stage.

19

There had been several points in *Siegfried's Death* which Wagner rightly felt would have to be elucidated for the spectator by means of a preliminary opera. Therefore a good deal of his space in *Young Siegfried* was taken up with explanation rather than action — at this point or that we in the theatre would have to learn from the mouth of one or other of the characters the episodes antecedent to the present action that had made this turn of events not merely possible but inevitable. Neither Wotan, Mime, the Nibelungs nor the Giants had appeared in *Siegfried's Death*. Alberich had figured there, his function being to explain to Hagen, and through him to the spectator, how he had robbed the Rhine of the Gold, how he had in turn been robbed of it to satisfy the Giants, Wotan having unwillingly surrendered it to them on the warning counsel of the Norns; how a Dragon now slept upon the Hoard; how Mime had schemed to acquire the Ring; how Siegfried had slain him and the Dragon and won him the Hoard and the Ring; and how he, Alberich, had begotten his son Hagen to wrest the Ring from this simple boy who does not know the virtue that resides in it. (In the corresponding scene of the *Twilight of the Gods* Alberich does not go into so much detail; it is unnecessary for him to do so, for it had all been set visibly before the spectator in the *Rhinegold*, the *Valkyrie* and *Siegfried*). But there still remained much to be elucidated, and to this task Wagner addressed himself in *Young Siegfried*. It marked the beginning, for him, of a new type of musical-dramatic construction which he was to employ most effectively later in *Tristan*, the *Mastersingers* and *Parsifal*; at a certain point in the action one or other of the characters would explain what had happened before the commencement of the opera, the narrative being made an organic part of the action, however, and raised to the emotional temperature of that, by means of Wagner's new art of the symphonic development of forward-reaching and backward-glancing "motives" in the orchestra.

The first thing he did in *Young Siegfried* was to explain in the opening scene, through Mime, how Siegfried had come into the world with the fragments of his father's sword as his legacy. Then came the skilful telling, in the colloquy between Mime and the Wanderer, of the story of the long-antecedent strife of Gods and Giants and Nibelungs for the Hoard and the Ring. Two other vital matters called for elucidation. First of all, how did Wotan come into the action which henceforth was to centre in Siegfried and Brynhilde? Wagner conveyed this information in the dialogue in the third act between the Wanderer and the Wala (Erda): there we learn that Brynhilde is the daughter of the pair, that she had disobeyed the God and been put to sleep on the fire-girt rock, and that Wotan had afterwards gone among men and bred the race of Volsungs from which had sprung a hero who should unconsciously take the guilt of the Gods on him. The troubled God asks the seeress what will be the end of it all. She tells him: the Gods must pass away, for their guilt lies heavy on them; they will be supplanted by something better than themselves. "Crazed are the Gods", says the Wala in the Sketch of 1851, "turned in their foolishness against themselves. They avenge guilt, yet are themselves all guilty. What they have profaned they still call holy: faith they break, yet faith they guard! What, you ask me, must the Gods now will? They must will what they will not: the end of the Gods, their passing away, I foresee."

20

But the moral problem at the very core of the drama needed even further exposition than this; and Wagner supplied that elucidation to perfection, in *Young Siegfried*, in the great scene of Alberich and the Wanderer outside Fafner's lair in the second act. The dialogue is a series of forensic pleadings in which the God comes off second-best, for Alberich has an effective counter to every one of his pleadings. The long colloquy may be paraphrased and summarised thus:

The Wanderer: I come to see, not to intervene. You are free, Nibelung, to act as you choose.

Alberich (with a bitter laugh):

Free, you say? Behold the shameless insolence of the master race! When you wrested my power from me did you leave me free? I am in a slave's bonds; and he who bound me now mocks me! Ye great and wise ones stole my power from me. You and yours came to me like thieves: first you stole from me my Tarnhelm, then you fettered me and dragged me to the upper earth. I offered you, for my freedom, the whole Hoard the Nibelungs had amassed for me; but nothing less would content you than my veriest own, my Ring. Was I "free" then to do as I would?

The Wanderer: You were as free as you deserved to be. You call the Ring your veriest own because you made it. But from whom, fool, did you ravish the Gold? Was *that* your own? Ask the Rhine-Daughters! Yours is the earlier and older guilt: blame that if now you are unfree.

Alberich: Shameless twister of the right! You reproach *me* with the guilt that served *your* ends so well? What *I* robbed from the Rhine, did *you* give it back to the Rhine-Daughters? No: you used it to pay the dull-witted Giants for building you the fortress from which you could rule the world in security. And now you reproach me for the deed that won you your power! How gladly would you yourself have ravished the Gold from the Rhine had you known how to smith it! But your craft did not extend that far at that time; now that you are older and wiser and you know more you chastise the guilt that serves you, but you yourself sin when it is to your advantage to do so!

The Wanderer: Pure and guiltless were we all until the Gold was smithed; but the race of the Giants murdered each other for the Hoard, till only one remains.

Alberich: But all that served your ends. So long as the Giants were slaying each other the Gods lived in bliss. But now that Fafner's end is near, who will inherit from him? That is the question that eternally gnaws at you. You have begotten and cherished a race of human heroes: will they, like the Giants, destroy each other for the Ring, or will it come back to the Nibelung again? Let it once come into my hands and I will lead the depths to storm the heights. I will make better use of it than the stupid

Giants could do. And then, thou holy shielder of heroes, tremble, for I shall be master of the world!

The Wanderer: The Gods do not covet the Ring. What they gave away they do not take back; but one who does not know its power, and wins it by his own deed, *he* will deal with it in his own fashion.

Alberich: Your sophistry does not deceive me! The heroes to whom you trust are beings of your own blood. You have raised a youth whom you are cunning enough to leave free to do the deed you dare not do yourself.

And so on.

Hardly anything of this magnificent dramatic give-and-take was carried over by Wagner later into the equivalent scene in *Siegfried;* there was no vital necessity for it there, for the spectator would already have learned most of it at first hand from the two preceding operas of the *Ring.* But now we have to piece it together bit by bit for ourselves, whereas in *Young Siegfried* it is given us in concentrated form at the precise moment when it is most essential that we shall know and understand the dilemma of the Gods, who cannot work the good they fain would work for the world because their moral authority has been cankered from the outset by that first piece of necessary wrong-doing.

One or two other points of difference between *Young Siegfried* and the present *Siegfried* may here be noted for completeness' sake.

In the former, Siegfried *twice* terrifies Mime, and at the same time demonstrates his own fearlessness, by bringing into the cave a wild animal he has captured — in the first instance a wolf, in the second a bear. It probably occurred to Wagner later that the rather extensive *Ring* menagerie might with advantage be thinned out a little; so he reduced the two episodes to one, dispensing with the wolf. In *Young Siegfried* it is no longer, as in the First Sketch of 1848, the forest birds in consort who direct Siegfried to Brynhilde's rock after the slaying of Fafner, but a single nightingale, which becomes, however, in the final *Siegfried,* a "wood bird" of no classifiable ornithological species. And in 1851, as in 1848, it is still the Giants *en masse* who had coveted and obtained the Ring, Fafner being the last survivor of the strife that had broken out among them afterwards for the possession of it.

21

In the Sketch of 1851, and in the poem of *Young Siegfried* based on this, we see Wagner coming up against one or two difficulties that cost him a good deal of trouble from time to time, and which he never overcame completely. The first of these was the handling of the "Fearing" motive.

We have seen him telling Uhlig, in May 1851, of a surprising discovery he had made — that his "Young Siegfried who wins the Hoard and awakes Brynhilde" has become identified in his imagination with the boy in the old folk tale who "sets out to 'learn what fear is' and is so stupid that he never manages to learn". What exactly does this mean? The more obvious explanation would be that about this time the old tale, of which he had always been fond, sprang up in Wagner's memory and grafted itself on the Volsung legend of Sigurd. It seems equally probable, however, that the reverse process may have taken place within him, that the fearing motive *per se* had already occurred to him in connection with the first act of his *Young Siegfried* and had afterwards linked itself up subconsciously with the tale of the youth who was anxious to learn what fear is but never could.

This was only one of the many difficult problems of new motivation and construction that confronted him when he began to elaborate *Young Siegfried* for the stage. In the poem of *Siegfried's Death* we had been told nothing more about the hero than was contained in Hagen's narration to Gunther and Gutrune in the first act: "From Wotan sprang Wälse, and from him a twin-pair, Siegmund and Sieglinde; the truest of Wälsungs they begat. His father's blood-sister gave him birth in the depths of a forest. . ." There is no mention here of his upbringing by Mime, who comes, however, into Alberich's later narration to Hagen: "Mime the false one brought up the hero in hopes to win through him the Hoard. A wise fool he! His trust in the Wälsung cost him his life!" All this, and more, had now to be set visibly before the spectator in the first act of the new drama, *Young Siegfried;* and at the outset it confronted Wagner with some difficulties.

In the opening scene he makes it clear to us that after Siegmund's death the dwarf had found Sieglinde in the forest, where she died giving birth to a son. She had told Mime her own name, but ostensibly he does not know that of the child's father; all he knows, he insists, is that with her last breath the woman had told him that the father had died in combat, and had asked that the boy should be called Siegfried, "for with that name he would grow great and strong". She had with her the pieces of a broken sword, relics of her husband's last fight; and these Mime had preserved. (Wagner fell into some confusion later with regard to these fragments. In *Young Siegfried* Mime tells the boy they had been given to him by the dying Sieglinde; but in the later dialogue with the Wanderer, after the latter has put to Mime the question he cannot answer — "Who will forge the sword anew?" — the dwarf cries out distractedly, "Accursed steel! would I ne'er had stolen it!" When Wagner came to write the present *Siegfried* he failed to remove this contradiction; he still made Mime tell Siegfried that the fragments had been given him by Sieglinde, yet still retained, in the scene with the Wanderer, the lines about his "stealing" them).

As the child grew up, his strength and courage had bred in Mime the hope that he might be trained to accomplish the deed for which the dwarf himself was too feeble. So he had brought the boy up in ignorance of everything but his foster-father and his cave and the nearby forest, and had tried to make him love him as his benefactor, to regard him as his father and mother in one. In this he had failed, the healthy natural instinct of the child making him loathe the evil dwarf and feel more companionship with the beasts of the forest. The dominant impulse of the boy had been to break away from the repulsive Mime and go out to learn something of the world, for which purpose he had kept on demanding that a sword should be made for him out of the fragments of his father's. Hence Mime's perpetual problem; he can neither forge the sword himself, cunning smith as he is, nor think of anyone who can, for the high-spirited boy has disdained to learn the hated old Nibelung's craft. Moreover, if by any chance the sword should be made, the first thing the boy would do would be to depart with it, which would put an end to the dwarf's dream of acquiring the treasure, the Tarnhelm and the Ring, and the world power inherent in them. At all costs, then, the boy must be kept in the cave until events somehow shape themselves in a way propitious to Mime's purpose.

22

For the solution of this problem Wagner fastened on the psychological motive of fearing. When *Young Siegfried* opens, Siegfried has once more been pestering the dwarf to provide him with the sword he desires. "If I did", asks Mime, "what would you do then?" "I have told you again and again", replies Siegfried; "I would go out into the world to learn fearing, since I will never learn it here with you." Now Mime had tried to instil fear of the unknown outer world into the boy in order to keep him to himself for his own ends. When Siegfried goes off into the wood in a temper he leaves Mime in sore perplexity, says the Sketch of 1851, "lest he will lose him before the boy has brought him the reward for all he has suffered on his account. . . Now he wants to depart; it is high time, therefore, to lead him to Fafner; the boy's foolish curiosity to learn fearing he must make use of to egg him on to Fafner."

Wagner's doubts as to how to handle the situation are shown by a supplementary note he has made in the Sketch at this point. "Merely this motive — Siegfried feels himself now quite free of Mime; he will leave him and go into the world; so now he asks him once more for the sword. Mime, in order to retain him in the forest, tries to instil fear of the world in him. He paints a picture of one terror after another beyond the forest, and asks, 'Don't you feel fear?' Argument about fearing. Mime is called upon to explain it. He describes fear. Siegfried cannot learn it, and will go away at once to do so. (Mime suddenly resolves to teach him it himself. Fafner? Later)". That is to say, Wagner must first have had the idea of bringing the action to its decisive point then and there; he would have Mime describe fear in detail to the boy. Later it occurred to him to make the dwarf give the boy the lesson himself, by means of Fafner; and then, still later, came the idea of postponing that lesson for a while — which is the meaning of the suggestion in brackets, "Later".

In the end he decided to make it "later". Having got thus far in the Sketch he now introduces the Wanderer, who plays his famous game of questions-and-answers with the dwarf. The God's final question, "Who will forge the fragments of the sword?", Mime, to his dismay and terror, cannot answer. The Wanderer does so for him: "Know then, doomed dwarf, that only Siegfried himself can forge the sword. As far as I am concerned you can keep your forfeited head; I have no use for it. But from now onwards have a care; indulge in no foolish chatter, for it may go badly with you if you do". And with a laugh he leaves him.

Siegfried now enters with the bear he has fearlessly subdued, which terrifies the dwarf. When he recovers from his fright, however, he thinks he sees the solution of his problem, for at last he knows the answer to the question that had always baffled him — who will forge the sword anew? "Mime pulls himself together", says Wagner in a marginal jotting: "he will make it appear that he has been doing something better than trying to make a sword himself [as the boy had ordered him to do before leaving him], — he has been pondering how to teach Siegfried fearing. He unfolds to him the plan with regard to Fafner. Siegfried accepts it." And Wagner makes the dramatic and psychological point still clearer for us by a gleeful aside which he puts into the Nibelung's mouth: "Oh clever Wanderer, see how dull-witted this bright sprig of humanity is; he himself puts into my hand the craft by means of which I will make him serve me!" He turns to Siegfried and offers to take him on the morrow to the dragon's lair, where his desire to learn what fear is shall be gratified. Siegfried, afire at the delightful prospect, once more demands the sword. "It is not yet ready", says Mime; "but I can tell you that you will learn fearing only with the sword you yourself have forged." Thereupon the boy brushes him aside and makes the sword himself, greatly to the delight of Mime, who, brewing a stupefying potion in a corner, gloats over the stupidity of Gods and heroes, who are all playing into his hands, and foresees his own winning of the Ring and with it world might. This brings the first act to a close.

23

This lay-out of the action was changed radically later. In the present *Siegfried* Mime's lurid description of fear is postponed to a later stage. In the poem of 1851 Mime had tried to teach Siegfried fearing *before* his colloquy with the Wanderer, his object being to prevent the impetuous boy leaving him. He argues, soundly enough, that without fear, and the caution it induces, existence is impossible in the great outer world. "Without it you will be lost; you will meet with your father's fate. He whose senses are not sharpened by fear goes about blindfolded. Danger lurks for you in all you do not see and do not hear. Just as steel has no cutting edge until it has been through the fire, so the man who has not been sharpened by fear is blind and deaf in the world; the waters will engulf him. So heed the old man's counsel, foolish boy; remain in the forest." Siegfried storms out in a passion, warning Mime of what is in store for him if the sword is not ready on his return. Mime broods sadly on the bitterness of his lot, and the Wanderer enters.

But in the present poem of *Siegfried* all this is altered. The Wanderer now does not tell Mime outright that it is Siegfried who alone can forge the sword; his parting words are these: "Hear this now, discomfited dwarf, Fafner's bold vanquisher! *Only he who has never known what fear is* [1] shall forge Nothung anew. Have a care for thy wise head from now on; I leave it to fall to him who has never learned fearing." This new turn of the phrasing led as a matter of course to further changes. In *Young Siegfried* it had been Mime himself who, having learned definitely from the Wanderer that it is Siegfried who will forge the fragments, eggs the boy on to attempt that feat. In the later *Siegfried,* however, the more ambiguous message of the Wanderer leaves Mime in great perplexity. When Siegfried returns and demands the sword the agitated dwarf can only express his despair in broken mumblings. "The sword? The sword? How could I forge it? (Half to himself): 'Only he who has never known fear can forge Nothung anew'. Too wise was I for such a work! . . . Where can I find good counsel? My wise head I wagered: I lost, and my head is to fall to 'him who has never learned fear'." He sees now that his policy with the boy has been the wrong one from the beginning; instead of teaching him fearing he had schemed to win his sole affection. That plan having failed, there is nothing for it now but to teach him fear. He slowly reassembles his scattered wits and tries another line. "For your sake", he tells the boy, "I have been thinking hard, trying to discover how I

[1] Italics mine.

could be of greatest help to you. For your sake I have discovered what fearing is, that I might pass my knowledge on to you"; and he launches upon the long description of the terrors of the forest—the spectral lights, the roaring winds, and so forth—with which the spectator of *Siegfried* is so familiar. The boy merely laughs at him. Then Mime promises to take him to a terrible dragon who will teach him fearing. Siegfried begins his forging of the sword, and Mime, aside, exults in his coming triumph over Alberich and the others—Siegfried having disposed of the dragon for him, he in turn will make an end of the ignorant boy with the potion he is now brewing, and make himself possessor of Tarnhelm, Hoard and Ring.[1]

24

Let us now take up again the chronological threads of the evolution of the *Ring* drama.

We have seen Wagner, in May 1851, happily convinced that with the writing of the poem of *Young Siegfried* he had reached the end of his labours in connection with the stage lay-out of his big Nibelungen drama. He was soon to discover that however hard he might try to persuade himself that, apart from the setting of the two texts to music, he had now finished with the subject, it decidedly had not finished with him. In July he could assure Liszt that he was going to settle down to the musical part of his task "next month", when, he hoped, his health would have taken a turn for the better. After making a copy of the poem of *Young Siegfried* for his own future use he presented the manuscript to his friend Frau Julie Ritter. In the copy he was keeping for himself he made a few alterations, which Uhlig transferred to Frau Ritter's copy. (This latter is now in the possession of Herr Fritz von Hausegger). Yet another copy—which later became the property of King Ludwig—he made about the same time for Liszt. But by now his restless imagination had evidently got to work afresh on the whole subject; for in September we find him telling Uhlig in one breath that he is about to set to work on the

---

[1] The ramifications of this "fearing" motive and of the difficulties Wagner had with it are endless. It is impossible to pursue the subject further here: for further light on it I can only refer the reader to my *Life of Wagner*, Vol. II, Chapter XVII.

music — which, he says, will give him little trouble, for the musical phrases are fitting themselves to the words almost without conscious effort on his part,[1] — and in the next that although he has finished the fair copy intended for Liszt it is doubtful whether he will send it to him just yet.

Why that hesitation? We have the explanation of it in a letter of his to Liszt of the 20th November: his intensive work at the Nibelungen subject during the last few months, it appears, has made him doubt whether a simple reading of the poem of *Young Siegfried* will make it all as clear to his friend as he could wish. More than a month before this, in fact, the conviction had taken root in him that he could give the spectator an adequate idea of the whole scope of the myth only by prefacing *Young Siegfried* and *Siegfried's Death* with two further operas, — or, in his own nomenclature, an opera (*The Valkyrie*) and a "big prelude" (*The Rhinegold*). He had broached this new scheme of his in letters to Uhlig of the 10th October and 3rd and 12th November. In the last of these, and again in the letter of the 20th November to Liszt, he brings out into the open, for himself and for others, what must have been fermenting for a long time in the depths of his subconscious mind. He had begun in 1848, he says, with a plan for a vast drama on the myth of the Nibelungen Hoard. Still thinking at that time in practical terms of the contemporary theatre, he had condensed the enormous material as best he could into a single opera — *Siegfried's Death* — embodying "one chief catastrophe" of the myth, i.e., the doom that at long last overtakes Siegfried and the Gods through the rape of the gold from the Rhine and the curse laid upon it by Alberich, certain antecedent matters that could not be included in the stage action being "indicated", as Wagner expresses it, to the audience at this point or that in narrative. Then he had realised that there was too much narrative — too much "epic", as he put it — in his drama; and to remedy that he had written *Young Siegfried*, in which some of these precedent matters were not merely told to the spectator but set visibly before him on the stage. And now, on further reflection, he has decided on two more preliminary operas, partly in order to get the whole myth on to the stage in plastic dramatic

---

[1] "I already have the opening in my mind; also various plastic motives, such as that of Fafner", he says.

form, partly because the more he has brooded upon the subject
the more fascinated he has become by the possibilities it opens
out to his imagination as poet-musician.

25

Though he could hardly have realised it to the full just then,
this resolution was the decisive turning-point not only of the *Ring*
and of his art in general but of his whole outer life. A work on
the huge scale he now had in mind would be a pure impossibility
in the German or any other theatre of that epoch. He was well
aware of this, and accepted it, and all its staggering implications,
with characteristic courage. As he put it to Liszt, the big tetralogy
he now had in view could be produced only at some "festival" or
other: "how and in what circumstances such a production can become possible is something I am not going to worry about at
present", he said blithely, "for the first thing for me to do is to
work out my big plan, and this, if I am to give due consideration
to my health, will take me at least three years." The Fates merci-
fully hid it from him that the last note of the tetralogy would not
be written until near the end of 1874 and the whole work not
performed until 1876, and then in a theatre of his own which he
had somehow managed to bring into being at murderous cost to
his happiness and his health: "every stone in that building", he
said to Cosima bitterly one day as they were returning from the
Bayreuth theatre after the first festival of 1876, "is red with my
blood and yours."

The practical man of the theatre in him had become critical of
the turn that *Young Siegfried* had taken towards epic rather than
drama. *Siegfried's Death* had been, as the present *Götterdäm-
merung* is, full of dramatic movement; it was only occasionally
that one of the characters launched into a narration of earlier
events, and even these passages fitted quite logically into the dramatic fabric; far from holding up the action of the moment they
helped it along and gave it greater point. But once Wagner had decided to set some of the events antecedent to *Siegfried's Death* on
the stage in *Young Siegfried,* the amount of material presented him
by the various myths became an embarrassment to him. The actual
stage action would permit of only so much; once more, as had been
the case with *Siegfried's Death,* there remained whole stretches of

the long story that would have to be communicated to the audience by means of narrative. In *Young Siegfried,* as Wagner must soon have recognised, there was comparatively little action after the first act, and even there a good deal of space had been taken up with acquainting the audience, by means of the series of questions and answers between Mime and the Wanderer, with the happenings that had led up to the scene now being shown on the stage. In the second act the action had been halted at this point or that for the enlightenment of the spectator by means first of all of the wrangle between the Wanderer and Alberich, then by a long survey of antecedent events in the colloquy between the Wala and the Wanderer. In the third act much space had been taken up by Brynhilde's acquainting the audience, *via* Siegfried, with the full story of the origin of the Volsungs, of Siegmund and Hunding, and of the death of Siegmund and the birth of Siegfried.

26

As has been pointed out already, Wagner had a double motive for deciding to replace these and other narrative episodes by a stage presentation of precedent events: the dramatic action would gain by the elimination or reduction of certain too "epic" elements, and the new dramas would provide him with a fascinating wealth of material for poetic characterisation and musical expression. Having resolved upon prefacing *Young Siegfried* with a *Rhinegold* and a *Valkyrie* he could now tighten up the action of *Young Siegfried* by taking out of the text of it a good deal of mere explanation. He began by shortening the scene of the exchange of recriminations between the Wanderer and Alberich, and then that between the Wanderer and the Wala. But the biggest cut of all was in the final scene on Brynhilde's rock between the Valkyrie and Siegfried. Some hundred and twenty lines of Brynhilde's narration — which, in a musical setting, would certainly have immobilised the stage action for a dangerously long time — were taken out at one slice and recast, to our eternal gain, as the three acts of the *Valkyrie.*

Having decided to complete his already double-barrelled scheme by writing two preliminary dramas, Wagner first of all drafted, apparently between the 3rd and the 10th November

1851, a short scenario for the *Rhinegold*. (For a while he could not make up his mind whether to give the new work that title or *The Rape of the Rhinegold*. It is obvious, by the way, that his first idea had been to make it an opera in three acts [1]). A few days later he made a tentative Prose Sketch for the first two acts of the *Valkyrie*. Why he did not draft the third act then we do not know; it may possibly have been because in the main the details of it were already too clear to him for him to need to put them on paper, and he was more immediately anxious to get to grips with the *Rhinegold*.

This preliminary Sketch bore the provisional title of "Siegmund and Sieglinde: the Chastisement of the Valkyrie". There are a few small differences between the plan for these two acts and that of the present *Valkyrie*. In the latter, the Volsung sword has been embedded by Wotan in the tree of Hunding's hut before the action opens; whereas in the Sketch, Wotan arrives in the hut while Hunding, Siegmund and Sieglinde are seated at the "guest meal". The stranger drives the sword into the ash-tree and departs: Siegmund withdraws it, whereupon Sieglinde surmises that he must be, like herself, a Volsung. (Here Wagner was proceeding on the lines of the Volsunga Saga). The second act was planned to begin with Fricka upbraiding Wotan for his condonation of the illicit love of the twin pair; judging from a marginal note in the Sketch it was only later that he decided to preface this episode with the present one, in which Wotan instructs Brynhilde to shield Siegmund in the coming fight. When Fricka, in the Sketch, asserts herself as the protectress of marriage vows, Wotan reminds her ironically that one of her sex, Grimhilde, had given herself to Alberich for gold: "he inveighs against Grimhilde and women". This little exchange of marital courtesies Wagner eliminated later, and it is not until we come to the *Twilight of the Gods* that we learn of the begetting of Hagen by Alberich upon Gunther's mother, the Gibichung Queen Grimhilde.

Wagner's bad health held him up for a time with his *Rhinegold*

---

[1] The oddest feature of this first *Rhinegold* sketch is that Wagner proposed to begin the opera with "Wotan bathing", and in that condition learning from the three Rhinemaidens the peculiar virtue of the Gold. Then Alberich was to appear, woo the Maidens in vain, see the glowing Gold, and learn that it could be won only by one who forswears love.

plan, though in a note book he drafted various little expansions of his first swift scenario. But as the days went by he realised, as he had often done before and was often to do in the future, that the best cure for his bodily malaise was not rest but creative work; and so, as the winter of 1851/2 drew to its close, we find him once more immersed in his great subject. In the spring of 1852, besides making a few jottings by way of elaboration of his first *Valkyrie* outline, he committed to paper within no more than eight days — from the 23rd to the 31st March — a long Prose Sketch, occupying today more than sixteen large pages of print, for the *Rhinegold*.

27

This had been preceded by a fair amount of tentative sketching of certain details. A jotting on the theft of the Rhinegold had run thus: "Wotan knows nothing as yet of the power of the Gold. Fasolt and Fafner demand it as the price of the release of Freia (the Rhinedaughters have already said that the Giants too had hungered after it),[1] but they [Fasolt and Fafner] do not know of Alberich's rape of it. Wotan and Loge go first of all [i.e., after the Giants have demanded the Hoard in lieu of Freia] to the Rhinedaughters; here they learn what has happened, and their help is asked for the recovery of the Gold. Then they [the Gods] go to the Nibelungs. . ." Wagner is evidently puzzled, as yet, how to launch the work. In this jotting, though Wotan knows nothing of the virtues of the Gold, Fasolt and Fafner do; indeed, they have at some time or other wished to gain possession of it [2] — which is a last rather blurred echo in Wagner's mind from the First Sketch of 1848, where the action begins with the robbery of the Gold by Alberich, a robbery of which the Giants are aware and the consequences of which they dread. Now, in 1852, Wagner shows them

[1] This, of course, does not appear in the present poem.
[2] Two passages in the present *Siegfried* shew Wagner unconsciously reverting to the abandoned plan of 1848. Mime jeers at Alberich in this fashion: "Where now is that Ring of thine? Thou coward, the Giants wrested it from thee"; whereas it was not the Giants but Wotan and Loge who had robbed him. Again, in reply to Mime's second question, the Wanderer says: "On the broad earth dwells the race of the Giants. Fasolt and Fafner, their princes, envied the Nibelung's power: the mighty Hoard they won for their own, and with it took the Ring." This is consistent with the original plan of 1848 but quite inconsistent with the present *Rhinegold*.

ignorant of the fact that Alberich has acquired the Gold, though they themselves have lusted after it in the past. Yet while the Giants had known all about the Rhinegold the Gods are still ignorant of it, or at any rate of the power inherent in it. In the end Wagner wisely deprived both Gods and Giants of pre-knowledge of the Gold and the Ring, and cut out his projected first scene of a colloquy between the Giants and the Gods and the visit of Loge to the Rhinedaughters, while a second jotting shows him to have already hit upon the right layout for his second scene — Wotan and Fricka, the castle completed and payment demanded, the return of Loge with the news of Alberich's rape of the Gold, the distress of the Gods over the loss of Freia, the Giants' demand of the Gold, and the journey of Wotan and Loge to Nibelheim.

28

Further note-book jottings of the spring of 1852 show him gradually beating the first act of the *Valkyrie* into its present shape, though he still clings to the idea of introducing Wotan in the scene in Hunding's hut and having him leave the sword in the ash-tree as a "guest-gift". Wagner even makes Wotan go to sleep there, "after a short address of urgent warning to Siegmund, who, however, in the impatience of his passion [for Sieglinde] pays no attention to him. When Wotan appears to be asleep (in a recess in the background), Sieglinde enters." Wagner's stage sense made him discard all this later, though apparently it appealed to him for a considerable time, as is shown by a jotting in the margin of his first rapid sketch (of November 1851) for the first two acts of the *Valkyrie*. Opposite the passage relating to the wrangle between Wotan and Fricka over the love of Siegmund and Sieglinde, he has crammed into the margin this suggestion for an effective riposte by the God: "Wert thou [1] witness of their love? What knowest thou, who saw'st and heard'st them not?" The handwriting of this jotting seems to indicate that it was not contemporary with the Sketch itself; perhaps it was added when Wagner, in the spring of 1852, made the further sketches with which we have just been dealing.[2]

[1] "As I was" is implied.
[2] A facsimile of the manuscript at this point will be found in Dr. Otto Strobel's *Richard Wagner: Skizzen und Entwürfe zur Ring-Dichtung*, p. 206.

The beautifully written manuscript of the full *Rhinegold* Sketch, which followed next, runs to some seventeen pages of print, and must have been the outcome of much concentrated thinking during the winter of 1851 and the spring of 1852, so complete is it in detail, and so correspondent to the present poem. The variants from the latter are few. Two vital features alone of the ultimate poem are lacking in the Sketch: there is no reference to Freia's apples as the source of the wellbeing of the Gods, and in the stage directions for the transition from the scene on the sunlit heights to that in Nibelheim there is no mention of the clangour of Nibelung anvils. On the other hand, Erda, when she rises to warn Wotan to give up the Ring, speaks in more detail than in the present poem. In the latter, all she says about the future at the point in question is:

> *All that exists endeth!*
> *A day of gloom*
> *dawns for your godhood:*
> *I charge thee, give up the Ring!*

In the Sketch she is much more explicit: "Hear the counsel of the Norns that I bring thee! Ill will it fare with you Gods if you are false to treaties, and yet more ill if you, Wotan, keep the Ring. Slowly to their ending the Gods will go, but swift your downfall if you do not give up the Ring." More she refuses to say, in spite of the God's anguished entreaty; and there can be no doubt that Wagner was right in leaving the matter, for the time being, veiled in a certain mystery. So with the later episode in which Wotan greets the resplendent Walhall and bids the Gods enter with him. In the Sketch he says, "Thee, majestic pile, I won for myself, paying the price with the accursed Gold. Now let the curse run its course; I cannot avert it, but within thy mighty walls I will gather round myself noble companions to uphold the world joyously with me. Let Dwarfs and Giants band themselves against me in envy and greed; there will I bring a new race into being." And a little later, when Fricka asks him the import of the name Walhall, he replies, in the Sketch, "When those are born whom I shall summon thither, then will the meaning of the name be clear to thee." In the present poem, however, Wagner wisely leaves the future enveloped in mystery; into Wotan's mouth he puts the studiously enigmatic words:

> *What strength 'gainst my fears*
> *my spirit has found,*
> *when vict'ry is mine,*
> *maketh my meaning clear.*

In all such contingencies as this, Wagner could rely on his music for a potency of suggestion beyond the scope of words.

29

By this time he had manifestly decided to cast the *Rhinegold* into one-act form; and we may be sure that even when he was drafting the Sketch he was seeing and hearing everything in terms of music. In a marginal note we see him hesitating for a moment over the names of the three Rhine Maidens, and finally keeping Flosshilde and Wellgunde but rejecting "Bronnlinde" — which perhaps came too near to "Brynhilde" — in favour of Woglinde. In the text of the opening scene of the Sketch he had merely specified that the swimming Maidens should sing "a joyous melody of the waves, without words". Then, in a later marginal note, he decided, after much scratching out, upon the half-words, half-nature-sounds of "Weia! Waga! Woge du Welle! Walle zur Woge! Waga! laweia! Wallala weia la wei!", which agrees as nearly as makes no matter with the song in the present opera.

For the rest, we see from the Sketch how far Wagner had travelled by now from the original scheme of 1848. There the drama had begun on a cosmic plane, with three primal forces — Gods, Giants and Nibelungs — locked in a combat upon which the future of the world depended. The Nibelungs aspire ceaselessly to power; the Giants seek only the safety of dull inaction; the Gods, seeing further and more nobly than the others, work for the making of a world in which everything shall tend towards ultimate righteousness. But in the full *Rhinegold* Sketch and the opera as we now have it the motivation of the Gods is something quite different. They have lost almost all their collectivity and with it their cosmic grandeur. In their collective place we now have the single God Wotan, half human in his qualities and motives. Like Alberich, he is possessed by the lust for world power. In pursuit of his aim he is none too scrupulous; for the building of the fortress that is to ensure his safety against all enemies he enters into a compact with the Giants which he never had any intention of carrying out, bartering Freia against their labour and trusting, when the hour of settlement should come, to the crafty and cynical Loge to find for him a way of evading his obligation. Nor is his wife Fricka any less free of ordinary human weaknesses. When she reproaches him for the levity with which he had placed Freia and them all in such peril he counters with the reminder that she herself had counselled him to build the castle. She, in her turn, rounds on him in purely human terms: Wotan is too fond of "ranging and changing" in the egoistic pursuit of love; and it was to bind him more closely to his own hearth that she had favoured the building of the fortress on which he had manifestly set his heart — only to find later that he had duped her into acquiescence, his immovable purpose all along having been to achieve through it domination of the world. And Fricka herself, when she hears from Loge of the treasure the Nibelung has accumulated by means of the Ring, is all for robbing him of it to turn it into trinkets for feminine adornment; gladly she seconds the proposal that Wotan and Loge shall descend to Nibelheim and despoil the too fortunate gnome.

This personalising of the force of the Gods in the single character of Wotan, and the humanising of him and Fricka, certainly presents Wagner with endless opportunities for musical expression; but it can hardly be denied that it deprives, for a while, the general scheme of the *Ring* drama of some of the ethical loftiness of the original plan. Wagner will reach his first far-foreseen ethical heights before the vast drama is over, but by a rather different route from the one he had first intended.

30

The full-scale Prose Sketch for the *Valkyrie,* made between the 17th and the 26th May 1852, runs to twenty pages of print. It is mostly in the first act that it differs occasionally from the present poem. It shows us Wagner still bent on introducing Wotan in person in the opening scene and striking the sword into the ash-tree in the presence of Siegmund, Sieglinde and Hunding. But in a couple of marginal jottings we see him hitting on the right course of procedure — Sieglinde is to tell Siegmund of a mysterious stranger who had once come into the hut and struck the sword into the tree. This new conception necessitated, of course, a re-handling of the scene in which the two Volsungs declare their love for each other. But it did more than that. Obviously the climactic point of the first act should be that in which Siegmund proves his Volsung blood by doing what none of the other heroes who had passed through the hut from time to time had been able to do — drawing the sword from the tree. In the Sketch this highly dramatic moment had come comparatively early in the act, just before Hunding retires to the inner chamber to sleep. The later plan enabled Wagner to postpone Siegmund's acquisition of the sword to the point at which it is most dramatically effective — the very end of the act, when Siegmund and Sieglinde rush out into the forest and to freedom together.

The end of the second act presents us with one of those curious instances in which Wagner, when he came to write his opera poem, modified the plan of the Sketch without taking sufficient care to eliminate all traces of the change. The reader who knows the *Valkyrie* will remember that at the end of the second act, after the death of Siegmund, the angry Wotan turns to Hunding with the words:

> *Get hence, slave!*
> *kneel before Fricka:*
> *tell her that Wotan's spear*
> *avenged what wrought her shame. —*
> *Go! Go!*

and strikes him dead with a contemptuous wave of his hand. More than one puzzled spectator has probably asked himself how a dead Hunding could go and kneel before a living Fricka. But if we turn to the Sketch we find at this point: "Wotan (bitterly): Go hence, and tell Fricka, on whom you called for help, that you have been avenged by my spear"; and the God strides away in fury to seek out Brynhilde and punish her, leaving Hunding still in the land of the living. This links up, of course, with Wagner's original intention that Siegfried's first act after the forging of the sword should be to track down his father's slayer and kill him.[1]

In the final *Valkyrie* Sketch, as in that for the *Rhinegold,* we see once again how changed Wagner's conception of Wotan now is from what it had been in 1848. More and more human elements have gathered about Wotan in the process of concentrating the Gods in his person. In his dialogue with Fricka in the second act we find him charged by her, as he is again in the present poem, with a number of marital infidelities; as the poem has it:

> *Thy own true wife*
> *thou oft hast betrayed;*
> *never a deep*
> *and never a height*
> *but there wandered*
> *thy wantoning glance;*
> *all the joy of change thou wouldst win thee,*
> *and grieved'st my heart with thy scorn.*
> *Sad at heart*
> *I saw thee forsake me,*
> *fly to the fray*
> *with the savage maidens*
> *whom thou in lawless*
> *love didst beget;*

and so on. Is this drastic humanisation of the God a final gain or loss to the drama? It is hard to say: it gives Wagner an opportunity to bring him nearer to us in his music, showing us the depths

---

[1] Discrepancies and loose ends are almost inevitable in the case of a vast design upon which a poet has worked for many years: changes are made at this point or that without the necessary adjustments being made at another. It was so with the *Aeneid.* The third Book is now in the form of a narrative told by Aeneas to Dido. But originally this tale of the voyage from Troy had been told not by Aeneas but by the poet himself, and the design of the Book — as, indeed, of the *Aeneid* as a whole — was altered later. The result is that it is sometimes difficult to square the course of events in the later Books with that suggested in the third. There are evidences, says Mr. W. F. Jackson Knight, "that Vergil wrote the Third *Aeneid* early, perhaps while he still designed a more historical poem than he eventually wrote, and that he did not finally adjust the book, either by revising it or by rewriting it, to the scheme which he finally chose". (*Roman Vergil,* pp. 71–2).

of tenderness there are in Wotan's heart for his beloved daughter, his second self, Brynhilde, and for the tragically fated Volsung race whom he had begotten in the hope that in some way of its own it would accomplish his frustrated will and redeem the world from the wrong he had brought into it; but at the same time no one who has studied the original scheme for the *Ring* can help feeling that something of its first grandeur and the high ethical impulse that brought it into the great company of the Greek dramatists has gone out of it.

31

Working with such passionate concentration that his health suffered for it, Wagner completed the long *Valkyrie* poem between the 1st June and 1st July 1852. In most essentials it agrees with the present poem, though he made some changes later in the handling of the scene between Wotan and Fricka in the second act.[1] His damaged health made progress on the *Rhinegold* poem rather slower than he had hoped, but the task was completed between the 15th September and the 3rd November 1852. It was during this time that he decided at last on the title for the huge drama: rejecting "Der Reif des Nibelungen"[2] and "Das Gold des Nibelungen" he finally settled, apparently in October, on *"Der Ring des Nibelungen,* a stage-festival-play to be produced on three days and a fore-evening". But his labours were still not at an end. The texts of *Young Siegfried* and *Siegfried's Death* had now to be altered in various ways to avoid repetitions of, or clashes with, the course of the action as set forth in the *Rhinegold* and *Valkyrie.* Two episodes in *Siegfried's Death* had to be re-written — the opening scene of the Norns and the scene of the visit of the

---

[1] When printing the *Valkyrie* poem in 1872 in the sixth volume of his Collected Works he added, at the foot of the relevant pages, the text as he had framed it in 1852, "before I had embarked on the musical setting". Even in 1852, indeed, he had re-written several passages when making a fair copy of the poem as it then was. Dr. Strobel gives us a facsimile of the page of the manuscript containing the words of Siegmund and Sieglinde at the close of the first act, showing the many alterations in the wording. It is rather puzzling at first to find this revised page dated by Wagner "11 May" — a time when he was engaged not on the poem but on the Sketch. As Dr. Strobel points out, however, "11 May" is obviously a slip of the pen for "11 June".
[2] "Reif" has the same meaning as "Ring".

Valkyries (now cut down to one of their number, Waltraute) to Brynhilde's rock. The colloquy of Alberich and Hagen in the second act of *Siegfried's Death* had to be radically recast, and, of course, a new ending to that drama had by now become necessary. It was not until the 15th December 1852 that he could write at the bottom of the last page of his manuscript "End of the stage-festival-play".

32

So much for the general chronological record. We have now to retrace our steps a little and glance at the artist Wagner in the process of completing his vast plan by the writing of two dramas to precede *Young Siegfried* and *Siegfried's Death*.

This enlargement of his original scheme landed him in difficulties of various kinds which he could not have foreseen. *Siegfried's Death* had been laid out on broad lines, the protagonists of it being to a great extent generalised, the Gods, the Giants and the Nibelungs confronting each other as ethical types, in the way they had done in the first Prose Sketch of 1848. Wotan had not appeared in person at all in *Siegfried's Death*. Of the personalities who play so large a part in the present *Ring* only Siegfried, Brynhilde, Gunther, Gutrune, Hagen and Alberich had figured in that first work. *Young Siegfried* had added Mime, the Dragon, the Wala and the Wanderer. With the addition of the *Rhinegold* and the *Valkyrie* to the plan a number of new characters had to be created — Wotan in his primal form as chief of the Gods, Loge and the minor Gods, Fasolt and Fafner, Fricka, Siegmund, Sieglinde and Hunding — and appropriate dramatic settings had to be devised for all of them; moreover, all that these new characters did and said had to be brought into logical relation with the final stages of the drama.

Wagner had now to make up his mind once for all as to certain factors which so far he had found it necessary only to treat in generalised fashion or refer to *en passant*. Here the myths could give him little help, for they are silent on several vital points and vague or contradictory on others. What, for instance, was the Gold that generated the Hoard? In different legends it comes into being and disappears again in different ways: sometimes it is associated primarily with the waters, sometimes with a mountain or

a cave. Precisely how a hoard came in the course of time to be the
Nibelung Hoard we do not know; nor do we know exactly who
the Nibelungs were. We are no clearer as to the building of Walhall. In one myth a certain master-builder offers to build the Gods
a fortress that will secure them against the Giants, naming as his
price the Goddess Freia. Loge, the most crafty of the Gods, persuades them to accept the offer, with the proviso that the castle
shall be finished by the first day of summer, a feat which appears
impossible. The master-builder, however, has a horse, Swadilfari,
which performs miracles in the way of conveying the necessary
stones. Only three days remain before the coming of summer, and
the fortress is complete except for the entrance. The artful Loge
saves the situation by turning himself into a mare, which entices
the horse into the forest; the builder loses a day and a night in
catching it, and so over-runs the time-clause in the contract. The
Gods now discover that he is an enemy of theirs — a Giant, — and
Thor disposes of him by a blow on the head with his hammer.
The legends, in forms as naïve as these, could not be of much use
to Wagner.

While for certain episodes of the *Rhinegold* and the *Valkyrie*
he drew upon the Volsunga Saga, they were not presented to him
there in a form that he could use for his drama. The Saga tells, for
instance, of a man called Otter, so named because he was skilled
at lying on the river bank and catching fish. One day, after having caught a fine salmon, he is slain by a stone thrown at him by
Loge, who happened to be passing with Wotan and another God.
Otter's father, Hreidmar, demands in atonement for the killing of
his son that the Gods, who have brought him the skin of the otter,
shall fill and cover it with gold. The ever-resourceful Loge goes
to the sea-goddess Ran, takes her net, and captures in a waterfall
a pike which is in reality the dwarf Andvari, whom he deprives of
all his gold, including a ring. Andvari lays a curse upon the treasure: it shall bring ruin on every future possessor of it. The Gods
go to Hreidmar and proceed to cover the otter-skin with the gold;
but Hreidmar cries out that he can still see a hair of the otter's
muzzle, and Wotan is compelled to part with the ring to cover the
chink. Andvari's curse soon begins to operate; another son of
Hreidmar — Fafner — murders his father to gain the treasure, and
changes himself into a *Wurm* so that he may lie brooding upon it

for ever. Once more we see that such an account as this of the origin of the gold and of the curse upon it, and of Fafner's changing himself into a dragon to guard it, could not furnish Wagner with more than a hint or two for the management of his drama.

33

It would take us too far afield, and fulfil no really useful purpose, to trace the various elements of Wagner's *Ring* to their sources in the myths. He has been reproached for not having kept more closely to these. The reproach has no justification. There is nothing sacrosanct about the legends themselves. They do not form a single organic work of art in which any single mediaeval writer could claim a proprietary right. They are simply a collection, or an amalgam, of stories of varying antiquity, with a touch here and there of the historical, as when the terrible figure of the Hun Attila, "the scourge of God", who destroyed the Burgundians in the mid-fifth century, enters on the scene under this name or that.

The three main sources for our knowledge of the story of the Volsungs and that of the Nibelungen Hoard are the Volsunga Saga, the Thidrek Saga, and the Nibelungenlied. Wagner took from each of them only what he needed for his own vast plan, and, as he was to do later with the Tristan and Parzival legends, condensed the material here, modified it there, and imposed his own ethical scheme upon it all. And out of it all he has made the most stupendous of dramas since the *Oresteia*.

In February 1853 he printed a private edition of the four poems, and he told his friends he hoped to set to work at the music in the coming spring. By July 1857 he had completed only the composition of the *Rhinegold*, the *Valkyrie* and the second act of *Siegfried*; then he laid the work aside to write *Tristan*, and, later, the *Mastersingers*. In April 1863 he brought out a public edition of the *Ring* poem, with a long preface setting forth his plan and hopes for a "festival" performance in some new theatre or other built specially for that purpose.[1] From his fellow-Germans *en*

[1] This imprint necessarily differed at many points from that of 1853, as Wagner incorporated in it the verbal alterations that had occurred to him, or been forced upon him, when writing his music. In the 1863 edition the

masse, he said, he did not expect much in the way of helping him to realise his ideal of music-drama; but he cherished the hope that some German Prince or other might come to his rescue. "Will this Prince be found?" he concluded. That preface was read and taken to heart by the ardent young Crown Prince Ludwig of Bavaria, then in his eighteenth year. He made a silent vow that if ever it should be in his power to do so he would place the resources of the Munich Court Theatre at Wagner's disposal; and when he ascended the throne in March 1864 he sent for the composer, assured him an existence free from ordinary material cares, and urged him to complete as soon as might be the great work which he had had to lay aside for so long.

34

The composition of the *Rhinegold* had occupied Wagner from the 5th September 1853 to the 14th January 1854, the full score being completed on the 28th May. The *Valkyrie* was composed between the 28th June and the 27th December 1854, and the orchestral score finished by the end of March 1856. The first two acts of *Siegfried* took him from the 22nd September 1856 to the 30th July 1857, the third act from the 1st March to the 14th June 1869. The full score was completed on the 5th February 1871. The dates of composition of the *Twilight of the Gods* were: act one, the 2nd October 1869 to the 5th June 1870, act two, the 24th June to the 19th November 1871, act three, the 4th January to the 10th April 1872. The full score was finished on the 21st November 1874.

The *Rhinegold* was first performed, in Munich, on the 22nd September 1869, with the following cast: Wotan — August Kindermann; Fricka — Sophie Stehle; Alberich — Karl Fischer; Mime — Schlosser; Loge — Heinrich Vogl; Donner — Heinrich; Froh — Nachbaur; Fasolt — Petzer; Fafner — Bausewein; Erda — Fräulein Seehofer. The *Valkyrie* followed on the 26th June 1870, the principal rôles being cast as follows: Siegmund — Vogl; Sieglinde — Therese Vogl; Brynhilde — Sophie Stehle; Wotan — Kindermann;

---

titles of *Young Siegfried* and *Siegfried's Death* are definitely abandoned for *Siegfried* and *The Twilight of the Gods*.

Fricka — Anna Kaufmann; Hunding — Bausewein. Both operas were conducted by Franz Wüllner.

The first public performances of the *Ring* in its entirety took place in Bayreuth, under Hans Richter, on the 13th, 14th, 16th and 17th August 1876, with the following casts:

Singer	Rhinegold	Valkyrie	Siegfried	Götterdäm-merung
Betz	Wotan	Wotan	Wanderer	
Gura	Donner			Gunther
Unger	Froh		Siegfried	Siegfried
Vogl	Loge			
Hill	Alberich		Alberich	Alberich
Schlosser	Mime		Mime	
Eilers	Fasolt			
Reichenberg	Fafner		Fafner	
Sadler-Grün	Fricka	Fricka		3rd Norn
Marie Haupt	Freia	Gerhilde	Wood-Bird	
Jaïde	Erda	Waltraute	Erda	Waltraute
Lilli Lehmann	Woglinde	Helmwige		Woglinde
Marie Lehmann	Wellgunde	Ortlinde		Wellgunde
Marie Lammert	Flosshilde	Rossweisse		Flosshilde
Niemann		Siegmund		
Niering		Hunding		
Scheffzky		Sieglinde		2nd Norn
Materna		Brynhilde	Brynhilde	Brynhilde
Antonie Amann		Siegrune		
Reicher-Kindermann		Grimgerde		
Johanna Wagner		Schwertleite		1st Norn
Siehr				Hagen
Weckerlin				Gutrune

The Rhinegold

1

THE FIRST sound we hear is a long-held E flat deep down in the double-basses, a primordial element, as it were, out of which the world of water represented by the Rhine will come into being by slow differentiation. At the fifth bar the next decisive note of the natural scale, the dominant, B flat, is added in the bassoons, and in the seventeenth bar the horns, in an ascending arpeggio, further add the third, G natural. The triad of E flat major is now fully defined, and out of that primal substance:

No. 1

Wagner proceeds to shape the 136 bars of the prelude proper. In the 49th bar the addition of intermediate notes of the scale gives us a motive more specifically that of the Rhine itself:

No. 2

though in the later course of the drama it will gather to itself other associations. In the episode of Siegfried's Rhine Journey in the *Twilight of the Gods*, for instance, it unquestionably refers to the river, while as accompaniment, later in the *Rhinegold*, to Erda's warning to Wotan, where she speaks of "the three daughters born to me ere the world was made", and of her knowing all things that were and shall be, the motive is manifestly associated in Wagner's mind with the primal element to which reference has just been made. It is one more illustration of the inadequacy of any one verbal label to cover all the significances which this or that motive originally had in Wagner's mind, or all the symbolisations that clustered about it as he sank himself more deeply into his subject.

The motion of the music gradually gains strength, and No. 2 floats now upon a series of arpeggio figures:

No. 3

suggestive of waves. While the tempo of the music remains always technically the same the sense of inner motion keeps on increasing, until the waters seem to be in full flood; and at this point the curtain rises.

Through a greenish twilight, that is darker below, lighter above, we see the bottom of the Rhine. In the lower depths the waters show more as a thin, humid mist, while in the upper part of the scene they are waves flowing in a mighty tide from right to left. Through the gloom of the lower mist craggy points of rock are visible jutting out everywhere, while in the enveloping darkness great fissures are suggested. As the flood of tone surges up in the orchestra to the highest point it has yet attained, one of the Rhinemaidens, Woglinde, comes into sight, swimming in a graceful circle round a rock that rises from the centre of the scene, the slender peak of it being visible in the clearer upper waters.

The E flat harmony that has run through the whole of the orchestral prelude so far suddenly shifts over, at the 137th bar, to the plane of A flat as Woglinde sings a greeting to the waters:

No. 4

Wei - a! Wa - ga! Wo-ge, du Wel - le, wal-le zur Wie - ge!
Wei - a! Wa - ga! Wander, ye wa - ters, lap me and lull me!

She is answered by the voice of her sister Wellgunde from above, then by that of Flosshilde; and the trio pursue each other in innocent merriment, though Flosshilde chides the others for losing sight in their play of what should be the object of their constant care — the sleeping Gold which it is their duty to guard.

2

While they are laughing and sporting the Nibelung Alberich has emerged from a dark chasm and clambered up to one of the rocks; himself hardly visible as yet in the darkness, he watches the gambols of the Rhinemaidens with growing pleasure. He hails the sisters in a raucous voice; he comes from Nibelheim, he says, and would gladly share in their sport. The Rhinemaidens dive deeper, see the uncouth creature who is addressing them, recoil from him in disgust, and dart upward again to swim in circles round the central rock: it was against some such foe as this, they remind each other, that their father warned them. The amorous Alberich begs them to descend again, that he may clasp the slender form of one of them in his arms. The grotesque spectacle of this repulsive gnome in love moves them to laughter, and they begin to tease him, swimming within clasping distance and then swiftly darting out of his reach, while he clambers awkwardly after now one, now another of them, slipping on the slimy crags and gasping and sneezing as he gropes his way through the mist. At last he loses his temper and tells the "cold and bony fish" who are laughing at him to "take eels for their lovers", since he is too ugly in their eyes for love.

Hitherto his attentions have been paid mostly to Wellgunde and Woglinde; now Flosshilde pretends to take pity on him, and in an enchanting lyrical interlude, in which the insinuating beauty of her song draws a corresponding sweetness of response even from the uncouth gnome, she promises him better fortune with her than he has had with her sisters. She maliciously simulates the passion and cajoleries and gallantries of genuine love:

> *Oh thy sharp-pointed glance*
> *and thy stiff scrubby beard,*
> *for ever to see and to hold!*
> *Might those bristles, thy curls,*
> *so wiry and wild,*
> *float round thy Flosshilde for ever!*

And thy form like a toad,
and the croak of thy voice,
Oh might I, mute and amazed,
nought else hear and behold!

For a moment she takes him in her arms, then breaks away cruelly from him and swims towards her sisters, and at a safe distance the three burst into heartless laughter at his expense. Goaded to fury, he swears he will capture one of them: he clambers with terrifying agility over the rocks, trying to seize now one of the Maidens, now another; but always they elude and deride him. At last he pauses, speechless, breathless, foaming with rage, and shakes a menacing fist at them:

No. 5

But his attention is suddenly drawn away from them by a glow that spreads gradually over the upper waters, finally concentrating itself in a dazzling gleam on the high point of the central peak. It is the sleeping Gold awakening, and through a gentle undulation of the strings we hear, in a horn, the motive of the Rhinegold:

No. 6

The Rhinemaidens hail the Gold joyously, and as the shimmer increases and No. 6 peals out again in a trumpet they break into a rapturous trio:

No. 7

as they swim gracefully round the rock. The orchestra seems to bathe the scene in a bright golden light.

3

The wondering Alberich asks the sisters the meaning of it all. They tell him what this golden glory is that floods the deeps with its radiance, and invite him to join them in their revels round it. He replies scornfully that if the Gold serves merely for childish games like theirs it has no attraction for him. But he would not talk like this, they assure him, if he knew the wonder that resides in the Gold: could anyone win it for his own and fashion a Ring from it he could make himself master of the world; and the wood wind give out softly the all-important motive of the Ring:

No. 8

Because of the virtue that is in the Gold, Flosshilde reminds her sisters reprovingly, their father has warned them to guard it watchfully lest some robber seize upon it. But Wellgunde and Woglinde in their turn remind her of what it is that secures the Gold against falling into hands that may use it to work evil: only one who had forsworn love could forge a Ring from it; and the motive of Renunciation of Love is heard for the first time as they sing:

> *He who the power*
> *of love forswears,*
> *from all delights*
> *of love forbears,*
> *alone can master the magic*
> *that makes a Ring from the Gold:*

No. 9

455

Secure they may be from care, then, "for all that liveth loveth, and no one in all creation will forswear delight of love". And least of all, Woglinde adds, this languishing, lusting imp here, visibly racked with love; and they ironically invite him to join them in their laughter, for the glory of the Gold has laid a touch of beauty even on his hideous form.

Soft enunciations of No. 6, followed by No. 9 in the darkest colours of the brass, show us what is passing through the gnome's brutish mind; with his eyes fixed on the Gold he says to himself:

> *The world's wealth*
> *can I win for my own then through thee?*
> *If love be denied me,*
> *delights by my cunning I'll seize!*
> *Mock as ye will!*
> *The Niblung neareth your toy!*

The Rhinemaidens scatter before him in terror as, with a supreme effort, he springs over to the centre rock and clambers to the summit of it. With a demoniacal laugh he stretches out his hand towards the Gold and cries:

> *Then frolic in darkness,*
> *brood of the waves!*
> *Your light lo, I put out,*
> *I wrench from the rock the Gold,*
> *forge me the Ring of revenge;*
> *for hear me, ye floods:*
> *Love now curse I for ever!*

While the terrified Rhinemaidens fly from him he tears the Gold from the rock and plunges with it into the depths, where he disappears from sight.

With the rape of the Gold the whole scene is suddenly plunged into darkness. The waters seem to sink into the depths below, and from the lowest deep of all Alberich's mocking laughter is heard. To a dark swirl of orchestral sound the rocks disappear in a billowing flood of black water that seems to sink and sink unendingly. The motive of Renunciation of Love strikes across it all like a sinister shadow, to be succeeded by the Ring motive in a new and broader form:

No.10 Bassoons

By this time the waves have gradually changed to clouds, and these to a fine mist, which slowly disperses as an increasingly bright light pierces through it from behind; and as the mist finally drifts away we see an open space on a mountain height.

4

Day is dawning. At one side of the scene are Wotan and his wife Fricka, both asleep on a flowery bank. As the light grows stronger there becomes visible, on the top of a cliff in the background, a majestic castle with glittering battlements; between this and the foreground where Wotan and Fricka recline we are to suppose the broad Rhine to flow.

From the orchestra the noble Walhall motive wells up in soft harmonies in trombones and tuba, with an occasional trumpet fanfare pealing out:

No.11

The conclusion of the motive:

No.12

is in the same rich colours. An immense peace seems to brood over the scene.

Wotan is dreaming blissfully of the splendid castle that has been built for him, a stronghold from which he sees himself, in imagination, ruling the world in unassailable might and to his own eternal glory; through the tissue of his dream, however, the theme of the Ring (No. 10) winds softly in the 'cellos. Fricka shares none of her spouse's illusions about the matter: she rouses him from what she calls his "deceptive dream" and exhorts him to take thought for the realities of the situation as it is bound to shape itself soon for him and herself and the other Gods. But for the moment reality has no meaning for the ecstatic, power-drunk dreamer. Raising himself slightly he catches sight of the majestic stronghold across the river, which he apostrophises: "'Tis completed, the everlasting work! There on the mountain top stands the citadel of the Gods with its stately soaring walls. In dreams I conceived it; my will called it into being; strong and fair it stands, fortress proud and peerless!"; and the trumpet hails it also with a final solemn gesture of its own.

But Fricka tells him that what makes his heart glow with pride of possession fills hers with dread. The fortress is indeed there, but the price has yet to be paid. The grave motive of Wotan's Treaty with the Giants, that has been engraved in runes on the God's spear:

No.13

p Cellos & Basses in 8ves

is heard in 'cellos and basses as she reminds him of his compact: Freia, the Goddess of youth and beauty and health and charm, had been promised to the Giants in payment. The infatuated Wotan waves her cares aside. Let her not fret over the price to be paid, he tells her; that is his affair — though manifestly he had hardly given it a serious thought, trusting to Loge, the nimble-witted and none too scrupulous God of fire, to solve his problem for him when the hour of reckoning should come. Fricka overwhelms him with reproaches for his levity: without ever consulting her and the other Gods he had callously bartered her sister Freia for the gratification of his lust for power.

Wotan ripostes that Fricka herself had been in favour of the building of the castle, and she explains why — heavy at heart over her spouse's infidelities she had thought to bind him to hearth and home by means of this splendid toy on which his heart had been set; and her sorrow finds expression in the gracious motive of Love's Enchantment:

No. 14

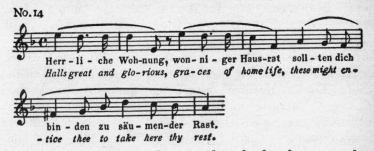

Herr - li - che Woh-nung, won- ni - ger Haus-rat soll - ten dich
Halls great and glo-rious, gra-ces of home life, these might en -

bin - den zu säu - men-der Rast.
- tice thee to take here thy rest.

But now, she continues, she sees that she has been mistaken; Wotan's one thought had been and is for power. With a smile, echoing ironically the gracious line of No. 14, he admits his double-dealing. "Ranging and changing" is his delight, as it is that of all who love, and he cannot desist from it; but if henceforth he is to be confined to his home, at least it shall be one from which he can subject the whole world to his rule. Again she reproaches him for his heartlessness in sacrificing love — here the orchestra breathes softly the melody of No. 9 — for "the tawdry toy of empire and power". The consummate casuist replies that to win her own love in days gone by he had forfeited an eye, so that her present reproof is unjust. In any case, it is because he prizes woman and woman's love so much that he will not resign Freia to the Giants; never, indeed, had that been his intention, he assures her.

5

A quickening of the tempo and a succession of urgent figures in the orchestra suggest hurried action behind the scenes. Fricka, looking off the stage, bids Wotan save Freia now, "for, defenceless and in grief, hither she hastens for help". Freia enters, as if in flight, to a motive that will always be associated with her later:

No. 15

(The segment of this marked A has been a source of much trouble to the analysts. They have dubbed it the motive of Flight, because it occurs now and later in some sort of connection with that idea. But we meet with it also in Wagner in quite other connections; and the truth seems to be that it was a musical *tic* into which he was inclined to fall on various occasions, sometimes, as here, with a specific purpose, sometimes without any).

In distracted tones Freia calls on Wotan and Fricka to save her, for Fasolt is hard on her heels for the payment promised to the Giants. "Let him threaten", says Wotan tranquilly; "saw'st thou not Loge?" Fricka scornfully upbraids him for putting his trust in that trickster; he has already done the Gods much harm, yet always Wotan is caught in his snares. Still tranquilly sure of himself, the God replies that his only need for and his only use of Loge are in cases like the present one, where wisdom fails and craft and guile alone will succeed; when Loge had counselled him to make his compact with Fasolt and Fafner he had promised to find him a way to cheat them out of Freia; and Wotan still has faith in the cunning rogue.

Freia calls desperately on her brothers Donner and Froh to come to her aid now that even Wotan has abandoned her. "They who wove this net of treachery about thee", Fricka tells her sombrely, "have all forsaken thee now!" At this tense point in the action Fasolt and Fafner enter, men of rough aspect and gigantic stature; their heavy tread and lumbering gait are depicted in their characteristic motive:

No. 16 *Pesante*

Quietly and patiently, for he feels he has right on his side, Fasolt, who is throughout of a milder nature than his brother, uncouth yet not essentially evil, brutish yet not brutal, states their case to Wotan. With endless toil, heavy stone they have piled on heavy stone, and now the fortress stands there, resplendent in the light of day: "pass thou in, and pay our wage!" What that wage is Wotan knows — "Freia the fair one, Holda the free one; [1] the bargain is that she goes home with us twain." Wotan contemptuously rejects the demand: "Crazed must ye be to talk of that bond! Other payment ask: Freia is not for sale!" Through all this conversation, of course, run the motives of the Treaty (No. 13) and Freia (No. 15).

6

Fasolt is for a moment speechless with amazement; then he asks the God if the solemn runes of treaty engraved on his spear are nothing more than a sport to him. The more realistic Fafner turns to his brother with a sneer: "My trusty brother, see'st thou not, fool, his deceit?" He sings the words to a phrase that is simultaneously outlined by the orchestra in this fashion:

No. 17

This is obviously a broadened version of a motive associated later with Loge (No. 23 below). That Wagner should employ it as he does here is one of several indications that when he was writing the *Rhinegold* he was not yet fully master of his new method of constructing his musical fabric out of leading motives; he was sometimes inclined to introduce them without reasons that we can now regard as valid. It is true that Wotan had relied on the guile of Loge to get him out of his difficulty on the day of reckoning; but as Fafner knows nothing of all this there seems to be no justification for the Loge motive to be anticipated here in connection with the Giant's remark to his brother. Wagner is obviously speaking to us here not as dramatist but *in propria persona*, telling us in the audience something *he* knows and feels we ought to know.

Fasolt solemnly warns Wotan of the consequences of a breach

[1] Holda is another name for the Goddess of youth in the mythologies. Wagner here plays antithetically upon the two names and adjectives — "Freia, die Holde, Holda, die Freie."

of faith on his part. "What thou art", he reminds him, "art thou only in virtue of treaties by which thy power is defined. We in our turn are bound to thee in peace. Cursed be all thy wisdom, perish all peace between us, if, no more open, honest and free, thou breakest the troth thou hast plighted." The Treaty motive (No. 13) here takes a slightly different form in Fasolt's mouth, and Wagner makes the 'cellos and basses imitate the vocal line at a time-interval of a minim:

It is not over-fanciful to assume that he intended to imply by this thematic dualism that the treaty was a bilateral one, for in order to force the accompanying orchestral part on our attention Wagner has marked it "staccato but with decision".

These, Fasolt concludes, are the words of a simple-minded Giant; "do thou, wise one, mind our words!" But Wotan waves the admonition airily aside:

> *How sly to take in earnest*
> *what but in sport was agreed on!*
> *The beauteous Goddess,*
> *sweet and bright,*
> *what need ye louts with her grace?*

Fasolt turns on him in anger. Is Wotan mocking them? he asks. "Ye who by beauty reign" (here the violas give out a soft reminiscence of the motive of Love's Enchantment), "ye, the regal, radiant race, yearn like fools for a fortress of stone, bartering for it woman's grace and charm. We dullards sweat with toil-hardened hands to win us a woman who, winsome and sweet, shall smile on our homestead; and now ye would break your own bond!" As Fasolt speaks of the charm of woman Wagner indulges himself in a stroke worthy of Mozart, who loved his characters so much and was so completely one with each of them at the moment he was describing him that he could not touch the humblest and awkwardest of them without a caress: Wagner here lays the gentlest of hands on the uncouth Giant who has a strain of tenderness in him:

No. 19

But the brutal Fafner strikes in with his usual realism. Why argue with these Gods? he asks his brother contemptuously. What, after all, is Freia to Fasolt and himself except as a means of putting pressure on the Gods? For it is they who need her most. In her garden grow golden apples:

No. 20

Gold' - ne Äp - fel   wachsen in   ih - rem   Gar - ten
Gold - en ap - ples   bloom with - in   her   gar - den

which she alone knows how to tend. They bestow on her kindred everlasting youth; without them — and here No. 20 takes on a darker tinge in bassoons and horns:

No. 21

the Gods will grow old and weak and waste away. Therefore let the Giants wrest Freia ruthlessly from this arrogant, faithless race.

7

Fear begins to take possession of Wotan. "Why tarries Loge so long?" he asks in an anxious aside. To the Giants he says, "Demand another wage!"; but Fasolt refuses, and he and Fafner make to seize Freia, who runs, crying for help, to her brothers Donner and Froh, who have now entered hastily. Froh throws a protecting arm round her, and Donner, the god of thunder, stands in the way of the Giants, brandishing his hammer and threatening to pay them in a coin for which they had not bargained. Freia wails "Woe's me! Woe's me! Wotan forsakes me!". Wotan, now thoroughly sobered, stretches out his spear between the disputants and bids Donner stay his hand. Force will not avail, he tells him; the treaty is engraved in runes on his spear-shaft, and he is bound by it. As he turns away in anger and disgust and with a secret fear in his heart he sees Loge approaching, coming up from the valley at the back. He is heralded by various motives associated with him at one time or another as the God of Craft:

and the God of Fire:

Wotan reproaches him for his delay in bringing news of the errand with which he had been entrusted — to find some means by which the fatal compact with the Giants could be evaded. Loge raises his hands in cynical protest: what compact had *he* ever entered into? It was Wotan who had pledged his word. For Loge himself is hardly one of the Gods, so different is he from the others. Donner and Froh, he says, dream of hearth and home, Wotan of the stronghold sure which he has now obtained (here the stately Walhall motive surges up in full in the orchestra), thanks to Fasolt and Fafner having carried out their part of the compact. As for himself, he lives in another element and is subject to none of the limitations of the other Gods; a restless, elusive spirit of fire, he sweeps homeless through the world, wandering wherever his fancy leads him.

Wotan reproves his flippancy. If he has been deceiving him all this time, he says, let him beware, for Wotan is his only protector among the Gods, who like not the vagrant and his shifty philosophy. Well he knows that when the Giants named Freia as the price of their labour Wotan would never have consented but for a promise by Loge that he would find a means to evade that article of the bond. To the constant accompaniment of the volatile motives associated with him Loge protests that all he had sworn was that he would ponder upon the problem:

> *But that I'd find thee*
> *some sure way forth*
> *where no way lies,*
> *could I such promise lay on me?*

The other Gods are revolted by his heartless cynicism: Fricka turns to Wotan with an angry reproach that he should ever have placed faith in this treacherous knave: Froh tells the God of Fire that he should be called "not Loge but Lüge" ("lies"): Donner, with a threatening gesture, swears he will put out his light: on all which Loge's sole comment is a contemptuous

> *Their disgrace to cover*
> *the gross fools curse me!*

Wotan steps between them as peacemaker. Let them not affront his friend Loge, he says diplomatically. "Ye know not his wiles; the slower he is to give his counsel the craftier it always is." But at a peremptory demand from Fasolt and Fafner for payment of their wage he calls on Loge to explain where and why he has lingered so long. The elusive one launches into the long scena known as "Loge's Narration", a gracious lyrical inset in an action that has latterly been carried on mainly on the lines of dramatic dialogue. Mockingly he reminds them that it is always his lot to get scant praise for what he does for them. The Freia motive (No. 15) takes on a particular grace and sweetness:

No. 25

as he tells how unceasingly he had searched through the world for a ransom for her that would be likely to satisfy the Giants. But all had been in vain: nowhere in the wide world, in water, earth or air, had he found anything that man valued more than woman's love; for nothing would anyone renounce it. But at last he had heard of one who had cast it aside in scorn, and that for gold. The sorrowing children of the Rhine had told him how the Nibelung Alberich, having sought their favours in vain, had abjured love and robbed them of the Gold with a curse; and they had implored Loge to carry the tale of their loss to Wotan and beg him to punish the thief and return the Gold to the waters from which it had been ravished.

8

It is at this point that Wagner begins to develop real mastery of the new system of leading motives with which he had endowed opera. So far he has employed his motives in more or less literal reproductions of them in their primary form — which was, indeed, to be expected, for as yet everything connected with the drama is in its primary stage of simple exposition, and his first task had been to define the melodic and harmonic and rhythmic shapes by which characters and things were to be identified. But now, when the action begins to be more subtilised, corresponding subtilisations of his thematic material are called for; and we see Wagner taking the first steps towards that psychological variation of the leading motives of the *Ring* that was to find its consummation, twenty years later, in the *Twilight of the Gods*. We see him beginning with the motive of the Rhinemaidens' song (No. 7). When Loge tells how "the lustrous children of the Rhine poured out their lament to me" the opening chords of No. 7 undergo this harmonic transformation:

No. 26

Bass: G

while at the words "For the glittering toy thus torn from the deep the Maidens are ever moaning" another harmonic change gives the motive, which in the beginning had been so symbolical of primal innocence and joy, a still profounder poignancy:

No. 27

A little later in the Narration the smooth thirds of the Ring motive (No. 8) take on a darker tinge and a sharper edge:

No. 28

Loge ends his story with a complacent and ironic assurance that he has now kept his promise to the Rhinemaidens to tell the story of their grief to the Gods. Wotan turns on him angrily: "Myself thou seest in need; what help have I to give to others?" But the story has struck deep into Fasolt and Fafner. "This Gold I begrudge the Nibelung", the former mutters; "much wrong he ever has wrought us, but always the dwarf has slipped away from our hold." "Some new mischief he will brew for us", replies Fafner, "if through the Gold he wins power." He asks Loge what is the greatness inherent in the Gold that the Nibelung lays such store by the possession of it. To the accompaniment of the Rhinemaidens' melody in its first innocent form, Loge tells him that when sleeping in the waters it is merely a toy, serving the laughing children of the deep for sport, but should it be rounded to a Ring it will confer measureless might on its possessor and give him dominion over the world.

"Rumours of this I already have heard", says Wotan reflectively, fitting the news into the pattern of his own thoughts. Fricka takes her own feminine view of it: would the golden toy, she asks Loge softly, serve as well for the adornment of women? More than that, replies the crafty God; she who possessed the golden trinkets which now the Nibelungs, slaves to its power, are making, could ensure her husband's faithfulness to her. She turns to Wotan, and, to the gracious strain of the Freia motive, says cajolingly, "Oh would that this Gold my consort could win!"

Unwittingly she has given utterance to Wotan's own secret thought. The Rhinegold motive (No. 6) peals out softly in the trumpet, then in quiet horn tones, as he says, half to himself, "To win the power contained in this Ring seems to me wise!" He asks Loge how the circlet can be made. Only by a magic rune, he is told; no one knows that rune, and none can learn it save by forswearing love. Wotan turns away in ill humour at this, and Loge remarks ironically, "That is not to thy liking! And indeed thou art too late. Alberich did not delay. Fearlessly he won him the magic spell, and already he has made the Ring."

9

The Gods are aghast. "Slaves shall we all be to the dwarf", says Donner, "if the Ring be not wrested from him." "The Ring I must have!" Wotan cries; while Froh is sure that now it is made it can be won easily without any of them forswearing love. Easily enough, replies Loge harshly: "by theft! What a thief stole," he explains to Wotan, "steal thou from the thief. Could aught be simpler? But Alberich guards himself with weapons of craft; shrewd and wary wilt thou have to be to overreach him and return the lustrous Gold to the Maidens whose cry for it goes up to thee." "Return it to the Maidens?" Wotan repeats incredulously; while Fricka sees no need to consider "that brood of the waves, who, to my grief, have lured many a man to their lair by their wiles." Silence falls upon the Gods; each of them, for reasons of his own, is ready to be an accomplice in the wresting of Gold and Ring and power from Alberich; but Wotan still shrinks from achieving that end by wrongdoing.

Their puzzled brooding is broken in upon roughly by the Giants. Fafner now lusts after the Gold not only because of the menace that Alberich's possession of it constitutes for them, but for its own sake. But to his brother he does not disclose all that is in his mind. He plays on what he knows to be Fasolt's weakness: the glittering Gold, he tells him, will serve them even better than

Freia, for it too will bestow eternal youth on whoever makes the magic of it his own. Fasolt, as the upsurge of the motive (No. 20) of Freia's apples in the orchestra indicates, finds it hard to give up the gracious Goddess on whom his rough heart has been set; and his demeanour shows that he is yielding to Fafner against his will. They lumber together towards Wotan, accompanied by the characteristic No. 16, and Fafner tells him the decision they have come to. They will not insist on Freia: an easier quittance of the debt will content them — "for us rough Giants the Nibelung's red Gold will do".

Wotan protests feebly: "Are ye mad? How can I give you what is not my own?" "With toil and moil", rejoins Fafner, "we built thee thy fortress. To subdue Alberich has always been beyond the power of us dull ones; but for you Gods it will be easy to master him by superior strength and guile." This is not to Wotan's liking: is he to conquer the Nibelung, he asks them all, half indignantly, half despairingly, only to satisfy the demands of this shameless pair? He sees now the net of his own careless duplicity beginning to close in on him. Freia he had never intended to give up, trusting to Loge's craft to find him a way out of his compact. His motive in making it had been to acquire a fortress from which he could hold sway over the world, bending both Giants and Nibelungs to his will. Another way of achieving that end has just been disclosed to him by Loge — the seizure of the Gold from Alberich, who will certainly use it to make himself master of the world; and no sooner has this way to the achievement of Wotan's purpose been pointed out to him than the Giants present him with his original dilemma in another form; he must give up either Freia or the Gold.

Fasolt breaks the tension by roughly drawing Freia to his side and bidding her come with them until the ransom is paid. Till nightfall, say the Giants, they will hold her as pledge; if when they return the Gold is not there for them, Freia will be forfeit. Screaming for help she is dragged away, and to graphic descriptive music in the orchestra Loge describes to the others how the rough pair stride away over stock and stone through the valley and across the Rhine by a ford, with the fair Goddess slung across their shoulders.

10

A change comes over the scene; a pale mist spreads over the stage, becoming gradually denser. The Gods look old and wan: in the orchestra the motives associated with Freia take on more sombre tints. At first only the cynical, detached Loge can find words for what is in the thoughts of all of them: they seem sick and withered, he tells them, the bloom has fled from their faces, dimmed is the light of their eyes; Froh's high courage has left him; Donner's arm is too feeble to hold up his great hammer; and Fricka — is she not grieving for Wotan, now grown old and grey in a trice? He sees it all: nothing of Freia's golden apples have they eaten today, the apples that renew their youth and strength; and now the Goddess herself is ravished from them, and without her the branches of the tree will droop and the decaying fruit fall to the ground. Loge does not spare them in their misery. He himself, he tells them, suffers nothing of all this; Fricka, who likes him not, has ever been sparing of the delicate fruit to him, nor does he miss it as they do, for by nature he is at best only half a God. But for the others the hour of doom has sounded, and the Giants know it and are calculating on it: "lacking the apples, old and grey, haggard, hoary, withered, the scorn of all the world, the race of the Gods is passing away."

Fricka's voice is raised in weary lament:

No. 29

Her reproach rouses Wotan. Starting up as a resolution suddenly shapes itself in his mind he bids Loge come with him to Nibelheim, where they will seize the Gold. Loge plays cruelly with him once more: he is going, then, after all, in answer to the prayer of the Rhinemaidens, to whom he intends to return the Gold? Wotan furiously bids him hold his peace. The Rhinemaidens do not concern him; all that matters is the ransoming of Freia. Loge suavely consents to go with him: "shall we descend to Nibelheim straight and steep through the Rhine?" "Not through the Rhine!" replies Wotan. "Not through the Rhine?" Loge echoes ironically, for he knows the God's reasons for not wishing to meet the Maidens now: "then swing we ourselves through the sulphur cleft there yonder; slip down it with me!" He disappears in a fissure at the side of the stage, from which a sulphurous vapour immediately rises. Wotan follows him, telling the others to wait there until evening, when he will return with Freia's ransom.

11

The long descriptive orchestral piece that accompanies the change of scene depicts the course of the two Gods to Nibelheim, and is necessarily constructed at first out of such motives as that of Loge and that of Alberich's Renunciation of Love (No. 9), the latter now in ominous dark brass colours. Then we hear what is generally described as a reminiscence of a figure:

which, in the opening scene of the opera, had expressed the gnome's anger and despair over his repulse by the Rhinemaidens. In the form it now takes:

it becomes a motive, usually labelled that of Servitude, which is put to important uses later. There is no necessity, however, to assume any hard-and-fast connection, on Wagner's part, between No. 30 and No. 31. A semitonal descent of this kind — naturally expressive of a wail or moan — appears in his works in all kinds of associations.

471

A figure that immediately follows No. 31 is usually described by the analysts as a development of the so-called Flight motive (No. 15 A), though just why this concept should be drawn upon here is not explained. We are on surer ground when we hear the Rhinegold motive (No. 6) in the bass trumpet, and then a hammering figure:

No. 32

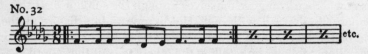

which we have already heard in Loge's Narration, at the point where he had told the other Gods of "the toiling dwarfs, slaves to the power of the Ring, who are smithing the Gold for Alberich". As with so many of Wagner's motives, this can be labelled in more than one way: primarily, as its rhythm implies, it describes the frenzied hammering of the enslaved dwarfs, and so constitutes what may be called a Smithing motive *per se;* and later in the *Ring,* as in the scene in *Siegfried* in which the hero forges his father's sword anew, Wagner employs it in this generalised sense. But in so far as the hammering is done in the *Rhinegold* by the Nibelungs the figure can with equal legitimacy be taken as *their* characteristic motive. It is an admirably malleable piece of musical material; it easily passes from the primarily rhythmical to the harmonic, and as easily combines with other motives, as in the following example at the point we have now reached:

No. 33

where, in the lower part, the lament of the enslaved Nibelungs is heard piercing through the rhythm of their hammering.

We can coldly dissect this orchestral interlude for purposes of anatomical demonstration, but it is an organic musical structure, developing according to its own laws at the same time that it tells in graphic form the story of the Gods' journey. After Wotan and

Loge have plunged into the fissure and disappeared from our sight a sulphurous vapour spreads rapidly over the stage in dense clouds. These ascend for a while, ultimately revealing a dark, solid rocky chasm which appears to be moving continuously upward, creating in the spectator the illusion that the stage is sinking deeper and deeper. Wotan and Loge, still unseen by us, are evidently nearing Nibelheim: a dark red glow becomes visible at various points in the distance, and on all sides we hear the clang of smithing: at the point denoted by our No. 33 the purely musical texture is reinforced by the smithing rhythm hammered out on eighteen anvils behind the scenes. The din increases, rising to a climax, and gradually dies away; and at last our eyes distinguish a great subterranean cavern that opens out on all sides into narrow shafts.

12

To graphic orchestral figures Alberich now appears, dragging his shrieking brother Mime out of one of the clefts in the rock. Mime, most skilful of smiths among the Nibelungs, has been trying a little sharp practice. Alberich has the Ring, which gives him the power to force his fellow-gnomes to tear the Gold out of the bowels of the earth for him. But what if Mime, whose cunning he knows well, should decoy him into some trap or other, or rob him of the Ring when he is asleep? To guard against this, Alberich has ordered him to make him a helmet which, he hopes, will enable him to be everywhere and at all times among his slaves, himself unseen, keeping them to their work, and secure against surprise when he sleeps. He knows, or strongly suspects, that Mime's craft has been equal to the task, but that he is concealing the Tarnhelm, hoping to use it himself to overcome his stronger brother. So now Alberich is urging the dwarf, with threats and blows, to give it up to him. Between his shrieks for mercy Mime makes stumbling excuses: the work is indeed finished, he admits, but he has been holding it back to see if it can be improved upon in any way. In his fright he lets the little piece of delicate metal work fall from his hand. Alberich pounces on it and examines it closely: it is the Tarnhelm, the characteristic motive of which, charged with mystery, is given out softly by the muted horns:

No. 34

It is quoted here in its full form. Only the first half of it is breathed by the orchestra as Alberich takes the work in his hand and studies it critically: the second section, from A onwards (where we see the so-called motive of Servitude in the upper part), appears a little later, when he places the object on his head and tests its powers by murmuring a spell: "Night and darkness — nowhere seen!" At once, to Mime's astonishment, Alberich disappears, only a cloud of vapour appearing where he had been standing. "Where art thou? I see thee not!" says Mime. "Then feel me, idle rogue!" replies Alberich; and we see the dwarf writhing under the blows from an invisible scourge.

Sure of himself now, Alberich, still invisible, imperiously apostrophises the Nibelung hordes: let them all kneel to him as their master, for now everywhere, at all times, himself unseen, he will be among them, keeping them to their work; slaves will they be to him for ever. The column of vapour that is Alberich disappears towards the back of the stage, and we hear his roaring and cursing receding into the distance; howls and shrieks come from the lower depths and die away from point to point as he makes his way further through the earth; and the hammering Nibelung rhythm in fortissimo combination with the Servitude motive (as in No. 33) tells us that the cowed slaves are being driven with a scourge to their work.

Mime has sunk to the ground in pain and terror; there, groaning and wailing, he is found by Wotan and Loge, who now enter on the scene from one of the clefts. Loge sets the whimpering dwarf on his feet again, and he tells them his sad story — how his brother Alberich had forged a Ring from the ravished Rhinegold and subdued the whole race of Nibelungs, who had once been so innocently happy working for themselves and making trinkets and toys for their womenfolk. Now this brutal brother of his has made vassals of them all: by virtue of the Ring he senses where gold lies, and for him they have to trace and track it, and dig and melt it, and cast it into bars and heap it in mounds. Mime he had compelled to make for him a magic helm, knowing the properties of which he, Mime, had intended to keep it for himself, to escape from servitude, and, perhaps, seize the Ring and so have Alberich in his power. But alas, though his craft was equal to making the object he did not know the spell that alone could animate it; and so it is now Alberich's, who had scourged him cruelly and vanished from his sight: "such thanks for my toil, poor fool, I won!" The opening words of Mime's narrative are accompanied by a figure in thirds in the bassoons:

No. 35

which will be used later by Wagner (in *Siegfried*) to depict the dwarf once more brooding upon the problems that confront him. It is generally referred to as the motive of Reflection.

The newcomers laugh at the lament of the grotesque little figure. This perplexes him, and he looks at them more attentively. Who are they? he asks. Friends, they assure him, who have come to set the Nibelungs free. But just then Alberich is heard approaching, and Mime runs hither and thither in helpless terror: "have a care", he tells them, "for Alberich nears." "Here will we await him", says Wotan tranquilly. He seats himself on a stone; Loge leans by his side. To the dual strains of No. 33 Alberich enters, now in his own shape again, with the Tarnhelm hung on his girdle, driving before him, with a whip, a multitude of Nibelungs who run up from the cave below: they are laden with gold and silver work of all kinds, which, under the compulsion of the whip, they pile up in a huge mound. Suddenly Alberich catches sight of

Wotan and Loge and halts suspiciously. With his scourge he drives Mime into the mass of the other Nibelungs, bidding them all get on with their tasks. He draws the Ring from his finger, kisses it, and stretches it out threateningly towards them as the orchestra gives out the Ring motive followed by that of Servitude:

No. 36

Loitering yet?
Linger ye still?
Tremble in terror,
down-trodden host!
Quick to obey
the Ring's great lord!

The gnomes, Mime among them, scatter in all directions, howling and shrieking, into the shafts.

13

Alberich scans the intruders warily and asks who they are and what they are doing here. Wotan tells him that they have come to see for themselves the wonders that have reached their ears of the great achievements of Alberich. To an angry outburst from the gnome, Loge replies that he should treat his guests with more courtesy. Who is it but he, Loge, who brings light and comforting warmth to the imp as he crouches in his sunless cave? Where would he be with his forging did not Loge light his fires? "I am thy kinsman and was thy friend: not lavish art thou with thy thanks." Alberich, however, is not to be duped by cajoleries. Loge was always false, he rejoins; once, it is true, he was his friend, but now he consorts with the light-elves [1] who dwell above: is he false to them too? But Alberich has no fear of him or them: do they see the Hoard that his host of toilers has heaped up for him over there?

[1] Lichtalben, the Gods: Alberich himself is a Schwarzalb, a black-elf.

And "that's only for today, a paltry measure. Day by day it shall increase my glory": and the sinister motive of the Hoard wells up in the depths of the orchestra in bassoon and bass clarinet:

No. 37

But what use is all this wealth to him, Wotan asks, here in joyless Nibelheim, where his treasure can buy him nothing? The treasure itself is something, Alberich replies; but it is more than its mere self — by means of it he will bend the whole world to his will. The beings who dwell in the upper air live, laugh and love, lapped in gentlest zephyrs (here the orchestra gives out the motive (No. 15) associated with Freia and her gracious charm); but he will wrench all this happiness from their grasp and make the Gods themselves his vassals. He himself has forsworn love, and at his bidding everything that has life shall forswear it too; by gold overpowered, for gold alone shall they yet hunger. There on the radiant mountain heights (here the Walhall motive rises in serene majesty in the orchestra) dwell the Gods in bliss, despising the black-elves below. But let them beware:

> *For first ye men*
> *shall bow to my might,*
> *then your winsome women,*
> *who my wooing despise,*
> *shall sate the lust of the dwarf,*
> *though love they deny . . .*
> *Beware of the night-nurtured host*
> *when the Nibelung Hoard shall uprise*
> *from silent deeps to the day!*

He is an impressive figure, the incarnation of envy and hatred and evil will, a force which Gods and men will have to reckon with.

He laughs savagely in Wotan's face. The outraged God vents his disgust on him, but Loge, stepping between them, counsels him to control his anger. Then he turns to Alberich with his usual smooth assurance. Who could fail to feel wonder, he asks, when faced by Alberich's wonderful work? If his craft can perform all he claims for it, what limit is there to his future power? Sun, moon and stars will all have to bow down before it. Yet, he deferentially hints, there may be just one thing it were wise to take into his calculations — the Nibelung host who are heaping up this treasure for him may possibly become envious of him and it; and by the slightest of harmonic turns to the Nibelung motive Wagner suggests the danger that may be lurking for Alberich in the dark places of Nibelheim:

No. 38

When he had held up the Ring to the gnomes, continues Loge, they had cowered before him. But what if a thief were to steal on him in his sleep and rob him of the Ring? What counter has he to that?

14

Alberich's vanity makes him fall into the trap. Loge flatters himself he is the cunning one, he says, but in his conceit he deems others witless. He, Alberich, had been clever enough to foresee the danger his kind friend has pointed out to him, and had provided against it. He has made the skilful Mime fashion for him the helm that is now hanging from his girdle, which enables him to change his shape or be invisible at will:

> *No one sees me,*
> *though he may seek;*
> *yet everywhere am I,*
> *though veiled from the view.*
> *So, free from care,*
> *I live secure, safe from thy craft,*
> *thou good, kind-hearted friend!*

Of all the many marvels he has met with on earth, replies Loge, this is the greatest. If Alberich speaks the truth, eternal might is indeed his. But who could believe in such a wonder except on the evidence of his own eyes? The vain gnome is willing and eager to prove it. What shape would Loge like him to assume? Loge has no choice, provided only the deed confirms the word. Alberich places the Tarnhelm on his head, murmurs a spell — "Dragon dread, turn thee and wind thee" — to the strain of No. 34, and instantly disappears: in his stead is a huge serpent writhing on the ground and stretching out its gaping jaws towards each of the Gods in turn:

No. 39

Loge pretends to be paralysed with terror; "Spare the life of poor Loge!" he cries. Wotan breaks into hearty laughter and compliments the gnome with an ironic "Good, Alberich! How wondrous quick the dwarf changed to a dragon!" The serpent vanishes and Alberich reappears in his own form, saying complacently "Hoho! ye wise ones! do ye believe me now?"

In a quaking voice Loge assures him that scepticism is no longer possible. Alberich has indeed changed himself into a big snake; but can he also accomplish the correspondingly small? That, surely, would be even more serviceable, for in case of danger he could slip away more easily. "As you will", says the vainglorious Alberich; "how small?" "Tiny enough", Loge replies, "to creep into the sort of crevice a toad makes for in its flight." "Pah! nought simpler!". The spell is murmured once more — "Crooked toad, grovel and crawl"; and in the gnome's place appears a toad. At a quick word from Loge, Wotan puts his foot on it; Loge takes it by the head and seizes the Tarnhelm, whereupon Alberich instantly becomes visible again in his own form, writhing helplessly under Wotan's foot and crying curses on him. Loge binds him hand and foot with a rope; despite his struggles he is dragged to the shaft by which the Gods had entered, and the three of them disappear, the orchestra breaking out into a jubilant fantasia on the Walhall motive, that of Loge (No. 22), and that of the Ring (No. 8). The triumph of the Gods seems complete.

The scenery now changes as before, but in the reverse order, as though Wotan and Loge were ascending. The motive of the Renunciation of Love is heard in quiet trombone tones: then, as the Gods may be supposed to be making their way past the forges, the Nibelung rhythm is heard once more hammering out on the anvils, but gradually sounding further and further away. For a moment the Freia motive rings out, as if announcing the triumphant return of the Gods from their mission, but, it is to be observed, in darker harmonies, hinting that there may be another side to the picture than the one on which the Gods' complacent gaze is just then fastened. The tone-painting continues with the motives of (a) the Giants, (b) Walhall, (c) Servitude, (d) Loge, (e) Freia's youthful charm, (f) the Rhinemaidens, and finally Servitude in the form (No. 30) in which, at the beginning of the previous scene, it had symbolised the subjection of the Nibelungs to Alberich. Now he himself is at the bottom of Fortune's wheel.

When at last the stage setting defines itself again we see the mountain height once more, still shrouded in the pale mist that had descended on it after the departure of the Giants with Freia. Wotan and Loge emerge from the shaft, dragging with them the bound Alberich. Loge loads him with sarcasms. "There, kinsman, take thou thy seat. Look, my worthy, there lies the world thou longedst to have for thy own: what corner wilt thou give me for my stall?" He dances round him in glee, snapping his fingers at him. Alberich curses him for a rogue and a robber and demands to be set free. His freedom he shall have, rejoins Loge, when he has paid ransom. The dwarf turns furiously on himself for his folly: "O thou dolt, thou credulous fool! to trust blindly this treacherous thief!"; and he vows revenge on his captors.

Wotan tells him what his ransom is to be — nothing less than his Hoard. Harsh as the terms are, Alberich, in an aside, comforts himself with the thought that if only he can save the Ring he can re-create the treasure, and the lesson will not have been too dearly bought if it teaches him to be wiser in future. He will summon the Gold for them, he says, if they will untie his hand. Loge sets his right hand free. The gnome puts the Ring to his lips and murmurs a secret command: a soft mysterious breathing of the

Ring motive in the orchestra is succeeded by the motive of Servitude in the dominating form it has assumed in No. 36: there is a moment of fateful silence, then we hear the various motives associated with the Nibelungs as slaves of Alberich. These sounds grow louder as the Nibelungs approach and at last pour on to the scene, running out from the clefts and bringing with them the Gold and treasures of all kinds that constitute the Hoard, which they pile up on the stage. Alberich, impressive even in defeat, writhes at the thought that his vassals should see him thus shamed, in bonds. Imperiously he orders them to be quick with their work and keep their eyes off him:

> *Then hence with you, rabble,*
> *haste to your tasks!*
> *Back to your burrows!*
> *Woe if idlers I find,*
> *for I follow hard at your heels!*

He kisses his Ring and holds it out commandingly. "As if he had struck them a blow", say the stage directions, "the Nibelungs rush in terror to the cleft, into which they gradually disappear below." This is one of the most tremendous episodes in the score, with the orchestra thundering out No. 36 in the loudest tones of trumpets and trombones.

16

The turmoil having died away, Alberich demands that he be released and allowed to take with him the Tarnhelm that Loge has thrown on the Hoard. The God contemptuously replies that this is part of the ransom. Alberich curses him, but then reflects that "he who made the one can make me another: still mine is the might that Mime obeys." Loge asks Wotan if he shall release their captive. But Wotan now demands also the Ring that gleams on the dwarf's finger. "My life take, but not the Ring!" cries Alberich in desperation. For life, he says, means nothing to him without it: hand and head, eye and ear, are not his more truly than this Ring. Sternly and bitingly Wotan asks him how he came to possess it. How did he get the Gold from which it is made? Was it not by theft from the Rhinemaidens? To Alberich all is now clear: the Gods are using him for a purpose of their own, and one no better essentially than his. "Do you, vile thief", he cries, "cast in my teeth a crime so welcome to you? You yourself would have robbed the Rhine of the Gold had you known how to forge the Ring from it":

> *How well, thou knave,*
> *it worked for thy purpose,*
> *that I, the Niblung,*
> *smarting with shame*
> *and with anger maddened,*
> *the terrible magic did win*
> *whose work now gladdens thy gaze!*
> *This curse-laden*
> *and monstrous deed*
> *of one wild with grief,*
> *wasted with woe,*
> *must now serve as toy*
> *for thy eyes to delight in,*
> *my curse prove a blessing to thee?*
> *Heed thyself,*
> *high-handed God!*
> *If I did sin,*
> *I sinned but against myself:*
> *but against all that was,*
> *is, and shall be,*
> *wilt thou, Wotan, sin,*
> *if basely thou seizest my Ring!*

Wagner, it will be seen, is holding the moral scales fairly between the two. For the first time, the central ethical problem of the great drama comes clearly into sight.

But it is too late now for Wotan, caught as he is in a net of his own weaving, to choose the right; he is irrevocably committed to a course of wrong-doing the consequences of which to himself and all of them he cannot foresee; and it is finely significant that Wagner leaves the fitting-in of this cornerstone of the great moral structure not to Loge — who has hitherto carried on most of the dialogue with Alberich — but to the more responsible Wotan. Ruthlessly he flings himself on the dwarf and tears the Ring from his finger; and while Alberich, with a horrible shriek, bewails his ruin, the God, possessed with but one thought — that of the acquisition of the power he has long desired — places the Ring on his own finger and contemplates it. " 'Tis mine now", he muses, "the spell of might that makes me lord of the world!" Curtly and contemptuously he gives Loge permission now to release the impotent gnome. Loge unties his bonds and tells him to "slip away home", for he is free.

Raising himself from the ground, Alberich echoes the God's last words with a wild laugh. "Am I then free? Really free? Then hearken now to my freedom's first salute!" He begins the tremendous monologue in which he lays a curse upon his lost Ring and upon everyone into whose hands it shall come:

> *As it gave me*
> *measureless might,*
> *let each who holds it*
> *die, slain by its spell!*

To no one on earth shall its radiance bring joy: care shall consume each wretched possessor of it, and envy gnaw at the heart of him who owns it not. No gain shall it bring to anyone, but murder shall follow it wherever it goes: the Ring's lord shall be the Ring's slave, till once more it shall return to Alberich's hands:

> *So, stirred*
> *by the direst need,*
> *the Nibelung blesseth his Ring:*
> *and now 'tis thine,*
> *look to it well!*
> *But my curse canst thou not flee!*

The monologue is dominated by two new motives of great importance in the later unfolding of the *Ring* drama, that of the Annihilation prophesied by Alberich:

No.40

and that of the Curse on the Ring:

No. 41

With a demoniacal laugh Alberich disappears into the cleft.

17

"The art of composition", said Wagner once, "is the art of transition". We have one of many examples of his own gift in this respect in the scene that follows Alberich's exit. The furious repetitions of the Servitude motive in the orchestra die down gradually into a succession of falling arpeggios that finally poise themselves on a few quiet, broad harmonies. "Didst thou hear his fond farewell?" asks the cynical Loge. "Let him enjoy his own slaver", Wotan replies quietly, lost in dreams as he contemplates the Ring on his finger. As the light slowly increases a series of tranquil harmonies ascending slowly in the orchestra depicts his satisfaction. But underneath them we hear pulsing insistently the rhythm of the motive of the Giants; and Loge, looking off stage, descries them in the distance, returning with Freia.

But for the present there is no cloud on the bland peace of the scene and the music. The mists disperse still further as Fricka, Froh and Donner enter. Fricka runs to Wotan and asks him anxiously for news of his mission. His answer is to point to the Hoard: "By force and guile our end we gained: there lies Freia's ransom"; but the muttering of the fateful Annihilation motive in the orchestra tells us something he himself, in his self-centred blindness, has not realised yet — that the Fates are brooding over the too complacent God, only waiting their opportunity to strike him down. Froh draws in a breath of ecstatic relief: how lovely is the smile of the earth, he says, how balmy the breeze; what would the Gods be without Freia and the "painless perpetual youth" she bestows on them?

As the light grows clearer still the Gods are seen recovering their old freshness of aspect; the castle, however, remains invisible in the mist that spreads over the Rhine and the heights beyond. (Wagner, like the good stage-craftsman he is, is reserving the sight of resplendent Walhall for a great dramatic stroke in the final moments of the opera). Fasolt and Fafner enter, bringing with them Freia, who runs to Fricka with a cry of joy. But Fasolt steps between them. Not yet, he reminds them, is she theirs; grieving he has brought her back to them; let the Gods now pay the price agreed on for her. Fasolt heaves a sigh: to part with Freia saddens his heart, but if he must lose her, at least let the treasure be heaped so high as to hide her from his sight. To this Wotan consents. The two Giants place Freia in the centre of the stage, and thrust their staves in the ground on either side of her so as to measure her height and breadth. Wotan, sick with a sense of soilure and degradation, bids them get on with their work. Assisted by Loge and Froh — the latter as anxious as Wotan to put an end to Freia's shame and theirs — the Giants heap up the treasure between the two poles, Fafner, in his greed for gold, roughly pressing the pile more tightly together and searching for crevices.

Wotan turns away in profound dejection: "Deep in my breast burns this disgrace!" he mutters. Fricka pours reproaches on him for his ambitious folly. "More! yet more!" cries Fafner. Donner rounds on him furiously, threatening him with his hammer; Wotan tries to pacify him, and Loge assures the Giants that the Hoard has given out. But Fafner, peering more closely, catches a glimpse of Freia's golden hair and demands that the Tarnhelm be thrown in to hide it. Wotan, more than ever weary of it all, tells Loge to add it to the pile. Fasolt, still grieving over the loss of Freia, peers more closely at the heap, and, as the orchestra gives out the gracious melody of No. 19, discovers a crevice through which he can still see her eye shining on him: "while its soft beauty doth charm me", he cries, "from the woman I cannot part." Loge protests that the Hoard is quite exhausted; but Fafner points to the golden Ring on Wotan's finger and demands that it shall go to stop the crevice. Loge assures him that Wotan intends to return it to the Rhinemaidens from whom the Gold was ravished; but Wotan swears vehemently that the prize he has won so hardly he will not part with. "But what of my promise to the Rhinedaughters?" asks the crafty, insincere Loge. "Thy promise binds me not;" rejoins Wotan: "the Ring I claim as my own. Boldly ask what ye will", he says to Fafner; "all else I'll give to you; but for all the world will I not surrender the Ring."

18

Fasolt's angry reply to this is to pull Freia out from behind the pile. "We end, then, where we began", he cries; "Freia is forfeit to us for ever!" He makes to leave the scene, but is held back by Fafner. Freia, Fricka, Donner and Froh appeal to Wotan to relent, but he is immovable: he is too deep now in the pit of his own digging to extricate himself by his own efforts. "Leave me in peace", he says moodily; "the Ring I will not yield!" And he turns away from them all in blind, futile anger. The knot of the drama cannot be untied now, but only cut; and that is done by the intervention of a world force greater even than the chief of the Gods himself.

By this time the stage has become quite dark again, and from the rocky cleft at the side there now breaks forth a bluish light, in which Erda suddenly becomes visible, rising from below the ground to half her height. She is the earth Goddess, the mother of the Norns who weave the threads of the world's destiny. Wagner symbolises her primal and eternal quality by a hardly perceptible but curiously significant mutation of the motive of primordial matter with which the opera had begun. (See examples No. 1 and No. 2). The theme is now in the minor, in the grave colours, first of all, of bassoon and tuba, and in a slow tempo:

The Gods stand awed and mute at the sight of this apparition. Erda stretches out her hand commandingly to Wotan and bids him relinquish the Ring and so evade the curse that lies on it; nothing but disaster will it bring him. "Who is the woman who brings me this warning?" he mutters. She tells him: "Whatever was, know I, whatever is, whatever shall be, I can see. The eternal world's Urwala,[1] Erda, 'tis who warns thee." By the most natural of transitions No. 42 resolves itself back again into No. 2:

as she tells him of the three daughters born to her before the earth was made; all that her eyes see is told to him nightly by the Norns. She has come to him now because he is in dire danger (here No. 40 projects its sinister shadow in the orchestra). "Hear me! Hear me!" she urges, to the falling figure seen in the bass part of No. 33 and the first bar of No. 36; "all that exists must come to an end. A day of gloom dawns for the Gods: again I charge thee, give up the Ring!" At this point a new motive appears, that of the Twilight of the Gods:

which concept Wagner symbolises by a simple reversal of No. 43. "Grave and mysterious are thy words", says Wotan thoughtfully; "tarry a while and tell me more that I would know." But already the bluish light has begun to fade, and Erda slowly disappears, with no further message for the tortured God than this: "I have warned thee; thou hast learned enough; brood now in care and fear." Wotan makes a desperate move to follow her into the cleft and ask her the meaning of this enigma: if henceforth he is to live in anxious fear, he cries, she must at least tell him all. But Froh and Fricka hold him back.

[1] It is as the Wala that Wotan invokes her in the first scene of the third act of *Siegfried*, "the eternal woman possessed of all the world's wisdom". Wagner seems to have taken over this concept from two of the Edda poems, the *Vegtamskvida* and *Balder's Doom*. More will be said on this point when we come to the *Siegfried* scene.

The God halts and stares thoughtfully before him, then turns resolutely to the Giants; they shall have their Gold, he tells them. We see him brooding profoundly on Erda's last words as No. 42 wells up in sombre orchestral colours. Then, rousing himself from his abstraction, he brandishes his spear as if he had taken a bold resolution, the trombones thundering out the commanding No. 13. Freia shall return to them, he says, bringing them their youth once more: the Giants can take the Ring and go. He throws it on the Hoard; Freia runs to the Gods, and the orchestra becomes all gladness and light as they load her with caresses. That Wagner, as a composer, was still to some extent the Wagner of *Tannhäuser* and *Lohengrin* is shown by the following phrase expressive of rejoicing:

No.45

Meanwhile Fafner has spread out an enormous sack, into which he begins to pack the Hoard. At once the Giants begin to quarrel over it. Fasolt demands measure for measure; Fafner reminds him that

> *More on the maid than the Gold*
> *thy lovesick eyes were set;*
> *I scarce could bring thee,*
> *fool, to exchange her;*
> *hadst thou won Freia,*
> *no share to me hadst thou given:*
> *now with the Hoard*
> *rightly retain I*
> *the greater half for myself.*

The sordid wrangle goes on. Fasolt appeals to the Gods for justice, but Wotan contemptuously turns his back on him. "Resign the treasure", Loge counsels Fasolt, "but make thyself sure of the Ring". The Annihilation motive (No. 40) mutters ominously in the depths of the orchestra, but Fasolt knows nothing of Alberich's curse. He throws himself on his brother, insisting on the Ring as compensation for Freia. They struggle for it, each seizing it in turn. At last Fafner fells Fasolt to the ground with a blow from his staff and wrenches the Ring from the dying Giant's hand: "Now glut thee with Freia's glance", he tells him grimly, "for the Ring seest thou no more!" He puts it on his finger and goes on quietly with his packing of the Hoard: the Gods stand around in horror-struck silence, and the Curse motive (No. 41) rends the air in the trombones. Alberich's curse has struck already, Wotan remarks in awed tones.

Loge, to the sinister throbbing of No. 40 in violas and bassoons, congratulates him on a good fortune with which nothing on earth can compare: great had been his luck when he won the Ring from Alberich, but greater still now he has lost it, for those who won it fight to the death for it. But one thought only is in Wotan's brooding mind. Live a slave to fear and care he cannot: how to end them no one knows but Erda, so to her he must descend. While the clarinets give out a reminiscence of the caressing No. 14 Fricka approaches him cajolingly: why does he not enter the noble fortress that awaits his coming? she asks him. "With evil wage I bought me that!" he answers sombrely.

The air is cleared by Donner, who, oppressed like the rest of them by the sweltering mists that envelop them, ascends a high rock that overhangs the valley, swings his hammer, and bids them disperse. Through swirling clouds of vapour a mighty horn call tears its way:

No. 46

He - da! He - da! He-do! Zu mir, du Ge-düft!
To me, all ye mists!

A vivid storm-picture ends in a convulsion, as it seems, of all nature as Donner crashes the hammer down on the rock and a blinding flash of lightning bursts from the clouds, followed by a violent thunderclap. For a moment Donner and Froh — the latter has run to his brother's side at his call — are invisible to the others. Then, almost in a moment, the clouds disperse; and when the pair become visible again we see, gleaming in the sunlight, a great rainbow bridge which they have thrown across the valley for the transit of the Gods to Walhall. During this storm episode Fafner has completed his packing up of the whole Hoard, and departed with the great sack on his back.

With the Rainbow motive:

No. 47

rising up from the depths of the orchestra in a great span, Froh points out to the others the way over the rainbow arch to the fortress where they can live henceforth, free of the terror that has descended upon them since the murderous strife over the Ring and Erda's solemn warning. The noble Walhall theme (No. 11) peals out in full splendour as the Gods gaze at the wonderful sight in speechless astonishment. Then, in a great lyrical harangue, Wotan greets the castle which that morning, lordless as it was then, had beckoned to him. From morn to eve, consumed with care, he had worked to make it his own; and now, as night is about to fall, he will enter its mighty walls to find shelter from his own troubled thoughts.

20

Suddenly a great idea strikes him. Snatching up a sword that had formed part of the treasure and had been left behind by Fafner, he hails the fortress, the trumpet giving out the last new motive of the *Rhinegold* score, that of the Sword:

No. 48

(In the stage directions in the score no provision had been made for this culminating point of the action; presumably Wagner's intention had been that Wotan should simply hail the castle with a gesture. But at the Bayreuth rehearsals of 1876 this course must have struck him as inadequate; and it was then that he hit upon the device with which we are now familiar). He turns slowly to Fricka, bidding her follow him into Walhall, there to dwell with him. What is the meaning of the name? she asks. His answer is en-

igmatic, because he himself is not yet sure what course he must
pursue to win back the Ring or frustrate the evil use of it:

> *What strength 'gainst my fears*
> *my spirit has found,*
> *when vict'ry is mine,*
> *maketh the meaning clear:*

but the ultimate meaning of it will be revealed to us in the later
stages of the drama. Taking Fricka by the hand, with all the others, except Loge, following him, he goes slowly towards the rainbow bridge.

But the last word is not to be with him, nor is the last thought
left in our minds to be that of Walhall and its supposed security.
First of all Loge turns the cold light of reason on it all. "They are
hastening to their end", he muses, "though they deem themselves
strong and enduring." As for himself he is ashamed to share any
more in their activities: he would prefer to transform himself
once more into a wayward flickering fire,

> *to burn and waste them*
> *who once held me bound,*
> *rather than blindly*
> *end with the blind,*
> *e'en were they of Gods the most godlike.*

He will think it over, he concludes; and putting on a careless manner he is about to rejoin the Gods when from the depths of the
valley comes the haunting song of the invisible Rhinemaidens. In
the first scene of the opera they had greeted the Gold with cries
of innocent joy. Now they look back sadly to the days when it was
theirs and pure: " Give us the Gold", they cry: "Oh give us its
glory again!"

The sound reaches Wotan's ear as he is about to set foot on the
bridge. Turning round, he asks who are these whose plaint ascends
to him. It is the Rhinechildren, Loge tells him, lamenting over the
stolen Gold. "Accursed nixies!" says Wotan: "stay them from pestering me!" Loge, calling down into the water, gives them the
message in his own ironical form:

> *Why wail ye to us?*
> *Hear what Wotan doth will!*

Gleams no more
on you maidens the Gold;
in the Gods' recovered glory
bask ye henceforth in bliss!

The Gods laugh at his humour and begin to pass over the bridge.
The Rhinemaidens break into a more poignant lament, ending
with

Tender and true
'tis but in the waters:
false and base
are those who revel above!

But the only response is the Walhall motive, growing more brilliant and more imposing bar by bar in the orchestra; and accompanied by a final *fff* restatement of the Rainbow motive the Gods
cross the bridge and the curtain falls.

It has been truly said that this final scene has a parallel in the
conclusion of the *Agamemnon* of Aeschylus. The murder of Agamemnon has been accomplished; Aegisthus and Clytemnestra confront the Chorus, angrily sure of themselves now and of the future, and the last word is given to the hard and ruthless Queen:
"Heed them not; let the pack growl as it will; thou and I will rule
the palace." But the Chorus has already hinted presciently at what
may happen some day if Orestes should return with vengeance in
his soul. In the *Rhinegold* Wotan and the Gods enter Walhall confident that henceforth they will be secure; but the doom foreseen
by the cynical Loge will for all that fall on them in the end.

The Valkyrie

THE COMPOSITION of the *Rhinegold* had thoroughly subdued Wagner's hand to the new kind of material he had come to work in. The result was that in the *Valkyrie* the musician in him opened out in all directions: he abandoned himself luxuriously to the sheer joy of music-making, both enlarging the scale of his design for each episode and delighting in fine filigree work from bar to bar; at the same time he has acquired a completer command of what is really the whole art of musical-dramatic composition of this kind — making his leading motives serve simultaneously a psychological and a musical purpose, in a more effective way than had been possible for him until now.

We have seen, at the end of the *Rhinegold*, a sobered, thoughtful Wotan retiring into Walhall, there to discover, if he can, some way of escape from the doom with which the curse on the Ring threatens the Gods. Wagner does not tell us directly, as yet, what has happened during the years that have elapsed between the last scene of the *Rhinegold* and the beginning of the *Valkyrie;* we learn that gradually as the action unfolds itself. Briefly, Wotan has realised that if an end is to be put to the evil that has stemmed inexorably, and will continue to stem, from the theft of the Gold from the Rhine, the concentration of its power in the Ring, and the curse that the frustrated Alberich has laid on this, the Ring must be returned to the primal innocence of the waters whence it had been ravished. As Wotan cannot deprive Fafner of it by force — for that would be to repeat the wrong he himself had committed by taking it from Alberich — the only hope for salvation for Gods and men resides in someone who, all unknowing, shall take on him the burden and the guilt of the Gods, winning the Ring for himself without their prompting yet remaining wholly ignorant of the power for evil that inheres in it; until, in some way or other which perhaps Wotan himself does not see clearly as yet, it will pass into the possession of the Rhinemaidens again. Wotan's first step towards the achievement of his aim has consequently been to create a race of heroes one of whom, by his own strength and virtue alone, will do what the Gods themselves are barred from doing. So Wotan has gone among men and allied himself with a mortal woman, a Volsung, by whom he has had twin children, Siegmund and Sieglinde. The former, he hopes, may be the instrument destined to accomplish the Gods' desire.

The opera opens with a great storm picture, in which we hear or see by turns the persistent bass of the storm wind:

No. 49

the crash of thunder, the lightning rending the clouds, and the furious swirling of the rain. The motive of Donner as the God of thunder (No. 46) peals out in the angriest tones of the heavy brass, and in the way in which Wagner combines this with the bass of No. 49 and the scurrying figures suggestive of wind and rain we see him already, before the new work is more than a few minutes old, on his way to that expressive contrapuntal handling of his thematic material that will become a more and more pronounced feature of the *Ring* scores.

As the storm shows signs of dying down in the 'cellos and basses the curtain rises on the interior of the forest dwelling of a Neiding warrior, Hunding. The room is built round the trunk of a mighty ash-tree which occupies the centre of it. In the foreground, to the right, is the hearth, behind which is a store-room. The great entrance door to the dwelling is at the back of the stage. On the left, steps lead up to an inner chamber. In the foreground, to the left, stands a table, behind which is a broad bench let into the wall, with some wooden seats in front of it.

2

The storm subsides to the last distant growlings of No. 49, which now flows quite naturally into:

No. 50

— the characteristic motive of Siegmund, who stumbles into the room through the great door giving on the forest. For a moment he stands immobile with his hand on the latch, looking warily round him: his appearance and his garb both suggest flight and suffering: his distress is particularly portrayed in the figure shown in the third bar of No. 50. As will be seen, it takes the form of those falling seconds which Wagner, in common with other composers, uses so frequently to express pain of body or soul that it is quite unwarrantable to pin them down rigidly to anyone or anything particular in the drama. Perceiving that for the moment, at any rate, he is safe from his pursuers, Siegmund closes the door behind him, staggers towards the hearth, and throws himself on a rug of bear-skin, saying wearily, "Whose hearth this may be, here must I rest me." He sinks back exhausted and remains motionless.

To the accompaniment of a final muttering of the storm Sieglinde enters from the inner chamber, imagining the newcomer to be her husband Hunding returned from the forest. Her mien is sombre; but her look changes to one of surprise when she sees a stranger stretched out on the hearth. Who can this weary one be, she asks herself, the orchestra giving out softly the motive shown in the bass of No. 50. As she bends over him to discover if he is still breathing, a wave of tenderness and pity sweeps over her:

No. 51

and in Wagner's combination of this with the Siegmund motive we once more see him using thematic counterpoint for the fusion of a musical and a psychological purpose.

It is left to the orchestra to express all the tenderness the sight of the weary man has awakened in Sieglinde as she goes out with a drinking horn and fills it with cool spring water, which she hands to him. He takes a deep draught of it and returns the horn to her with a glance of silent gratitude. He fixes his gaze on her, feeling dimly that there is a bond of sympathy between them that comes from something more than a simple kindness bestowed and accepted; and an expressive 'cello solo carries No. 50 to a new conclusion:

No. 52

that indicates the dawning of something like love between them. The two limbs of this motive, marked A and B, will become the material for a great symphonic development in the duet that concludes the first act.

Who is his benefactor? Siegmund asks her. Sadly she replies, "This house and this wife call Hunding master; take thine ease as his guest; tarry till he return." Surely her husband would not deny guest-right to a wounded and weaponless man, says Siegmund. Yet wounded as he is, he is still hale; and as for his weapons, if they had served him as well against his enemies as his arm and his spirit had been willing to do there would have been a different story now to tell. But shield and spear had been shattered in the fight, and the enemy pack had hunted him hard through the tempest. But all that is over now: his weariness has gone, and after the dark night that had fallen on his eyelids there has come the sunlight of the presence and the kindness of this woman. The whole of the orchestral tissue during this episode and what immediately follows is woven out of the tiny motives Nos. 50, 51, and 52; Wagner's new craftsmanship enables him to weave and re-weave them to any extent he desires, and always the mutations of the music go hand in hand with the changing thoughts and emotions of the actors.

3

Going to the store-room, Sieglinde returns with a horn filled with mead, which she offers to Siegmund. He refuses to taste it, however, until her lips have touched it; then he takes a long draught of it, his gaze all the while fixed on her with growing warmth, while the orchestra muses softly upon No. 52 B: something stronger than sympathy and gratitude is beginning to stir in both of them. But the unexpected tenderness that has come suddenly into his life of constant warfare brings Siegmund only pain; and by the tiniest of touches — by introducing a stabbing minor ninth into the harmony — Wagner gives a poignant turn to the original mood of No. 52 A:

No. 53

as Siegmund lowers his gaze gloomily to the ground. "Thou hast solaced an unhappy one", he says in a trembling voice; "sorrow would he ward from thee!"

Declaring himself rested now he starts up and goes to the door, but at a word from her he halts; ill fate, he warns her, pursues him wherever he goes, and he would not bring unhappiness on her and her house by staying. He raises the latch, but at an impulsive cry from her of "Abide thou here! No ill fate canst thou bring where ill fate has made its home!" he looks searchingly into her face, and, reading what he does there as she lowers her eyes confusedly and sadly, he returns to her. The sorrow-laden motive of the Volsungs' Woe:

No. 54

wells up in the orchestra, followed by that of Sieglinde's pity (No. 51) and that of Siegmund (No. 50). " 'Woeful' ", he says, is my own name for myself; Hunding here I will await." He leans against the hearth, looking intently at her with calm sympathy. She turns her gaze on him again, and during a long silence, during which the orchestra muses softly on the motives associated with the pair, they look into each other's eyes with an expression of deepest emotion.

Suddenly an ominous figure in the horns:

No. 55

announces the nearing of Hunding, who is heard outside, leading his horse to the stable. Sieglinde, recalled with a start to reality, goes to the door and opens it; and Hunding enters, armed with shield and spear, the orchestra thundering out his motive, which is as dark and dour as the man himself:

No. 56

Catching sight of a stranger, Hunding turns to Sieglinde with a look of stern enquiry. She explains that she had found the man on their hearth, faint and weary, and had tended him as guest. Siegmund has been looking hard at Hunding all this while: "Rest and drink the woman has given me", he says; "wilt thou chide her therefor?" "Sacred is my hearth", replies Hunding, "sacred hold thou my house"; and doffing his armour and handing it to Sieglinde he bids her set out the meal. She hangs the arms on the branches of the ash-tree, then brings food and drink from the store-room and prepares the table for supper. While doing so she involuntarily turns her eyes on Siegmund again, the orchestra giving out softly but with intensity Nos. 51 and 52 A.

Intercepting the glance, Hunding scans Siegmund's features keenly, and then, with some surprise, compares them with those of Sieglinde. "How like the two are", he says in an aside, "and in his eye too there gleams all the guile of the serpent." Concealing his astonishment, however, he turns once more with an assumption of unconcern to Siegmund, who, in reply to his enquiry, tells him that he had made his way thither through field and forest, bramble and brake, driven by storm and direst need: his way he had lost, nor does he know where he now is. Motioning to him to take his place at the table, his host tells him that he is under the roof of Hunding, whose kinsmen hold sway over all the lands around. And now, what is the name of this guest of his? The bass clarinet gives out the darkened outline of No. 54, to which the wood wind reply softly with No. 51 and No. 52 B as Sieglinde's eyes turn in tender sympathy to Siegmund, who is apparently reluctant to answer. Perhaps he would not deny the woman here, his wife? says Hunding, whose eyes have never left the pair: "see how eagerly she asks." Sieglinde, at once embarrassed and interested, asks the question on her own account, and Siegmund begins his story, which is prefaced by the motive of the Volsungs' Woe (No. 54) in the 'cellos.

4

Neither "Peaceful" (Friedmund) nor "Joyful" (Frohwalt) can he call himself, Siegmund says, but rather "Woeful" (Wehwalt). His father was named Wolfe, and he himself had a twin sister; but mother and sister he had lost so young that he had hardly known either of them. Wolfe was strong and warlike, and of enemies he had many. One day father and boy had returned from their hunting to find the wolf's nest empty: the hall was in ashes, the great oak-tree only a stump; the mother lay dead, the sister had vanished without leaving a trace; and it was the brood of the

Neidings that had wrought this ruin and woe. (Here the orchestra gives out the Hunding motive). After that, father and son had lived year in year out the life of the hunted, but always they were formidable in fight. "A Wölfing it is", Siegmund concludes, "who tells thee this. As Wölfing is he well known."

Wolfe and Wölfing he has never known, says Hunding, but of the warrior pair he has heard much talk. Urged on by Sieglinde, Siegmund continues his story. One day the Neidings had made a furious onslaught on them. Well the pair had fought, and the foe had been scattered in flight. But the boy had been separated from his father, and nowhere could he come upon his traces: "only a wolf-skin found I deep in the forest; my father never more did I find"; and the orchestra, with the softest of reminiscences of the Wotan-Walhall motive from the *Rhinegold* (No. 11), tells us who this Wolfe had been. Then Siegmund had left the forest behind him and fared among men and women; but where'er he went, whatever he did, no friends, no trust, could he find:

> *Ill fate lay on me.*
> *Whate'er to me seemed right,*
> *others reckoned it ill;*
> *what I held to be foul,*
> *others counted as fair.*
> *In feuds I fell*
> *wherever I dwelt,*
> *wrath ever*
> *'gainst me I roused;*
> *sought I for gladness,*
> *found I but grief;*
> *and so must I "Woeful" call me;*
> *for woe still walks in my wake.*

From Sieglinde comes a look of warm understanding, accompanied by a tender breathing of No. 52 B in the orchestra: the grim Hunding merely comments that manifestly the Norns who wove this man's fate had small love for him. At Sieglinde's request Siegmund goes on to tell them how it had come about that he is now hunted and weaponless. A maid in distress had cried to him for help against her brutal kinsmen who wished to give her in a loveless marriage. He had fought and killed her brothers, and then the maiden's wrath against them had turned to grief: she had clasped the bodies in her arms and bathed them in bitter tears. A wailing figure that is repeated several times in the orchestra depicts her grief:

No. 57

The slain men's kindred had gathered from all quarters and fallen on Siegmund and the maid: for as long as he could he had defended her with shield and spear, until at last these were hewn from his hands. The maiden died on her brothers' bodies; he himself, weaponless, had been forced to flee. "Now knowest thou, questioning wife", he concludes, turning a look that is at once sorrowful and ardent on Sieglinde, "why I may not name me 'Joyful' ". Here the orchestra gives out for the first time the important motive of the Volsungs, the tragic race doomed to suffering:

No. 58

He rises and walks to the hearth. Sieglinde, pale and deeply moved, does not raise her sad eyes from the ground. Hunding rises, suppressing his black anger with difficulty. A turbulent breed he knows, he tells Siegmund, hated by all and by him because it holds nothing sacred that others revere. He himself had lately been called upon to take toll for kinsmen's blood that had been shed: he had been too late, but now, when he returns, he finds his flying foeman's traces leading to his own hearth. For this day and the night Siegmund shall have guest-sanctuary, but in the morning he will have to defend himself in combat: "no longer truce I allow; for murder toll will I take." Sieglinde steps anxiously between the two men, but Hunding roughly orders her to leave them; she is to prepare his night-draught and wait for him within.

To a new mutation of her Pity motive (No. 51) in the clarinet (afterwards in the cor anglais):

No. 59

she stands for a while irresolute, then goes with faltering steps towards the store-room; there she pauses again, with half-averted face, as if turning something over in her mind. During the long silence that follows, the orchestra plays softly but significantly with the motives already associated with herself and Siegmund. A purpose seems suddenly to have taken shape within her: with quiet resolution she opens the cupboard, fills a drinking horn, and shakes into it some spices from a box. She looks at Siegmund, whose eyes have never turned away from her. Perceiving that Hunding is watching them intently she goes with the drinking-horn to the inner chamber; but on the steps leading up to it she once more turns round to Siegmund, looks yearningly at him, and then, by the fixity of her gaze at a particular spot in the ash-tree, makes him too look in that direction; and as he does so the Sword motive from the *Rhinegold* (No. 48) peals out, quietly but markedly, first in the bass trumpet, then in the oboe. Hunding, roused from his dark brooding, starts up and makes a violent gesture to her to leave them; and with a last look at Siegmund she goes into the inner chamber. The harsh No. 56 shatters the silence as Hunding takes his weapons down from the tree: with a last ominous word to Siegmund to prepare himself for the combat to the death on the morrow he goes into the chamber, and the bolt is heard shooting from within. Siegmund is left to his own melancholy brooding.

5

By now the room has become quite dark, only a faint glow from the fire enabling us to see him sink despairingly on to the couch by the fire. The Hunding motive, reduced now to not much more than an ominous insistent rhythm, hammers its unrelenting way through what follows, as if it were a thought that allows Siegmund no peace of mind. No. 48 projects itself, still quietly, in the bass trumpet as he begins his long monologue. His father, he recalls bitterly, had promised him that in his direst need he should find a sword; yet now he is weaponless in an enemy's house, a mere hostage awaiting vengeance. A winsome woman has gladdened his eyes, but she is held in thrall by the very man who now mocks his impotence to defend himself. In his frenzy he gives a great cry to the father who seems to have abandoned him:

No. 60

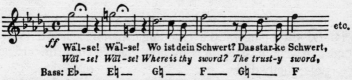

ff Wäl-se! Wäl-se! Wo ist dein Schwert? Das star-ke Schwert,
Wäl-se! Wäl-se! Where is thy sword? The trust-y sword,
Bass: Eb___ E♮___ G♮___ F___ G♮___ F

"Wälse! Wälse! where is now the trusty sword that shall serve me in my need, when the rage that is boiling in my breast shall break forth and consume me?" The trumpet, projecting the Sword motive in a bolder line and a brighter colour than before, gives him the answer as a flicker from the fire on the hearth suddenly lights up the spot in the ash-tree trunk that had been indicated by Sieglinde's parting glance, where the hilt of a sword is now faintly visible. Siegmund does not perceive it as yet; he is intent on the gleam from the hearth, which he sees, in fancy, as the last look of Sieglinde still lingering in the room to gladden his heart:

> *Darkening shadows*
> *sank on mine eyes;*
> *but her lustrous look*
> *fell on me then:*
> *summer and sunlight it brought.*

Wagner now opens the floodgates of his lyrical inspiration, but organically inwrought with the new musical material we hear the Sword motive taking new and gracious shapes:

No. 61

The radiance has departed, sings Siegmund:

> *Yet once more, ere 'twas lost,*
> *fell its light on me here;*
> *e'en the ancient ash-tree's stem*
> *shone forth with a golden glow:*
> *the flush is fading,*
> *the light is low;*
> *darker the shadows*
> *fall on my eyelids:*
> *deep in my heart there glimmers now*
> *but a faint, dying glow.*

The orchestra sinks to a double pianissimo through which only the fateful throbbing of the Hunding rhythm is heard in the kettledrums. The hearth-fire is by now completely extinguished; the stage is wholly dark.

Sieglinde, robed in white, enters and advances lightly and rapidly to the hearth. Hurriedly she bids Siegmund listen to what she has to say to him. Hunding lies in a deep sleep, for she had mingled a drug with his draught. Siegmund is to fly in the night. But first she will show him a sword of might: would that he could make it his! Could he do so she would call him the noblest of heroes, for only the strongest may win it; and a new motive, that of Victory, is heard in the wind, in combination with the theme of the Sword:

No. 62

She tells him how the weapon had come there. At her wedding Hunding's kinsmen had filled the hall, drinking to him and to the maiden who had been shamefully sold to him for wife. As she sat there in silent sorrow a stranger strode in; and the Walhall motive (No. 11), welling up in the soft dark tones of horns, bassoons and trombones, tells us who it was — an old man robed in grey, says Sieglinde, whose great hat hung so low that it hid one of his eyes, though in the other gleamed a menace that struck terror in all on whom it lighted. She alone had felt not fear but a sweet yearning and pain, "sadness and solace in one". Then the Sword motive comes to the forefront as she tells how the stranger, glancing at her and glowering at the others, had swung a great sword and struck it up to the hilt in the ash-tree's trunk, saying that it should be his who could withdraw it. All tried, but it baffled the strength of everyone; and there, in silence, it still remains. "Then I", continues Sieglinde to the soft accompaniment of No. 11, "knew who this stranger was who was thus greeting me in my grief; I know, too, who is he for whom the weapon doth wait."

The Sword motive rings out imperially in the trumpet, and then, accompanied by the Victory call (No. 62), Sieglinde sings:

No. 63

of her hope that this day she may find the friend come from afar to bring her comfort after all her sufferings and all the ignominies that had been put upon her:

> whate'er I've borne
> in my bitterest woe,
> whate'er I have suffered
> in shame and disgrace,
> sweetest of vengeance
> soon should I know then!
> Retrieved then were
> whate'er I had lost,
> again I would win
> all I have wept for,

> *found I this holiest friend,*
> *and folded the hero to me!*

Siegmund takes her in his arms and replies with an intensity of emotion equal to her own. He is the friend, he tells her, who shall win both weapon and wife. His own sufferings among men have matched hers; but

> *joy of vengeance*
> *gladdens our hearts now!*
> *So laugh I*
> *in highest delight,*
> *holding thee, noblest and dearest,*
> *feeling the beat of thy heart.*

6

At this point the great door flies open, for no better reason, one is inclined to think at first, then a desire on Wagner's part to create a striking stage effect. We soon realise, however, that the flinging open of the door, revealing a beautiful spring night with the full moon flooding the pair with its radiance, is symbolic rather than realistic. At the flying open of the door Sieglinde had started back in alarm and torn herself away from Siegmund: "Who has passed? Who has entered here?" she cries. He draws her to him again with tender compulsion and leads her to the couch, where they sit down together. "No one passed", he assures her, "but one has come: see now how Spring smiles in the hall." Soft orchestral throbbings fill the air, and Siegmund launches his Spring Song:

No. 64

Win - ter - stür - me wi - chen dem Won - ne - mond, in
Win - ter storms have waned in the win - some May, in

mil - dem Lich - te leuch - tet der Lenz,
gen - tle ra - diance spark - les the spring,

It tells how the storms of winter have waned to the winsome May: Spring has come, to nature as to them, and makes his laughing way through the land, with birds singing and flowers coming to

life again after their long frost-bound sleep. To his sister Spring
flies, and she leaps with a laugh to greet him, "for Love did lure
the Spring". Siegmund and Sieglinde too have found each other
and are made one now; Love and Spring have met in them and
kissed each other.[1]

Wagner luxuriates in the opportunity to give the musician in
him full freedom of wing. No. 52 B takes on a new sweetness and
loveliness as Siegmund sings of his own coming to Sieglinde being like that of Spring, drawn by love, to the earth. She answers
him, "Thou art the Spring that long I had sighed for through
winter's ice-bound days" — to an expansive version of No. 52 A,
followed by 52 B. Friendless and alien, she says, was all around
her until he came. She had recognised him for her own the moment she had set eyes on him: what had lain hidden in darkness
in her starved and thwarted soul then became clear as light and
sang in her ear. A motive of Bliss:

No. 65

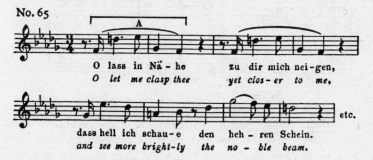

O lass in Nä - he   zu dir mich nei - gen,
O let me clasp thee   yet clos - er to me,

dass hell ich schau - e   den heh - ren Schein.
and see more bright-ly   the no - ble beam.

seems an anticipation of *Tristan* as they sing, in modulation after
modulation of it, of their joy in each other. The strain ends with
a rapturous cadence:

[1] Both words and music of the Spring Song went through many changes
before reaching their present form. Wagner's original draft for the melody
was in C major, in 3/4 time:

Win-ter-stür-me wi-chen dem Won-ne-mond, in lin-den Lüf-ten wiegt sich der Lenz.

The obvious faults of this melody were corrected later, and as Wagner developed the song along its purely musical lines he made several alterations
in the words to make them fit in with the melody.

No. 66

denn won - - - nig wei - -
in rap - - - ture feast

- - det mein Blick.
— I my gaze.

that prolongs its dying fall through voices and orchestra. The rapture of the pair finds expression in modifications of No. 65 that bring us still nearer the *Tristan* idiom:

No. 67

while their common inheritance, now joyously recognised by them both, is symbolised by elaborations of the Wotan-Walhall motive. They understand now why their hearts had been filled with sympathy and tenderness at the first sight of each other; and luxuriant reminiscences of No. 52 pack the orchestra. Sieglinde knows now that he, like herself, is a Volsung, Wälse's child, and names him "Siegmund". He accepts the name, springs towards the ash-tree, and seizes the hilt of the Sword: this was indeed the weapon his father had promised should be his in the hour of need! The orchestral tissue is throughout an organically woven web of motives, each of them carrying its own clear meaning — with, however, one exception. When Siegmund sings

Holiest love's
most mighty need,
passionate longing's
feverish need,

brightly burns in my breast,
drives to deeds and death,

it is to the strain of No. 9, the motive to which, at its first appearance in the *Rhinegold*, the commentators have all attached the label of "Renunciation of Love", because it is to this melody that Alberich avows the renunciation that had won him the Gold. Manifestly there can be no "renunciation" of love implied in the episode in the *Valkyrie* at which we have now arrived; rather is it an assertion of love. Here is yet another warning of the dangers attending the labelling of a Wagnerian motive, however convenient it may be for us to do so, according to the words or the situation in connection with which it makes its first appearance in the opera. For the composer, the range of psychological reference of a motive was far wider, and the terms of reference far subtler, than our ready-made tickets can provide for: the musical idea came from a psychical complex within him that may take on an infinity of nuances in the course of the drama. It becomes clear to us now that when No. 9 first appears in the *Rhinegold* it should be taken as signifying not so much Alberich's renunciation of love as the Love itself, universal, omnipotent, which the gnome, in his lust for power, has decided to renounce.

With his hand on the hilt of the sword Siegmund names the weapon Nothung (that which shall serve him in his need):

No. 68

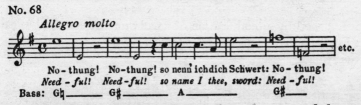

then, with a mighty effort, he plucks it from the tree and shows it to the astonished and ecstatic Sieglinde, the orchestra giving out No. 48 with the full power of the brass. He has won her, he tells her, he, Siegmund the Volsung, and this is his bride-gift to her. Together they will flee from the foeman's house to the laughing house of Spring, where Love shall hold her and Nothung ward her. She answers him in words of equal passion, and as the orchestra executes an excited fantasia on a combination of the Sword motive and that of Love (No. 52 B):

No. 69

the two fall into each other's arms, and the curtain falls to a final cry from Siegmund,

> *Bride and sister*
> *be to thy brother;*
> *so flourish the Volsungs for aye!*

7

The second act opens with an orchestral prelude of immense energy, woven for the most part out of motives with which we are now familiar. First of all the Sword motive, in a new rhythmic form, rings out in the trumpet:

No. 70

It is followed by a modification of what we must continue to call the Flight motive from the *Rhinegold* (No. 15 A):

No. 71

for no better reason than that it was first heard in connection with the flight of Freia from the Giants. Precisely what significance it had in Wagner's mind at the present juncture it is difficult to say. A little later it takes a broader form:

No. 72

Later still No. 65 A, in the shape it had assumed in No. 67, reminds us of the love of Siegmund and Sieglinde:

No. 73

Bass: G♮

Even in the condensation of this last example for purposes of quotation we can see the motive combined contrapuntally with that of Flight: the whole tissue of the prelude, indeed, is symphonic, the short motives cohering into an organic whole. The general purport of it cannot be expressed in terms of a set "programme"; what we are conscious of is an atmosphere of tremendous excitement, in which the past drama of the Volsung pair is moving towards a new and greater tension.

In that drama a fresh figure, that of the Valkyrie [1] Brynhilde — the daughter of Wotan and Erda, and his favourite among his nine Valkyrie daughters — is to play a prominent part. We find her first characterised in the prelude by a figure that will always be typical not only of herself but of the Valkyries in general:

[1] The "Wal-" of "Walküre" comes from an old German word signifying battlefield, and the remainder of the word from an old verb "küren" (to choose: cf. the present German verb "erküren", p.p. "erkoren", to choose, elect). The duty of the Valkyries was to carry the valiant slain to Walhall, there to form a bodyguard of heroes for Wotan. "Wal" (modern German "Wahl") itself really means "choice", "election"; it survives curiously in such words as "Walstatt" and "Walplatz", signifying a field of battle. It was during and after battle that heroes were "chosen" to people Walhall.

The reader, by the way, must beware of associating some of the names in the *Ring* with modern German words similar in form but different in meaning. The "mund" of "Siegmund", for instance, has nothing to do with the modern "Mund" (mouth): it comes from an old root meaning guardian or protector, which survives today in such words as "Vormund" (guardian, trustee), "Vormundschaft" (trusteeship), and "Vormundschaftsgericht" (Court of Chancery): "Siegmund" is the guardian of victory ("Sieg"). The "Hund" of "Hunding", again, derives not from "Hund" (dog) but from "Hüne" (a giant), which may be related to "Hunne" (a Hun).

The names of Brynhilde and her eight sisters — Gerhilde, Ortlinde, Waltraute, Schwertleite, Helmwige, Siegrune, Grimgerde and Rossweisse — are all composites; Schwertleite, for instance, signifies "sword wielder", Siegrune "the one who knows the runes of victory". The word "Walküre", by the way, is accented by Wagner on the first syllable.

No. 74

(Rarely, and least of all in the concert piece known as "The Ride of the Valkyries", do we hear the theme played as Wagner conceived it. By scamping the short note of each bar the brass almost invariably convert the melody into:

No. 75

Further, Wagner always insisted on sharp definition being given to the first note of each bar, not to the fourth, as is the way with our orchestras).

8

As No. 74 grows more and more jubilant the curtain rises, showing a wild mountain pass, with a gorge in the background rising to a high ridge of rocks. Wotan and Brynhilde enter, she fully armed, the God also in war array, carrying his spear. In energetic tones he bids the Valkyrie harness her horse, for soon there will be work for her to do: there will be a combat between Hunding and Siegmund, in which she is to aid the Volsung; as for Hunding, he may go where he belongs, for in Walhall the God needs him not. Elated at the news, Brynhilde, giving glad repeated cries of "Hojotoho! Heihaha!":

No. 76

springs up the rocks, accompanied by orchestral figures that convey a remarkable impression of the wild energy of the Valkyries. Pausing on a high peak she looks down into the gorge at the back, and gaily warns Wotan to look to himself, for a storm will soon burst on him — the furious Fricka is coming in her ram-drawn chariot, scourging the terrified beasts in her wrath, eager for the fray with her spouse. Though she herself, says Brynhilde, revels in the strife of heroes, in a combat of this kind she has no part to play; she will leave her father to face the storm alone as best he can; and with another volley of joyous "Hojotohos!" she disappears behind the mountain height at the side of the stage.

Fricka appears in the gorge, dismounts from her car, and, accompanied by a motive expressive of Wrath:

No. 77

strides impetuously towards Wotan, who turns to face her with a resigned aside: "The old disputes, the old annoys! Yet firmly I must stand and meet them!" Fricka pauses in front of him and begins her harangue with quiet dignity.[1] She has sought him out in the wilds of which he is so fond, she tells him, because she must exact a promise from him. Hunding has brought his plaint to her as the protectress of marriage and cried out for vengeance; and she has sworn to punish the pair who have betrayed him. Wotan asks quietly what wrong they have done, these two who in Spring had bowed to the magic power of Love: "not lord over love am I". If anything is unholy it is the oath that binds lives together without love; and as for himself he cannot intervene, for his heart is always with the brave, whom he ever spurs on to strife. That he has small regard for wedlock she knows, Fricka rejoins; but does

[1] In the first form of the poem the dialogue between Wotan and Fricka ran along somewhat different lines from Fricka's words (in the present poem) "Wie thörig und taub du dich stellst" down to her "So ist es denn aus mit den ewigen Göttern". When printing the final text of the *Ring* poem, in 1872, in the 5th and 6th volumes of his Collected Works, Wagner gave also, at the foot of the relative pages, the text as it originally was between these two points.

he go so far as to condone the union of sister and brother? [1] When was that known before? "Thou knowest it now", is Wotan's reply; "that these twain are lovers thou seest for thyself. So hear my frank counsel — give them thy grace and bless Siegmund and Sieglinde's bond."

Fricka flames into anger at this. The honour and glory of the Gods, she says, has been a small thing to him since he begat these turbulent Volsungs; and now the eternal laws of right and wrong are to be flouted for their benefit. She reproaches him with his infidelities to herself:

No. 78

O_____ was klag'ich um E - he und Eid, da zu-
O_____ why weep I for wed-lock and troth, which thy-

- erst du selbst sie ver-sehrt.
- self wert first to pro-fane!

> *Thy own true wife*
> *thou hast oft betrayed;*
> *never a deep*
> *and never a height*
> *but there wandered*
> *thy wantoning glance;*
> *all the joy of change thou wouldst win thee,*
> *and grieved'st my heart with thy scorn.*

She had been forsaken while he flew to the fray with the lawless Valkyries of his own begetting, whom he had even given as handmaidens to his consort; and later he had left her to dwell in the forest as Wälse:

[1] The concept of a sister-bride has its roots deep in some of the old sagas; it goes back to primitive notions of bisexual deities as principles of nature. Wagner was compelled, willy-nilly, to adopt the idea of the blood unity of Siegmund and Sieglinde for his drama, though it hardly bears transplantation from the world of the sagas to that of the modern stage. It has always been something of a stumbling-block for some listeners to the *Ring*. The more lunatic among Wagner's critics of the 1870's went so far as to accuse him of "glorifying incest".

> *from common mortal*
> *this twin-pair begetting,*
> *at the feet of these wolf-whelps*
> *throwest thou, base one, thy wife!*
> *Then finish thy work!*
> *Fill up the cup!*
> *Let them trample on the betrayed one!*

9

Her eloquence is lost on Wotan. "Ne'er didst thou learn when I would teach thee", the hard-pressed sophist replies tranquilly; "ne'er canst thou comprehend till clear as daylight it lies before thee. Only custom canst thou understand; but my own thought reaches out to what ne'er yet has befallen. A man we need, one neither bound by the laws of the Gods nor sheltered by the Gods; he alone is

> *meet for the deed*
> *which, though the need of the Godhead,*
> *a God of himself may not do".*

She rejects the notion that a hero can do what the Gods themselves cannot. "For who breathed this fire into men? Who gave them the light of their eyes? Without thy shield, what are they? Without thy spur, to what would they aspire? But this new trick thou shalt not work on me! This thy Volsung thou shalt not have from me: in him I find but thee, for only through thee does he dare."

"In deepest sorrow himself did he mould", replies Wotan; "to my protection he owes nothing." But in the anguish of his love for Siegmund he has now made a false move, and Fricka is quick to seize her advantage. "Then leave him now to his own devices", she answers; "shield him not today; take back the sword thou didst bestow." Siegmund had won it himself in his need, says Wotan vehemently. From now onwards the direction of the argument passes more and more into the hands of Fricka; she speaks with mounting passion, while "Wotan's whole demeanour", as the stage directions have it, "from this point onwards expresses a profound and ever-increasing uneasiness and dejection." He listens for a while in silence, only a motive of Dejection in the bassoon and bass clarinet:

No. 79

Bass: *f* E

revealing the completeness of his bafflement and the depth of his despair. "Who was it who planned that need for him", Fricka insists, "and the sword that should serve him in it? Didst *thou* not strike the sword into the tree trunk? Didst *thou* not lead him where he would find it? Didst *thou* not promise it to him?" Touched to the quick, Wotan springs up with an angry gesture, but dares not speak. Perceiving his discomfiture, Fricka grows still more confident and aggressive. With bondsmen, she says scornfully, she disdains to battle; from the free man the felon gets only scourging. Against the power of Wotan she would wage war if need were, but this Siegmund shall be punished only as a slave. Shall such a slave command Wotan's spouse, making her a shame and a scoff before all?

"Wotan", Wagner's stage directions run, "makes another passionate gesture, then sinks down, realising his impotence"; the orchestra underlines the gesture with a vehement statement of No. 77. Fricka presses her advantage home, and Wotan, with the 'cellos and basses muttering the motive of Dejection (No. 79), asks gloomily "What desir'st thou?" "Shield not the Volsung!" is the sharp reply. "His way let him go", says Wotan in a choked voice. But this is not enough for Fricka: she demands that he shall look her straight in the eyes and promise that neither will he aid Siegmund nor — thus shattering the God's last secret hope — allow the Valkyrie to do so. Wotan makes a final passionate effort to ride the storm. "I cannot forsake him", he cries; "he found my sword." "Then withdraw its magic", replies the pitiless Fricka; "let the blade break; let him be helpless against his foe!"

10

Just then Brynhilde's joyous "Hojotoho!" peals from the adjacent heights, and she herself comes into sight. Perceiving Fricka she suddenly breaks off, slowly and silently leads her horse down the rocky path, and leaves it in a cave. The increasingly sombre orchestral mutations of her call depict her growing realisation of the gravity of the situation:

She stands silent as Fricka majestically orders Wotan to bid the Valkyrie vindicate the honour of the Gods by withholding her aid from Siegmund. Wotan, now utterly defeated, throws himself on a rocky seat in the profoundest dejection, muttering, "Take my oath!" Fricka strides towards Brynhilde and pauses for a moment before her; "War-father doth wait for thee", she tells her calmly; "let him instruct thee how the lot is to fall"; and the Curse motive (No. 41) raises its head ominously in the quiet tones of the trombones. According to Wagner's directions, she enters her chariot and drives swiftly away. But this rather inconvenient piece of realism is generally dispensed with in performance: Fricka walks slowly away from the pair, giving the player of the part a superb opportunity to show us how charged with meaning a mere slow walk can be, provided she has the dignity of mien and gait to enable her to seize the opportunity — which few Wagnerian singers have. Two or three realisations of the difficult episode linger in the older opera-goer's memory.

After Fricka's departure the tense silence is broken by Brynhilde, who goes anxiously to the suffering Wotan and asks him the meaning of it all. The God's head sinks heavily on to his breast: "In my own fetters fast am I held"! he ejaculates mournfully; "I, the least free of all that liveth!" His brooding ends in a terrible cry of "O shame! O distress! Gods' extremity! Wrath and Grief without end! The saddest am I of all living!" [1] The terrified Bryn-

---

[1] In his first swift Sketch of November 1851 for the *Valkyrie,* Wagner's plan for the scene immediately following the exit of Fricka had run thus: "Wotan's profound grief that he must ever find himself in opposition to himself; there must be beings freer than the unhappy Gods are. He longs for the land of Forgetfulness." (Then comes the scene between Wotan and Brynhilde). This plan was not carried out either in the more detailed Sketch of the 17th May 1852 or in the poem, in both of which it is replaced by Wotan's ejaculation, "In my own fetters fast am I — the least free of all living". Apparently the long Narration to Brynhilde only took its present shape in Wagner's mind some time between the above two dates, for in the first Sketch we have merely this: "Brynhilde [after the departure of Fricka] ca-

hilde throws away helmet, shield and spear and sinks down at his feet, laying her head and hand lovingly on his breast and knee and imploring him to confide in her, the truest of his children. The motive of Siegmund and Sieglinde's love (No. 52), threading its melancholy way through the silence in the veiled tones of the bass clarinet, reveals to us what is passing through Wotan's tortured mind. For a moment he communes softly with himself: if he were to tell her all, so runs his thought, would he not loosen the inmost hold of his will? Brynhilde reassures him; speaking to her, she says, he will be speaking to Wotan's own will, for what is she but that? When he does so it is indeed, he muses, to himself, for to all others but himself and her his thought must remain for ever secret. It is a point that needs to be remembered by those who find the Narration that follows over-long and repetitive: the God is not so much speaking to another as brooding within his secret self upon the dilemma in which he now finds himself, and retracing in his imagination the stages by which he has brought himself to his present sorry pass.

11

He begins in a hollow, stifled voice, looking steadfastly all the while into Brynhilde's eyes. It is not the impersonal Wotan of Wagner's first cosmic conception of 1848, but the more human Wotan of a later date, who makes his way, as it were, across the screen that gradually unrolls itself before our eyes, the Wotan whose lust for power had led him to the first false step on a path the end of which would be the downfall of the Gods. One passage alone in the monologue is sufficient to show the difference between the two conceptions. As the reader will recall, in the "Sketch for a drama on the Nibelungen myth" (1848) Wotan, standing aloof from both the Giants and the Nibelungs, had en-

---

joles and tries to console him. Wotan, without willing it, discloses his secret object with regard to the Volsungs, his offspring. Brynhilde understands him completely: she offers to protect Siegmund. Wotan is angry with her, and, mastering himself by a supreme effort, wrathfully commands Siegmund's death. He goes away in a passion. Brynhilde perceives Siegmund and Sieglinde in flight", etc. In the later Sketch these half-dozen lines are expanded to seventy-six, which give us the dialogue between Wotan and the Valkyrie as we have it now.

gaged the former to build him a fortress "from which he could govern the world in peace and order"; for the Gods had planned a world subject to good laws, and had devoted themselves to the bringing into being of a worthy human race: "the object of their lofty ordering of the world is moral consciousness". Wotan had gradually become involved in a network of evil, though his intentions from the first had been good. In his present Narration to Brynhilde, however, he depicts himself as morally flawed from the beginning, aiming only at power and stopping at nothing to achieve it:

> *all whom by our laws*
> *we had held in bondage,*
> *the mortals whose spirits*
> *proud we had curbed,*
> *whom by guileful agreements'*
> *craft and deception*
> *we bound in a blind*
> *and servile obedience,*
> *these ye were to spur*
> *to storm and to combat,*
> *their desires goading*
> *to grimmest war,*
> *that hosts of hardy heroes*
> *should gather in Walhall's halls.*

He now begins his quiet retrospect at the very beginning:

> *When youthful love's*
> *delight from me fled,*
> *my soul grew athirst for power:*
> *by wildest wishes*
> *blindly impelled,*
> *I won myself the world.*
> *Fraud and deception*
> *unwitting wrought I,*
> *binding by treaties*
> *what threatened harm:*
> *craftily lured on by Loge,*
> *who flick'ring fled away.*

He goes on to tell how "the baffled Nibelung Alberich" had forsworn love and so won the Rhine's pure Gold, and with it measureless might; how he himself had wrested the Ring from him by craft, paying for Walhall with it instead of restoring it to the Rhine; how the wise Erda had counselled him to give up the Ring, warning him of the fate of the Gods if he retained it, but had refused to tell him more; how, in the chill of his fear, he had followed her into the womb of the earth, mastered her in love, and "learned much from her counsel"; how she had borne him his beloved Brynhilde, his second self, whom he had nurtured with eight sister Valkyries; how they had brought him the spirits of heroes who had fallen in battle, to be a guard for him against his foes. Forever lurking in the shadows is Alberich, racked by rage and envy; Wotan does not fear an assault on Walhall by him and his "night-begotten forces", but should the Ring come into the gnome's hands again he would rouse all creation against the Gods. Against Fafner, who now sleeps upon the Ring, Wotan himself is powerless:

> *But I bargained with him,*
> *and may not attack him;*
> *powerless 'gainst him*
> *would prove all my might: —*
> *these are the fetters*
> *that confine me:*
> *I, who by treaties am lord,*
> *to my treaties now am a slave;*

and the weary motive of the Need of the Gods drags its slow length along through the 'cellos:

No. 81

It will be seen that halfway through the second bar this continues with the Dejection motive (No. 79), while at the end of that bar the Sword motive is heard in the bass trumpet.

To one alone can he look for salvation — to a hero strange to him, free of his will, in no wise helped by the Godhead, one who will fight even against Wotan, as God, yet accomplish what the God himself must not do. For this purpose he had reared Siegmund, giving him the Sword that should do the deed longed for by the Gods. But Fricka had pierced through his deceit and overwhelmed him with shame: to her he must yield. Flee as he will from Alberich's curse, everywhere it pursues him; and his heart's beloved, his Siegmund, he must now abandon and betray.

In his despair he invokes the ruin of the Gods; let all their glittering, shameful pomp pass away. All is in vain: for one thing only he now longs — an end to it all. Then he reflects that it is for that ending that Alberich works unrestingly. Erda had warned him that when "the night-born foe of love" should beget a son the doom of the Gods would be nigh; and of late the rumour had reached his ears that Alberich had bought with gold the love of a woman in whose womb now lies "the fruit of hate, grim envy's son". This wonder, he wails, befell

> *to him, the loveless,*
> *yet of my love so boundless*
> *the free one was born not to me.*

In bitter wrath he gives the Nibelung's son his blessing; let him sate himself on the prize that is to fall into his hands. For himself, he can struggle no more: Brynhilde, in the combat between Siegmund and Hunding, is to fight for Fricka and for wedlock's vows:

> *what she doth choose*
> *is also my choice:*
> *of what avail were my own will,*
> *since the free one I cannot fashion?*
> *to Fricka's vassal*
> *give thou thine aid!*

Brynhilde strives in vain to persuade him to alter this decision of despair, even vowing that she will never fight against the hero whom Wotan loves. But he turns on her in devastating fury. Who is she, "the submissive blind slave of my will", to flout his commands? Let her provoke him to wrath and his lightning will blast her; his breast is filled with "a rage that could lay woeful and waste the world that once delighted my heart". He warns her, then, not to rouse his anger: "Siegmund is to die; this be the Valkyrie's work!" He rushes away, blind-mad with the fury of frustration and despair, and disappears among the rocks, leaving Brynhilde terrified and bewildered.

12

The tremendous monologue, that seems long only to those who merely feel that Wotan is telling them something they know already and have no inward eye and ear for the drama that is being played out in the God's tortured soul and for the new emotional life given to it in his tragic retrospect of it, is necessarily built up, for the most part, on reference after reference to the motives associated with each person, each episode of the story told. But they are not merely pasted in at the appropriate spots; they have a psychological life of their own, and take on new musical forms and colours now in congruence with Wotan's changing emotions. At the point, for instance, where he foresees the doom that will fall on the Gods when a son is born to Alberich, the Walhall motive undergoes this sombre mutation:

No. 82

Musing affectionately on the distress of "War-father", Brynhilde, sad at heart, takes up her weapons, dons them again, and sighs for the Volsung hero whom she must abandon to his fate. Slowly she makes her way to the back of the stage, to the melancholy strain of No. 81. As she reaches the mountain summit the

Flight motive comes out hurriedly once more in the orchestra:
Brynhilde has caught sight of Siegmund and Sieglinde approaching through the gorge. She watches their movements for a moment, then disappears into the cave in which she had left her
horse.

The Volsung pair enter. Sieglinde, flying in blind terror from
the pursuing Hunding, would press on, exhausted as she is, but
Siegmund tries gently to restrain her. At last he succeeds in bringing her to the stone seat, where she throws her arms passionately
round his neck, remains thus a moment, and then breaks away
from him again in panic, wildly urging him to leave the woman
who has brought this woe on herself and him. To the first rapture
of love has succeeded horror and self-loathing: "scorn I bring on
my brother, shame to the friend who freed me". For any shame
she may feel, Siegmund replies, Hunding shall pay with his life
"when Nothung at his heart shall gnaw". The horn-calls of the
pursuers are heard, pounding out the sinister Hunding rhythm;
the kinsmen and the bloodhounds are on her track, she cries distractedly, and some rending dissonances in trumpets and horns
graphically depict her frenzy. Then, in sheer exhaustion, she melts
again and throws herself on his breast, but once more starts up in
terror as the ominous calls boom out again. In imagination she
sees the hounds tearing at Siegmund's flesh, their fangs fastened
in him, the Sword in splinters, the ash-tree splitting and crashing;
and with a last cry of "Brother! my brother! Siegmund!" she sinks
fainting into his arms. While the orchestra gives out poignant reminiscences of their love music in the first act (No. 52) he bends
over her anxiously, finds that she is still breathing, presses a long
kiss on her brow, and seats himself on the rock with her head rest-
ing on his lap, in which position both remain during the scene
that follows.

13

After a long, expressive silence Brynhilde comes out of the cave,
leading her horse by the bridle, strides slowly and solemnly towards them, and pauses to contemplate the man whose fate lies in
her unwilling hands. The brass gives out quietly the solemn motive of Death:

No. 83

The chords marked A, with their curiously impressive crescendo and diminuendo, are more particularly associated in the sequel with the Annunciation of Death which it is the duty of the Valkyrie to bring to the hero at Wotan's command. As she stands gazing earnestly at him, holding shield and spear in one hand while the other rests on the neck of her horse, the orchestra gives out the quietest of reminiscences of the Walhall motive — that Walhall in which the Volsung will soon join the ranks of Wotan's brave and faithful ones. When at last she addresses Siegmund by name it is to an arresting modulation in the wood wind. She bids him look at her; she has come, she tells him, to summon him hence. With the orchestra playing incessantly on No. 83 and the Walhall motive she answers the questions he puts to her:

> *Death-fated men*
> *alone behold me;*
> *who sees my face*
> *must forth from the light of life.*
> *On the war-field alone*
> *I come to heroes;*
> *him whom I greet*
> *I choose him for my own.*

Question and answer succeed each other until the whole story is told: she is going to take him to Walhall, to join the hallowed band of fallen heroes about Wotan; there he will find his father Wälse, and smiling Wish-maidens who will hand him the festive cup; but Sieglinde he will see no more. At these last words of hers he bends gently over Sieglinde, kisses her softly on the brow, then turns tranquilly to the Valkyrie again:

> *Then greet for me Walhall,*
> *greet for me Wotan,*

greet for me Wälse
and all the heroes;
greet too the gracious
wish-maidens: —
to them I'll follow thee not!

Gravely she reminds him, to an impressive modification of No. 83:

No. 84

that having seen the Valkyrie's withering glance he must now fare
forth with her: all his courage will be of no avail, for death always
prevails, and it is death that she is bringing him. To what hero
must he fall? Siegmund asks. "Hunding's hand deals the blow", is
the reply. He smiles scornfully at her: it is Hunding who will die,
and Hunding whom, if she lusts for strife and death, she can take
with her to Walhall. Gently and solemnly she once more bids him
hearken to her: it is he who must die today: the Sword on which
he counts will fail him, for he who gave it now withdraws the
spell from it.

Siegmund bends tenderly over Sieglinde again in an outburst of
grief at his father Wälse's betrayal of him:

O shame on him
who bestowed the sword,
to make me my foeman's scorn!
If I must fall then,
I go not to Walhall:
Hella [1] *take me to her!*

. . . .

Yet if on my anguish
thine eyes would feast,
then gloat upon my grief now;
let my pain comfort

[1] The Goddess of the underworld.

thy pitiless heart:
but of Walhall's paltry raptures
prithee speak not to me!

14

This is the turning-point in the action. Brynhilde, deeply moved
by this devotion, begs him to give Sieglinde into her protection:

thy wife trust to me
for the babe's dear sake,
the pure pledge of her passion for thee.

His reply is that no one shall protect her but himself, and if he
must die he will slay her first. As he draws his sword to kill her,
Brynhilde's sympathy overmasters her. In a passionate outburst,
to the accompaniment of a striking orchestral foreshadowing of
the idiom of *Tristan,* she declares that Sieglinde shall live, nor shall
Siegmund be parted from her. She will thwart the death-doom;
he shall triumph in the fight. As the ominous horn-calls peal out in
the distance again she tells him to take up his sword and strike
without fear, for the steel and the Valkyrie's help will both prove
true. She rushes away with her horse and disappears in the gorge
on the right, Siegmund looking after her with joy and relief, while
the orchestra pours out an excited and exultant flood of tone.

The stage darkens, heavy thunderclouds descending upon the
background and gradually enveloping the rocks, the gorge and
the hills. Siegmund broods tenderly over the sleeping Sieglinde:
"so slumber still", he says, "until the fight be o'er and peace doth
end thy pain"; while the orchestra breathes softly some of the
themes associated with the pair in the first act, such as No. 52 and
No. 64 (the Spring Song). But the sounds of the pursuers have
meantime been drawing nearer and nearer, until at last a cow-
horn (behind the scenes), blaring out the rhythm of No. 56, rouses
Siegmund from his dreams. He starts up resolutely with drawn
sword, hastens to the background, and at the mountain top disappears in the dark thunderclouds, from which a flash of lightning
breaks. The cow-horn sounds again, more insistently than before.

Sieglinde begins to move restlessly in her dreams. The violas
give out a short melody:

No. 85 *Lento*

which the sufferers from Wagnerphobia assure us Wagner borrowed from Liszt. Memories of her childhood, her wedding, and
the destruction of the Volsung home rise in her: "Would that our
father were home!" she mutters: "with the boy he still roams in
the woods. Mother! Mother! I tremble with fear: how harsh and
hateful seem all these strangers! Misty vapours darken the air;
fiery tongues are flaming towards us; the house is burning. Brother!
Siegmund! Siegmund!" A crash of thunder and a vivid lightning-
flash awake her; she leaps up and gazes round her with increasing
terror as the storm lashes the scene and Hunding's horn-call
sounds again, this time quite close. His hoarse voice is heard from
the pass at the back, calling on Wehwalt to stand and face him.
He is answered by the voice of Siegmund, who, further away in
the gorge, asks this enemy of his where he is hiding. Not weaponless is he now, he cries, for from the ash-tree's great stem he had
plucked the Sword he now wields, a Sword that will make a mock-
ery of Fricka's protection of his foe.

15

In another lightning-flash the two men become visible, locked
in combat. Sieglinde gives a despairing cry of "Stay your hands,
ye madmen! Slay me first!", and runs towards the pass; but another flash that breaks out over the two men makes her reel back
as if blinded. Through the mounting excitement in the orchestra
the Valkyrie motive (No. 74), accompanied by the Sword motive
in the trumpet, tears its way in the trombones as Brynhilde suddenly becomes visible, hovering above Siegmund and guarding
him with her shield. But just as he is aiming a blow at Hunding a
red glow appears in the clouds to the left, and by the light of it
we see Wotan standing over Hunding and holding out his spear in
front of Siegmund. At his angry "Recoil from my spear! Splintered
be the Sword!" Brynhilde shrinks back in terror: Siegmund's
sword snaps on the God's spear, and Hunding buries his own
weapon in the unarmed man's breast. Wotan, as the Treaty motive (No. 13) striding downwards in the bass instruments of the

orchestra reminds us, has remembered and is keeping his pledged word, upon which his moral power is based.

Through the vague light that now takes possession of the stage we dimly see Brynhilde running to Sieglinde, who, hearing Siegmund's death sigh, has fallen to the ground as if lifeless, while the orchestra throws together in stark apposition the opening of the Volsung motive (No. 58 A) and the fateful form of the Annunciation of Death motive shown in No. 84. She lifts Sieglinde on to her horse, which is standing near the gorge at the side, and disappears with her. When the clouds that envelop the stage divide, Hunding is seen driving his spear into the breast of the dead Siegmund, and Wotan standing by his side on a rock,[1] leaning on his spear and gazing with infinite sadness at the hero's body. He has done what Fricka had exacted of him, as the Treaty motive making its slow way down in 'cellos and basses again reminds us, and is now free once more to feel and act for himself. "Get hence, slave!" he says with bitter scorn. "Kneel before Fricka: tell her that Wotan's spear has avenged what wrought her shame. Go! Go!", and at a contemptuous wave of his hand Hunding falls dead.[2] Wagner has marked the whole passage double piano and piano; but some singers make the mistake of hurling the "Go! Go!" at Hunding's head in a vehement forte. They have missed the psychological nuance of the situation: at that moment Wotan is too sunk in grief at his own betrayal of Siegmund to do any storming. The tempest breaks a little later: he remembers Brynhilde's flouting of his will, and in an access of rage cries woe upon her: "harshly will I punish her crime, if my steed be as swift as her flight!" He disappears in thunder and lightning in pursuit of her, a brief orchestral postlude depicting the fury of his purpose.

16

From the Prose Sketch we learn that the wild landscape in which the opening scene of the third act is set is the customary

[1] In the Prose Sketch of 1852 Wagner says that at this point Wotan appears to Hunding "as Wälse". This little touch was of course not carried over into the poem. The reader will recall that in the Sketch Wotan had appeared as Wälse in the first act, "in the form of an oldish man with grey hair and beard and only one eye, with a round hat and a grey cloak".

[2] As has been pointed out earlier, Wagner has carelessly carried over into the poem here a feature that was valid only for the Sketch.

rendezvous of the Valkyries "when they return from their various expeditions in order to ride back to Walhall".

Wagner takes advantage of the picturesque opportunities pre-sented by this conception to write a large-scale piece of descriptive music. The thematic bases of it are naturally the Valkyries' motive (No. 74), the characteristic "Hojotoho!" (No. 76), and a pictorial figure, suggestive of the mad course of the Valkyries through the air:

No. 86

that had been already hinted at in the orchestra at Brynhilde's first appearance in act two. (What was probably the full theme of the Valkyries in its earliest form has come down to us on a fragment of music paper presented by Wagner on the 23rd July 1851 to a young Swiss enthusiast, Robert Radecke, whose acquaintance he had just made. There the words and the melody run thus:

No. 87

The reader who knows his *Ring* will not need to be told that these words do not appear anywhere in the *Valkyrie* poem. They come from the *Siegfried's Death* of 1848, in which, it will be remem-bered, there was a scene (not carried over into the present *Twilight of the Gods*) in which the Valkyries visited Brynhilde's rock *en masse* to condole with her on her punishment by Wotan; and the words of No. 87 are the first two of the four lines they sing as they ride away again into the storm. It would be interesting to know how many more of the musical motives of the present tetralogy were conceived for use in *Siegfried's Death*).

These three motives, together with such realistic effects as the thunderous gallop and the panting and whinnying of the horses, are all that Wagner requires to build up the huge structure of the exciting first scene of the third act.

The stage shows us the summit of a rocky mountain, with a pine-wood on the right, and on the left the entrance to a cave; the background is occupied by rocks of various heights that form the verge of a precipice. When the curtain rises, Gerhilde, Ortlinde, Waltraute and Schwertleite are already assembled on the rocky point above the cave. They hail each other, and are answered by a Valkyrie on horseback in the air, who, as a lightning-flash rends the clouds, becomes visible in the distance with a slain warrior hanging across her saddle. One by one the sisters arrive and are greeted joyously by those already on the scene. They indulge in savage merriment; the horses with the bodies have been left in the adjacent wood, and the lifetime enmity of the dead heroes now communicates itself to the animals, who, we gather, have to be separated to keep them from attacking each other.

17

The eight Valkyries are on the point of riding off together to Walhall when they observe that one of them, Brynhilde, is missing:

> *Till she comes hither,*
> *here must we bide:*
> *War-father grimmest*
> *greeting would give,*
> *saw he not her in our midst.*

At last they catch sight of her in the distance, spurring her panting horse Grane towards the rock. There is something with her on her saddle, but this, to their astonishment, proves to be a woman. At last she enters on foot from the wood, leading and supporting Sieglinde, and breathlessly appealing for aid in her need: for the first time, she tells them, she is not the pursuer but the pursued, for War-father hunts her close. They do not understand; but Ortlinde and Waltraute, looking from the summit of the mountain, see a thundercloud approaching from the north, and in it War-father driving his steed furiously towards them. He is accompanied all the time by the pounding of the motive of the Need of the Gods

(No. 81); it is destiny, more than personal anger, that is urging him on relentlessly to punish his rebellious child.

Brynhilde hurriedly makes clear to the others what has happened: the fainting woman with her is Sieglinde, Siegmund's sister and bride; Brynhilde had disobeyed War-father's command to desert Siegmund in his fight with Hunding, and now retribution is about to fall on Sieglinde:

> *Woe to the woman*
> *if he find her here;*
> *to all of the Volsungs*
> *ruin he threatens!*
> *Who'll lend me the swiftest*
> *horse in my need,*
> *to bear the woman away?*

The horrified Valkyries refuse to lend her a horse, for fear of Wotan. Sieglinde breaks in on her piteous appeals for help; she repulses the protecting arm that Brynhilde would throw round her, reproaches her for saving her life when Siegmund had died, and implores her to strike her sword through her heart. But Brynhilde exhorts her to cling to life for the sake of the child that Siegmund has left with her as a pledge of his love; "a Volsung thou bearest to him!" Sieglinde starts violently, then turns in exaltation to Brynhilde: "Rescue me, brave one", she cries; "rescue my babe! Shelter me, o maids, with your shields!"

The clouds pile up at the back, the thunder rolls nearer, and the terrified Valkyries distractedly urge Brynhilde to fly with the woman, for help her themselves they dare not. Sieglinde falls on her knees to Brynhilde, who raises her as a resolution suddenly takes shape within her; she bids her fly to safety, while she herself will stay and face Wotan. But where is Sieglinde to go? The Valkyries tell her of a wood that stretches away to the eastward, where Fafner, changed into a dragon, lies in a cavern guarding the Ring. It is no place for a suffering woman, they say; but Brynhilde remembers that Wotan dreads the spot and shuns it. As the God draws nearer she tells Sieglinde hurriedly to fly to the wood, be brave and defiant there, enduring hunger and thirst, thorns and rough ways, for in her womb she bears "the world's most wonderful hero". She gives her the fragments of Siegmund's sword

which she has carried under her armour, and exhorts her to preserve them for the child, whose name is to be "Siegfried, who
shall rejoice in victory"; and the vigorous motive that is to be
identified with the future hero of the *Ring* is heard in the horns:

No. 88

Sieglinde responds with a great cry of thankfulness, to a melody:

No. 89

which will be used in the closing bars of the *Twilight of the Gods*
to symbolise Redemption by Love. For Siegmund's sake, she says,
she will save the child; then she bids Brynhilde farewell and hastens away to the wood.

18

The storm has increased in violence, and the approach of Wotan is heralded by a fiery glow that breaks out in the background,
to the right. His voice, magnified by a speaking trumpet, is heard
through the thunder, bidding Brynhilde stay and face him. For a
while she had stood watching Sieglinde's flight; now she returns,
full of anxiety, to the centre of the stage. In response to a last desperate appeal to her sisters to shield her from the wrath of the
God they draw themselves up in a body on the rocky peak, concealing her in their midst. In mounting excitement they describe
the coming of War-father, breathing revenge. At last he enters
from the little wood and strides furiously towards them, asking
where is Brynhilde, and threatening them with his anger if they
conceal her from him. In a brief ensemble in which their agitated
cries ascend in wave on wave they try to appease his wrath, but in

vain. He upbraids them for their womanish weakness: was it from him, he asks, they got this craven spirit, from him, who had reared them to be hard and ruthless, to fare with joy to the combat:

> *and ye wild ones now weep and whine*
> *when my wrath doth a traitor chastise?*

He tells them, to the accompaniment of the tragic motive of the Need of the Gods (No. 81), what Brynhilde's crime has been:

> *No one but she*
> *knew all the depths of my musing;*
> *No one but she*
> *saw to the spring of my spirit!*
> *'Twas she shaped*
> *into deed what I had but wished: —*
> *and now our holiest*
> *bond hath she broke,*
> *the faithless one*
> *my own will hath defied,*
> *my sacred command*
> *openly scorned,*
> *'gainst myself the weapon she turned*
> *that my will alone made hers!*

He summons her to come forth and meet her accuser and receive the scourging she has earned.

The music softens suddenly as Brynhilde emerges from the midst of the Valkyries, comes down humbly, but with firm steps, from the rock, and pauses a short distance from the God: "Here stand I, father", she says quietly; "pronounce thou my punishment." Her sentence she herself has shaped, he tells her passionately. His will alone had brought her into being, and against his will she had worked; her sole duty had been to carry out his commands, yet she had dared to command against him; his Wishmaid she had been, yet against his will she had dared to wish; Shield-maid she had been to him, yet against him she had raised her shield; Lot-chooser she was, yet a lot against him she had chosen; Hero-stirrer he had created her to be, yet against him she had stirred up heroes. "What once thou wert, I have told thee;

what now thou art, that say to thyself: Wish-maid and Valkyrie thou art no more."

We catch a glimpse of the heartbreak at the core of his anger as he goes on to pronounce sentence on her. The motive representative of her as the Announcer of Death (No. 85) receives a great lyrical expansion:

No. 90

Nicht weis' ich dir mehr Hel-den zur Wal; nicht
No more farst thou forth war-riors to seek; no

führst du mehr Sie-ger in mei-nen Saal:
more bringst thou her-oes to fill my hall:

as he tells her, in lines of much poetic beauty, that no more will he send her out to find him heroes and bring them to him in Walhall; no more, at the Gods' festal banquet, will his best-loved one fill his drinking-horn; no more his dear child's mouth will he kiss; the company of the Gods will own her no longer; she will be an outcast from them, "for broken now is our bond, and thou for ever art banned from my sight"; and the theme of Wotan as the guardian of treaties (No. 13), tearing its way downwards in trombones and tuba, gives us the clue to the compulsion under which he is now acting as he does.

"All thou hast given, then, thou takest away?" asks Brynhilde sadly. No, he replies; one who shall come shall take it all, for here on this rock shall she await the fate he has decreed for her;

> *defenceless in sleep*
> *bound shalt thou lie:*
> *that man shall master the maid*
> *who shall find her and wake her from sleep.*

The Valkyries break into a wail of protest; coming down from the rock they group themselves round Brynhilde, half-kneeling before Wotan and imploring him to relent. Angrily he repeats his decision: their faithless sister shall be found and mastered by a husband,

by the hearth to sit and spin,
to all mockers a sport and shame.

His anger mounts as Brynhilde sinks to the ground with a cry and the Valkyries recoil from her. Harshly he bids them leave her to her fate, unless they wish to share her punishment with her. They separate with wild cries and run into the adjoining wood, from which there soon comes a great clamour (No. 86 in frenzied waves). Black clouds gather about the cliffs; and by a lightning-flash the Valkyries are seen, with loose bridles, crowded together and riding away, to the strains of No. 74.

19

Gradually the tempest dies down, the clouds disperse, and the calm of twilight, merging gradually into night, descends upon the scene. Wotan and Brynhilde are now alone, she lying in utter abasement at his feet. A long and solemn silence is broken first of all by the melody of No. 90 in the veiled melancholy tones of the bass clarinet, then by a new motive, beginning in the same instrument and continuing in the 'cellos and basses and then in the cor anglais, symbolical of the Volsung Love that lies deep down in Wotan's hurt and angry heart:

No. 91

The final limb of the long melody:

No. 92

will rank later as an independent motive. (Both No. 91 and No. 92 derive from No. 79, which at its first appearance in the scene between Wotan and Fricka has been styled the motive of Dejection. Once more we realise the absurdity of trying to fasten a Wagnerian motive down to a fixed verbal formula. The phrase is psychologically complex in the way that only music can be; it voices the grief of Wotan, evoked at one time by the call on him to abandon Siegmund and surrender his dream of a rescuing Volsung hero, at another time his sorrow both at the shattering of his hopes in that respect and at the necessity of eternal separation from Brynhilde. So again with the figure of No. 84, which reappears, in the course of the present scene, in the 'cellos at one point: it has nothing to do now, as it formerly had, with the Annunciation of Death, but recurs spontaneously to Wagner as the most fitting expression of Brynhilde's grief at her banishment from Wotan and Walhalla).

During the sad dialogue that follows, Nos. 91 and 92 keep winding their melancholy way through the orchestral texture in one instrument after another, but mostly in the poignant timbres of oboe or cor anglais. The Valkyrie timidly asks if her deed was in truth so shameful as to merit such a scourging, such abasement:

> *Look in my eyes then:*
> *silence thy rage,*
> *master thy wrath,*
> *make clearer to me*
> *the hidden guilt,*
> *that thou set'st thy face like a stone,*
> *and dost turn from thy favourite child.*

"Ask of thy deed itself", the God replies gloomily; "thy guilt it will show thee." She urges that she had but carried out his order to fight for the Volsung; it was true that he had revoked it, but, she pleads, only after Fricka had imposed her will on him and made him false to his purpose. In her mutinous pride, he rejoins, she had presumed to substitute her own wisdom for his. Gradually gaining confidence, she tells him how she had pierced beneath his words to what lay in his heart; her love had seen what he had striven to hide even from himself — that he desired the victory of Siegmund; and when she had looked into the hero's eyes and seen the distress of his soul at the thought of parting from Sieglinde she had been filled with pity and love for him, and felt that for her to disobey the God's command would be the highest form of obedience to his secret will. Wagner's imagination strikes out a new figure of grief (not a motive):

No. 93

upon which he allows himself the luxury of playing for a considerable time as Brynhilde describes the emotions that had possessed her in her dialogue with Siegmund. When she tells how she had disobeyed Wotan's decree because she had recognised that the love that filled her own heart was one with the love of Wotan for the Volsungs, No. 92 suddenly becomes luminously transfigured:

No. 94

And when the God says "So didst thou do what myself would fain have done, yet what ne'er could be, by fate doubly forbid", we find Wagner unexpectedly taking up again the figure shown in No. 85, where it had accompanied Sieglinde's words "Would that our father were home! With the boy still he roams in the woods!" It now assumes the following form:

No. 95

being combined, as will be seen, with No. 94. Precisely what psychological significance Nos. 85 and 95 had for Wagner it is impossible to say.

20

Wotan opens out his whole heart now to this beloved child of his. He tells her of his own distress all this long while; he had sought to bury his sorrow for ever under the ruins of the world he so loved; she, not knowing, not understanding, had listened only to the voice of love,

> *while I, gall of the Gods'*
> *bitterest anguish must drink.*

For a time the music is of a melting tenderness: then Wotan resumes more drily. She must follow her heart's own folly now to the end; from him she had turned away, and he can no longer work through her or take counsel with her. Her reply is quiet and simple. Unfit was she for him, for to her foolish mind one thing only had seemed good — to love whatever he loved. Yet she asks him not to forget that in dishonouring her he will dishonour the immortal part of himself, soiling himself in shaming her.

Still hard and unrelenting, he tells her that as she has chosen love, now she must follow as her master the man who shall compel her love. Then let it be, she begs him, no common, worthless man who shall take possession of her. The more bitterly he refuses, the more ardently and intimately she pleads. She reminds him of the Volsung race he had bred, which she had preserved from destruction by saving Sieglinde and her child, together with the Sword the God had shaped for Siegmund. At this last reminder of his hopes and his frustration his anger rises again. He will hear no more, he says; she must submit to her fate; he cannot choose for her:

> *as from me thou didst turn,*
> *I turn from thee;*
> *I may not know*
> *what now thou dost wish:*
> *thy chastisement*
> *must I see fulfilled.*

Her punishment is to lie bound and weaponless in deep slumber and become the wife of the man who shall find and waken her. The orchestra gives out softly the mysterious, lulling motive of Magic Sleep:

No. 96

She falls on her knees before him and breaks out in passionate protest: if she is to be bound in fetters of sleep, let him surround the rock with such terrors that only the freest and greatest of heroes will brave them. Foreshadowings in the minor:

No. 97

of what will develop later into the motive of Brynhilde's Slumber play continuously about her words. Wotan refuses her request: "Too much thou cravest, too great this grace!" She repeats it more urgently: let him slay her with his spear, let him destroy her utterly, but not inflict woeful shame on her. Then, in wild exaltation, she asks him to surround the rock with a fire that will consume any craven who dares approach it. Fire motives from the *Rhinegold* (Nos. 22 and 24) combine with the Valkyrie motive (No. 74) to give point to her appeal.

At last Wotan's heart melts. To a mighty surge of orchestral tone, in which we hear the Slumber motive now defining itself in its true form:

No. 98

he raises Brynhilde to her feet, gazes, profoundly moved, into her eyes, and begins his great farewell to her:

No. 99

Leb' wohl,   du küh - nes,   herr - lich - es   Kind!
Fare - well,   thou val - iant,   glo - ri - ous   child!

If he must really part from her:

No. 100 *Appassionato*

Muss ich dich mei - den, und darf nicht
Must I then leave thee, my lov - ing

min - nig mein Gruss dich— mehr grüss - en,
greet - ing no more may I give thee,

if no more she shall hand him the mead-cup at the banquets of the Gods, he will at least engirdle her rock with "such a bridal fire as ne'er yet has burned for a bride", a fire that will strike fear into the heart of all but the boldest:

> *For one alone winneth the bride,*
> *one freer than I, the God!*

The flames seem already to leap out from the orchestra: and as he speaks of the one who alone shall win her the Siegfried motive (No. 88) raises its head prophetically.

While the orchestra luxuriates in developments of No. 98 he folds her in a loving embrace, and suddenly all becomes tenderness again as the Slumber motive takes on a new form and now runs a long symphonic course:

No. 101

pp   etc.

as the God savours for the last time the honey of this vast love of his:

> *Thine eyes so lustrous and pure,*
> *that, smiling, oft I caressed,*
> *when my fond kiss*
> *thy courage won thee,*
> *when heroes' laud*
> *from thy honied lips*
> *in childish lispings flowed forth:*
> *these unclouded, glorious eyes,*
> *that oft have lightened my gloom,*
> *when hopeless longing*

my heart had wasted,
when worldly pleasures
I wished to win me,
by fear fettered and maddened.

Till there comes the motive of the Last Greeting:

No. 102

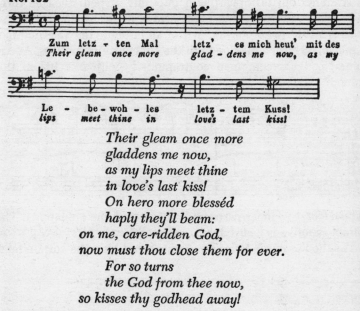

Zum letz - ten Mal   letz' es mich heut' mit des
Their gleam once more   glad - dens me now, as my

Le - be - woh - les   letz - tem Kuss!
lips   meet thine in   love's last kiss!

Their gleam once more
gladdens me now,
as my lips meet thine
in love's last kiss!
On hero more blessèd
haply they'll beam:
on me, care-ridden God,
now must thou close them for ever.
For so turns
the God from thee now,
so kisses thy godhead away!

"He imprints a long kiss on her eyes", say the stage directions, "and she sinks back in his arms with closed eyes, unconsciousness gently stealing over her." For some time not a word is spoken, the orchestra saying all that is in the heart of each of them in a quiet meditation on Nos. 96 and 98. "He leads her tenderly to a low mossy bank underneath a broad-branched fir-tree, and there lays her down. He contemplates her, then closes her helmet. His eyes rest for a time on the form of the sleeping maiden, whom he now covers completely with the great steel shield of the Valkyrie. He moves slowly away, then turns round once more with a sorrowful look. He goes with solemn decision to the centre of the stage and turns his Spear-point towards a large rock." He strikes it three times with his Spear and summons Loge to appear and encircle

the fell with his fire, which at once, to the characteristic Loge motives, flames out on all sides. With a final command:

> *He who my spear-point's*
> *sharpness feareth*
> *ne'er breaks through this fierce-flaming fire!*

he stretches out his Spear, as if imposing a spell: then he turns
and departs, twice looking back sorrowfully at his child. The last
word is left to the orchestra, first of all intoning the Siegfried motive (No. 88), then playing with the lambent Fire motives. At one
point No. 98 is combined contrapuntally with No. 102 in this
fashion:

(The decorative inner parts are omitted from the quotation). The
Slumber motive is heard again, followed by the fateful No. 83 A,
and as the fire music fades away in the orchestra the curtain falls.

Siegfried

1

O F all the characters who had figured in the first drama of the *Ring* only one, Alberich, was destined to play a part in the last. In the new world in which *Siegfried* is set, Wotan appears not *in propria persona* but only as the Wanderer. Mime survives for a while from the *Rhinegold;* so also does Fafner, but in his changed form as Dragon. Alberich remains what he was at the beginning and will be to the end. Brynhilde is taken over from the *Valkyrie,* but psychologically transformed, though the transformation is not as complete as it will become in the *Twilight of the Gods.* Erda, as before, is less a character than a nature-symbol. Siegfried, on whose unconscious shoulders now falls the burden Wotan had laid down, is entirely new.

The prelude to *Siegfried* is psychological; it reveals what is passing, not only at the moment when the new work opens but always, in the mind of Mime,[1] who has never ceased to brood on

---

[1] Mime should not be the feeble, pitiful, sympathy-cadging figure that is made of him in most of the performances we see. He is a thing of evil, and, in his debased way, of power for evil. Wagner's conception of him is to be seen in a passage in the stage directions of *Young Siegfried* that was not reproduced in the present opera. "He is small and bent, somewhat deformed and hobbling. His head is abnormally large, his face a dark ashen colour and wrinkled, his eyes small and piercing, with red rims, his grey beard long and scrubby, his head bald and covered with a red cap. He wears a dark grey smock with a broad belt about his loins: feet bare, with thick coarse soles underneath. *There must be nothing approaching caricature in all this:* his aspect, when he is quiet, must simply be eerie; it is only in moments of extreme excitement that he becomes *outwardly* ludicrous, but never too uncouth. His voice is husky and harsh; but this again ought of itself never to provoke the listener to laughter." (Italics mine).

Nor must Alberich be the purely grotesque figure we generally see on

the problem of the Ring — how to gain possession of it and make himself master of the world. In the Nibelheim scene of the *Rhinegold* we saw him musing mournfully on his subjection to Alberich, on the cause of it, the possibility of escape from it, to a curious little figure in thirds in the bassoons. It is with this motive of Reflection (No. 35), still in the bassoons, that Wagner begins the prelude to *Siegfried:*

No. 104

The dwarf's thoughts are fixed, as always, on the Hoard (see No. 37):

No. 105

as he goes on with his smithing to the familiar motive from the *Rhinegold:*

No. 106

to which, as will be seen, is conjoined the motive of the Servitude of the Nibelungs (No. 33). This latter swells to a great moan as Mime reflects on his unhappy lot and his impotence to remedy it. Then his thoughts turn to the all-important Ring (No. 8 in the wood wind). If only he could possess himself of that! But how? Only a stronger arm than his, and a weapon better than any he has ever succeeded in making, will ever subdue the monstrous Dragon; and the bass trumpet, giving out the Sword motive (No. 48) softly, hints at what that weapon shall be.

---

the stage: for all his ugliness there must be a certain grandeur about him. "He resembles", says Wagner in *Young Siegfried,* "Mime in every respect [i.e. in that they are brothers]; only his appearance and his expression invariably make a more serious and indeed nobler effect."

As he plunges afresh into his work with the frenzy of despair the curtain rises, showing a rocky cavern with two natural entrances from the forest, one in the background (right), the other, a broader one, also at the back but sideways. On the left, against the wall, the rocks of the cave shape themselves into a great smith's forge, the chimney of which, also natural, goes up through the roof; only the bellows are artificial. Near by are a big anvil and other smith's implements. At the anvil sits Mime, tapping away with a small hammer at a sword in the making. He is manifestly uneasy and out of spirits. At last he gives it up. All is in vain, he complains; the youth whom he harbours in his cave has once again commanded him to make him a sword, but the best that Mime has hitherto been able to make, though fit for any giant, has been shattered by the malapert boy at a single stroke, as though it were a toy for a child! Peevishly he throws the sword down on the anvil, puts his arms akimbo, and, to the accompaniment of No. 104, stares moodily at the ground. "I know no sword", he says, "that the boy could not break, except one forged from the fragments of Nothung. But all my skill does not suffice for the welding of that; and even could I achieve it it would bring me nothing but shame." The old torturing thought of his impotence fills his mind as the Dragon motive heaves like a brute mass in the depths of the orchestra in the tuba:

No. 107

There in the dark forest lurks Fafner, his huge bulk stretched across the Hoard. Only Siegfried could slay him, and he only with the so-desired sword: "and I cannot weld it", Mime wails shrilly, "this sword!" Once more he sets to work in hopeless dejection at the steel on the anvil:

> *I tinker and hammer it*
> *at the boy's behest;*
> *one blow and he'll break it to bits,*
> *and scoff and scold at the smith!*

and again he lets the hammer fall from his poor puny hand.

2

As he does so a merry "Hoiho!" is heard from without, and the young Siegfried, accompanied by a motive that will henceforth characterise him to the end:

No.108

enters impetuously from the wood. He is wearing a rough forester's dress; a silver horn hangs on a chain from his neck; he is leading a great bear by a bast-rope and setting it with wanton boyish humour at the frightened Mime. The dwarf drops the sword in terror and cowers behind the forge, the boy pursuing him with gay laughter: he has brought the bear, he explains, to ask in person for the sword. He releases the brute, gives him a stroke on the back with the rope, and sends him lumbering off into the wood, whereupon Mime, trembling all over, comes out from behind the forge: he never objects, he tells the boy, to his killing bears, but to bring them alive into the cave is going a little too far.

Sitting down to recover from his laughter, Siegfried explains that he had gone out into the wood hoping to find some companion more to his liking than the dwarf; he had sounded his horn (No. 108), and out of the bush had come a bear and growled at him; and, for lack of something better, Siegfried had accepted him as at any rate an improvement on the dwarf; so he had bridled him and brought him to ask about the sword. His usual self again now, Mime takes the sword from the anvil and hands it to the boy, singing its praises as sharp enough even for him. But sharpness and brightness are nothing, Siegfried tells him, if the steel be not hard and true. Passing his hand over it he rejects it as merely a useless toy, not a sword but "a pitiful pin"; and smiting it on the anvil he breaks it into splinters. Then, to a lively new motive, characteristic of his youthful impetuosity:

No.109

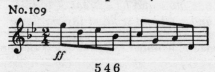

which accompanies him all through his harangue, he vents his rage on the terrified Mime. What does the wretched boaster and bungler mean by fobbing him off with a piece of trash of this sort? He is always prating of battles and giants and great deeds and weapons of might; yet when Siegfried essays the swords he has made for him they break in twain at his first grip on them. Were not the pitiful old imp, he continues, too vile for his hate he would break him in pieces, him and his sword. "Then would my torment have an end!"; and he throws himself in a raging temper on a stone seat.

Mime has prudently kept out of his way during this tempest, which goes on raging in the orchestra (No. 109) after Siegfried has ceased railing. He tries the line of suave cajolery. Why is the boy so petulant? he asks him. How is it that he, Mime, can never please him, try as he will? To a new motive, a rhythmical modification of No. 32:

No.110 *Moderato*

he appeals to his sense of gratitude: "thou shouldst be obedient to Mime, who always thinks but of thee". The sulking boy turns to the wall, presenting his back to the dwarf, who stands for a moment perplexed. Then he goes to the pots on the hearth and coaxingly shows Siegfried the meat and the broth he has prepared for him out of pure affection. Without turning round, the boy knocks meat and bowl out of his hands: "meat did I roast for myself", he says; "and slake thy own thirst with thy swill!" Still to the accompaniment of No. 110, Mime reproaches him in high-pitched querulous tones. So this is the sorry wage he gets for all his love and devotion! In a whining voice:

No.111 *Allegro*

Als zul-len-des Kind zog ich dich auf,
A whim-per-ing babe brought I thee up,

he reminds the boy how he had brought him up, a whimpering little brat, given him warm clothes and food and drink and a soft bed which he used to smooth with his own hands, and many a toy, including a ringing horn — and all for pure love of him. He had worked for him, thought for him, quickened his wits with wise counsel, given him the golden key to knowledge. He stays at home and toils and moils while the boy wanders at will in the woods; the poor old dwarf withers and wastes for the lad, and all he gets for his work and worry is torment and hatred: and overcome by his own pathos he breaks down and sobs.

But when Siegfried at last turns round and fixes his eyes searchingly on Mime's face the dwarf evades his look. To the accompaniment now of No. 109, now of No. 110, Siegfried, beginning steadily and quietly but soon working himself into a passion again, gives him his frank opinion of him. "Much indeed hast thou taught me, much from thee have I learned; but what thou didst most desire to teach me, that have I tried in vain to learn — how to endure the sight of thee! Thou givest me food and drink, and I feed on loathing alone; my pillow thou makest, but no sleep can I get; when thou wouldst teach me wisdom I remain deaf and dull. I have only to glance at thee, and everything thou dost becomes evil in my eyes." His temper rises as he goes on:

when thou dost stand,
shuffle and scrape,
crouching and slinking,
with thine eyelids blinking,
by the neck I long
to take the nodder,
an end to make
of the misshaped fumbler!
So learned I, Mime, to love thee.

Let the dwarf, if he is as wise as he claims to be, solve this puzzle for him if he can — why is every beast he meets in the forest, and the trees, and the birds, and the fish in the brook, all dearer to him than Mime? Why, indeed, once having left him, does he ever return to him?

3

Mime is confident he can answer this. As a new motive of great beauty, that of Love, which brings for the first time a note of profound feeling into the score, wells up in the 'cellos:

No. 112

he carefully explains — still keeping at a safe distance, however — that it is only the boy's wilful tongue, not his heart, that makes him talk like this. "Always the young yearn for the parents' nest, and the name of this longing is love. Thus thou dost love thy Mime, and cannot help loving him; for what the parent bird is to the fledgling, nourished in the nest ere he can fly, such to his boy, his bantling, is the sage and unselfish old Mime." Again to the accompaniment of the tender No. 112, Siegfried asks him to explain something more. "When the birds sing for happiness in the spring, each of them calls enticingly to the other; and thou thyself hast told me that they were husband and wife. They caressed each other and built them a nest, and brooded there over their little ones until these could spread their wings:

No. 113

So it is too with the deer in the woods, and even the wild wolves and foxes: the father brings the food to the nest, the mother suckles the young. And thus I learned what love is, and from the mother I never took the cubs. Where then is *thy* wife, Mime, that I may call her mother?"

Ignoring a peevish interjection from the Nibelung, the boy goes on, in a derisive imitation of the words and the tune of the latter's first recital of the kindnesses he had shown him: "The whimpering babe thou broughtest up, fed it and gave it warm clothes. But what wind had wafted the whelp to thee? Didst thou make me, perchance, without a mother?" Mime, greatly embarrassed, assures him that he is his father and mother in one. Siegfried gives him the lie direct. For he has observed that the young of a brood are like the old; he has seen his own face in a brook, and he is no more like Mime than a shining fish is like a toad, and no fish ever had toad for its father. With the orchestra returning to the impetuous figure shown in No. 109 he asks again if the dwarf can tell him why, having fled from him into the forest as he so often does, he ever returns to him; and he answers his question himself — he returns solely to learn from him who his father and mother were, and this he will know if he has to tear it out of him by force, as he has had to wring the knowledge of everything else out of him, even speech.

He seizes him by the throat. Mime, half-choked, at last regains his liberty; and after another lament over the boy's ingratitude he begins to tell him what he knows. Though, it is true, he is neither father nor mother to him, it is to Mime that Siegfried owes everything: "but a fool was I to count on thy thanks!" he wails. The orchestra gives out softly the motive of the Volsung Woe (No. 54); and to modifications of that and other motives associated in the *Valkyrie* with Siegmund and Sieglinde, such as:

he tells how long ago he had found a woman weeping in a desolate wood, how he had brought her to his cave, where he gave her warm shelter, how she had given birth to a child — Siegfried — and died. "So died, then", says Siegfried slowly and sadly, "my mother of me?" Mime starts off again with his hypocritical "A whimpering babe brought I thee up"; but Siegfried cuts him short

and demands to be told more. Why, he asks, is he called Siegfried? It was his mother's wish, Mime replies, that he should bear
that name, "for as Siegfried shouldst thou be fair and strong". The
mother's name he never knew, he says; but under a new threat
from the boy he reveals that it was Sieglinde. But the father's
name the dwarf had never learned; all he knew of him was that
he had died in combat. Once more his attempt to go on in the old
whining, canting vein is cut short by Siegfried: what proof, he
asks, has he that Mime is telling him the truth?

After some pondering, the Nibelung produces the two fragments of a broken sword, while the Sword motive (No. 48) comes
out quietly in the orchestra, over a bass formed from the Nibelung smithing motive (No. 32). These, says the dwarf, were all
the pitiful pay he got for his kindness to the woman — a shattered
sword which, she told him, the boy's father had borne in the last
of his fights, in which he was killed. At once the boy leaps to the
right conclusion: it is out of these fragments that the smith shall
forge him the sword he desires — his own rightful weapon; and a
phrase that begins as the Sword motive but continues as No. 108
symbolises the bond between the old and the new possessor of
the Sword:

No. 115

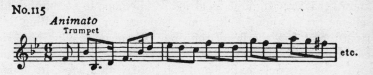

To insistent repetitions of the eager No. 109 he bids Mime set to
work without delay:

> *Trick me no longer;*
> *no more of thy toys;*
> *in these fragments alone*
> *put I my faith!*
> *Find I a fault,*
> *forge thou it feebly,*
> *bungling and botching*
> *the sturdy steel,*
> *thou hound, thy hide will I baste,*
> *I'll burnish thee brighter than steel!*

He will have the sword this very day, and with it he will leave the wood and go into the world, never to return:

No.116

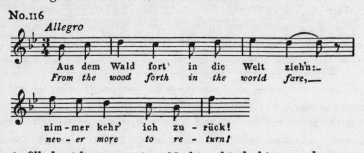

He is filled with a great joy. Nothing binds him any longer to Mime and his cave. "My father art thou not; thy hearth is not my house, nor thy cave my rightful roof". He will be free, like the fish in the stream, the bird on the wind; and the hated little Nibelung he will see no more. He rushes impetuously into the forest, executing a joyous fantasia on the theme of No. 116, and leaving Mime in the utmost confusion and terror.

4

For the dwarf is now a prey to a new anxiety. He has always known that only through Siegfried can he hope to accomplish his scheme for subduing Fafner and winning for himself Ring and Hoard; and now the headstrong boy is bent on leaving him. He goes back to the forge and seats himself by the anvil. "He storms away", he says dejectedly, "and I sit here, with a new care added to the old one! What way out is there for me? How hold this wildling to me and lead him to Fafner's lair? How forge me those baffling splinters — for no forge-fire can melt them, no dwarf's hammer conquer their hardness"; and he ends with a wail of "The Nibelung's hate, need and toil ne'er can knit Nothung anew, make me the sword as it was!"

As he collapses in despair by the anvil, Wotan enters slowly from the forest by the door at the back of the cave. He is now the Wanderer, wearing a long mantle of dark blue and a large hat that comes low down over the eye that is lacking. With a sudden dramatic change the orchestra slows down to a tempo befitting the gravity of the God, whose characteristic motive, as Wanderer, is intoned solemnly by the brass:

No.117

It has a broad pendant that is like the unhurrying tread of a God:

No.118

and a majestic ending:

No.119

He greets the cowering Nibelung courteously, asking the customary grace of house and hearth for a weary wayfarer. In reply to Mime's timorous enquiries he says he is known to the world as Wanderer, always receiving guest-greeting from good men, learning from them and speaking wisdom to them; for few are wise enough — the shaft is directed covertly at Mime — to know the true nature of their own need, and out of his own store of wisdom he has often been able to help them. All this while he has been steadily approaching Mime, and now he has come right down to the hearth. The dwarf protests that he is wise enough for his own purposes and needs no counsel from strangers, and tells the intruder to go on his way. But the Wanderer calmly seats himself

by the hearth and proposes a combat of wits: he stakes his head
on his ability to answer whatever question the Nibelung may ask
him.

5

The Reflection motive (No. 104) is murmured by the bassoons
as Mime ponders within himself how to get rid of this intrusive
spy, as he regards him. In the end, confident of his own cunning,
he decides to accept the challenge — his hearth against the other's
head. He will ask him three questions. This Wanderer boasts of
having gone far and wide over the earth's back. Very well; can
the wise one tell him what race it is that dwells in the caverns of
the earth? To the accompaniment of the familiar motives at the
appropriate points (Nos. 32, 8, 33, 105 etc.) the Wanderer replies
that it is the Nibelungs, whose home is Nibelheim. Slaves they
were to Alberich, who had won power over them and amassed
great treasure by a magic Ring. The same procedure then follows,
with the same reference to characteristic motives. Mime, after further reflection, asks what race it is that dwells on the surface of
the earth. It is the Giants, is the answer, whose home is Riesen-
heim. Two of them, Fasolt and Fafner, envying the Nibelung's
power, made Ring and Hoard their own: then strife broke out between the brothers, Fasolt was slain, and Fafner, transformed into
a Dragon, now guards the treasure. And now, what is the dwarf's
third question?

Mime, rather baffled by this omniscience, reflects more deeply
than ever, and at last asks, "What is the race that dwells on cloud-
covered heights?" To a stately enunciation of the Walhall motive
the Wanderer replies that it is the Gods. Walhall is their home;
the highest of them is Licht-Alberich, Wotan.[1] From the stem of
the world-ash-tree he had made himself a Spear, and by virtue
of the runes he had carved on it he governs the world: the Giants
he curbed, the Nibelungs kneel before him; "ever they bow and
obey him, the Ring's most mighty Lord!" As if by accident he lets
his Spear touch the ground; there is a light rumble of thunder,
and Mime shrinks back in terror. "Now tell me, thou wise dwarf,
have I true answers given? My head can I have and hold?"

[1] Alberich himself, as has been pointed out earlier, is Schwarz-Alberich
(Black Alberich). The antithesis is that of the power that works in the light
and the power rooted in darkness.

Timidly and and ingratiatingly Mime assures him that his head
is safe and exhorts him to go on his way; but the Wanderer, to the
accompaniment of the stately No. 118, tranquilly reminds him
that by the rules of wagering it is now the dwarf's turn to back
his own wisdom with his own head. Mime is scared, but pulling
his wits together and gaining confidence as he proceeds he prepares to put his first question. A motive that will always characterise him later in his moments of satisfaction with his own slippery craft:

accompanies him as he mock-modestly disparages his own poor
knowledge. It is a long time, he says, since he left his mother and
his homeland, and his mother-wits are a little moidered. But he
will do his best; perhaps his luck will be in and the poor dwarf
will save his head.

What is the race, asks the Wanderer, the orchestra giving out
the Volsung motive (No. 58), that Wotan wreaked his wrath on,
though he loved it more than all others in the world. Little does
he know, replies Mime, of heroes in general; but this question at
least he can answer fully — it is the race of the Volsungs, which
Wotan begat and cherished, though he chastised it too. To Wälse
were born Siegmund and Sieglinde, a wild twin pair, and the offspring of their love was Siegfried, of all the Volsungs the strongest. "Now tell me, Wanderer, if so far I have saved my head?"
The Wanderer compliments him genially on his knowingness, and
poses the second question: Who is the wise Nibelung who harbours Siegfried, to fight Fafner for him and win him the Hoard;
and by what sword will Fafner die? This, Mime, feels, is almost
absurdly easy. He rubs his hands in glee as he answers, to the accompaniment of No. 120, "Nothung is the name of the sword: in
an ash-tree's stem it was struck by Wotan, and Siegmund alone
could draw it forth. He wielded it in his last fight, but it was shattered on Wotan's spear; and now the fragments are in the possession of a cunning smith, who knows that only with this Wotan-
sword can a brave but witless boy, Siegfried, slay the Dragon."

The slippery No. 120 comes out boldly in the orchestra as he asks again, highly pleased with himself, "Has the dwarf saved his head?"

Wotan breaks into a peal of laughter. Nowhere on earth, he assures him, is the like of Mime for wisdom to be found. But since he is so wise as to mould this stripling hero to his own ends, perhaps he is wise enough also to answer this third question: By whose hand shall the mighty pieces of the Volsung sword be made afresh into Nothung?

6

Mime starts up in the wildest terror, and with the boisterous No. 108 seeming to mock him all the time in the orchestra he screams, "The pieces! The Sword! Woe's me, I know not! What shall I do? Where shall I turn? Accursed steel! Would I ne'er had stolen it. Nought has it brought me but care and fear! It is too hard for me, hammer and rivet and solder it as I will! The craftiest of smiths here comes to shame!" In a paroxysm of despair he throws his tools about as if demented, crying, "Who'll shape me the Sword that baffles my skill? Who can achieve this marvel?"

Tranquilly, accompanied by the dignified No. 117, the Wanderer rises from the hearth. "Three questions of thine I suffered, three I answered. But as for thee, vain is thy knowledge: what it most behoved thee to know, because it would have served thy need, that thou knewest not." While the Nibelung motive (No. 32) chatters distractedly in the upper part of the orchestra and the Treaty motive (No. 13) goes thundering down against it in the trombones, the Wanderer speaks his final words. "I have won the wise one's head: now, bold destroyer of Fafner, listen to what I have to tell thee. He who knows not what fear is alone shall forge Nothung anew! Thy wise old head ward well from today. I want it not: I leave it to him who has never learned to fear!" He turns away with a smile and disappears into the forest.

Mime has sunk on to his stool, as if crushed. The Wanderer's words are an enigma as well as a threat; for if Siegfried has any fear in him he will never be able to overcome Fafner, while if, unfearing, he should achieve that deed, then, according to this mysterious Wanderer who appears to know all secrets, the dwarf's own head will be forfeit to him.[1] There now follows a piece of orchestral painting of extraordinary power. As Mime stares in desperation at the sunlit forest it seems to him to be alive with menacing lights, flickering and flashing, glittering and swirling, quivering and darting. Loge (Nos. 22 and 23) is filling it with flame, and from the depths of the orchestra comes a roar as of monsters opening their maws to seize on their prey. With a shriek of "Fafner! Fafner!" Mime collapses in terror behind the great anvil.

7

As he does so the Sword motive (this time in the minor) rings out in the trumpet; then the atmosphere suddenly changes, the motive of Siegfried's cry for freedom (No. 116) begins its lively chatter again, and the boy's voice is heard from the wood, hailing Mime with a shout of "Ho there! thou idler!" When he enters the cave he is surprised to find it apparently empty. Gaily he searches for the dwarf, whose voice is at last heard from behind the anvil, asking feebly if the boy is alone. Siegfried humorously suggests that perhaps he is sharpening the sword. The word plunges Mime into confusion once more. How can he forge it? he asks; and half to himself he repeats the Wanderer's closing words — "He who knows not what fear is alone shall forge Nothung anew." Hardly conscious of the boy's presence, he continues to muse aloud on his own baffling problem: his wise old head he had wagered and lost — forfeit to him "who never fear has learned". He sees now the mistake he had made in his bringing-up of Siegfried:

> *Him would I fly*
> *who fear has known!*
> *But that truly ne'er taught I the stripling;*
> *I fool-like forgot*

[1] This question of "fearing" is the knottiest psychological and dramatic problem with which Wagner has confronted us in the *Ring*. He himself never succeeded in steering a quite logical course between the various possible handlings of the motive that occurred to him from time to time. A full discussion of the complicated matter, however, is impossible here: I can only refer the reader who wishes to track it out in all its windings to my *Life of Wagner,* Vol. II, pages 307–318, where I have gone into it at tedious length. In the present analysis we can only keep to Wagner's libretto.

the one thing good.
Love for the dwarf
was his lesson;
but alas, no luck had I!
How now put this fear in his heart?

Recovering something of his composure, he assures Siegfried that his thoughts had been wholly turned on him during his absence, and the things of weight he might perhaps teach him:

> *What fear is learned I for thee,*
> *that I, thou dunce, might teach thee.*

He begins the lesson. The thoughtless boy means to go out into the world without having learned fear; but without that knowledge the sharpest of swords will not protect him. Approaching the wondering and impatient Siegfried and speaking more and more confidently as he regains his self-possession, he assures him that he had only been keeping a promise of his to the child's mother in preserving him from the guile of the world until he had learned fear.

"What is this fearing?" Siegfried asks; "is it a craft? If so, why have I not been taught it?" The orchestra becomes a pictorial instrument again as Mime asks him if, when night falls on the forest, he has never seen and heard horrors and terrors crowding round him, so that he quaked with fright and it seemed as if his throbbing heart would burst. "Feltest thou never that, then fear is far from thy soul". Mime himself quakes with terror as his imagination plays upon the picture he is conjuring up. But Siegfried merely remarks reflectively, "That must be the strangest of feelings, all this shivering, shuddering, glowing and trembling, burning and fainting, and for these delights do I long. But always my heart beats soundly in my breast. Can you, Mime, teach me?"

Mime's great moment has now come. He will teach the boy fearing, he says, if he will accompany him to Neidhöhle, at the east of the wood, where there is a dragon (here No. 107 heaves up its cumbrous bulk in the depths of the orchestra), who slays and devours men; it is "not far from the world", he assures Siegfried, for he knows that to leave the wood for the world is the heart's desire of the boy. To this Fafner he will go gladly, says Siegfried, so let Mime make him at once the sword he needs. To the rhythm of No. 109 he urges the dwarf to set to work. But Mime wails once more that, alas, the task is beyond his strength, though within the power of one who has never known fear. At this, Siegfried brushes the puling little gnome aside and strides to the hearth, saying that he himself will forge afresh his father's blade.

To a vigorous transformation of the Siegfried horn motive (No. 108):

No. 121

Allegro

he begins by pitching Mime's tools about. The dwarf tells him that had he been more willing in the past to learn the smith's craft he would find his labour lighter now; but the boy replies that when the master does not know there is not much chance of the apprentice learning from him. He makes a face at Mime and tells him to take himself off and not meddle, lest he fall in the fire. By now he has piled a great heap of charcoal on the hearth: he blows up the fire, fixes the fragments of the sword in the vice, and files them vigorously. Mime watches him, from time to time offering a piece of advice that is contemptuously rejected, and wondering more and more at the success of Siegfried's unorthodox methods: "My wisdom fails, that see I clearly; the fool is favoured by folly alone! See how he works! The steel is in shreds, yet cool is he yet. Old am I, as old as the cave and the wood; yet aught like this never before have I seen!".

8

As he realises the likelihood of the boy succeeding, as the Wanderer seemed to have hinted he would, fear steals again into Mime's heart:

> *where now to hide*
> *my hapless head?*
> *To the valiant boy will it fall,*
> *learns he from Fafner not fear!*
> *But woe is me still!*
> *If Siegfried learns fear,*

> *how then shall the dragon be slain?*
> *Can he win the dwarf the Ring?*
> *Oh fate accurst!*
> *I'm fettered fast:*
> *where shall I counsel find*
> *how to master this fearless boy?*

By this time Siegfried has filed the fragments away and put them in a crucible, which he places on the forge fire. He turns to Mime and asks what name the sword once had. "Nothung", is the reply; "'twas thy mother told me its name". The characteristic interval (the raised fifth) that has differentiated No. 121 from No. 108 now serves to shape the Nothung motive, which is first of all foreshadowed thus:

No. 122
Allegro vigoroso

before assuming its final form as Siegfried invokes the weapon:

No. 123
No - thung!   Neid-lich-es   Schwert!

He blows up a roaring fire with the bellows:

No. 124
Animato

as he goes on with his lusty song to the Sword:

No.125

It continues to an orchestral accompaniment that seems to belch fire as the labouring bellows rise and fall. "Hoho! Hohei!" Siegfried sings; "bellows blow, brighten the blaze!" Once he had felled a tree in the forest and burned the good grey ash to charcoal, that now flares and sparkles and fuses the shreds of the steel:

No.126

All the while Mime is watching him closely and thinking aloud: "He'll forge him the sword and fell grim Fafner, that see I clearly now. Hoard and Ring will fall to him; but how shall I make them mine?" He has hatched out a plan. He will brew a broth which he will give to the boy when he is faint after the combat with the Dragon; in it he will put herbs that will send him into a sound sleep; and then he, Mime, will kill him with Nothung itself, and Ring and Hoard will be his. He rubs his hands, delighted with his own cleverness: "Hei, wisest Wanderer, deem'st thou me dull now? What think'st thou of my subtle wit? Have I found the way to peace?"

Meanwhile Siegfried continues with his work and his song. He pours the glowing contents of the crucible into a mould, which he plunges into the trough, where the steaming steel hisses under the shock of the cold water. Exultantly he thrusts it into the fire and tugs again at the bellows, singing his joyous greeting to "Nothung, the masterful sword, that will soon make hot blood flow", and his good spirits find expression in an exuberant motive of Joy in Victory in the orchestra:

No. 127

During his work he has kept an interested eye on Mime, who, beside himself with delight at his own cleverness, has been shaking herbs and spices into a cooking-pot which, standing on the opposite side of the hearth, he now puts on the fire. What is the booby doing there with his sauces? asks Siegfried. Hypocritically the dwarf congratulates him on his skill as a smith: the master is learning now from the man, who puts him to shame. Henceforth it is Siegfried who shall do the smithing, while Mime will boil the eggs for his soup. But the boy's healthy instinct bids him beware: he will take care that he eats or drinks nothing of Mime's cooking.

9

He takes the mould from the fire, breaks it, lays the glowing steel on the anvil, and after a derisive comment on the dwarf's incompetence in his craft he launches into the second phase of the forging song. A vigorous new motive pounds out in the orchestra:

No. 128

as he rains blow after blow on the steel with his hammer and exults in the new life that he can feel springing up in the fragments of his father's sword: he has tamed its stubborn pride, he cries. Unobservant of Mime, who has been pouring the contents of the pot into a flask and gloating in anticipation over his own triumph, the boy hammers away at the sword, until at last he takes it from the anvil, brandishes it, and plunges it into the water trough, laughing boisterously at its hissing there.

While he is fitting it into a haft, Mime, to the accompaniment of No. 32, works himself into an ecstasy over the coming success of his plan. He has a vision of a glorified Mime bestriding a subject world. Once he had been slave to Alberich; but soon the Gold will be his, and then the poor despised dwarf will be master of the Nibelungs, with the whole world prostrate at his feet, Gods and heroes cringing before him:

> *Mime, the daring,*
> *Mime is king now,*
> *prince of the Nibelungs,*
> *ruler of all!*
> *Hei, Mime, what brought thee this luck?*
> *Who counted that this would come?*

He leaps about and laughs delightedly:

No. 129

By this time Siegfried has riveted the handle with his last blow. He brandishes the sword, greeting it with a final great cry of "Nothung!", the phrase beginning, as it has always done until now, with a suggestion of the coming of the minor, but changing unexpectedly into the major towards the end, with electrifying effect:

No. 130

(Wagner's 2/4 notation may perhaps conceal the actual rhythm of this from the reader; the effect on the ear is):

No. 131

Dead the Sword had lain in splinters, Siegfried sings, but now he has brought it to life again, glorious and proud:

> *Show thou the dastards*
> *how thou canst shine!*
> *Cut through the false heart,*
> *strike at the knave!*
> *See, Mime, thou smith:*
> *so severs Siegfried's sword!*

He aims a mighty blow with it at the anvil, which splits from top to bottom, while the orchestra rushes on with an exuberant combination of No. 115 and No. 108. The curtain descends with Mime, who has been dancing on his stool in rapture, falling off it in terror as Siegfried exultantly holds the Sword aloft.

10

The prelude to the second act prepares us for a different atmosphere from the one that Siegfried has filled with the gladness of his youth in the first act.

Under shuddering tremolandi in the lower strings we hear the motive of Fafner in his re-incarnation as Dragon; it will be seen that the fall of a full fourth that characterised the Giants in the *Rhinegold* (see No. 16) has now become an augmented fourth, giving the motive an added cumbersomeness:

No. 132

The tuba, which plays a large part in the prelude, then gives out the motive (No. 107) which had represented Fafner as he figured in the imagination of Mime in the prelude to the first act; and it links up with No. 132 in this fashion:

No. 133

Through the subterranean gloom of the orchestral picture the Ring motive pierces occasionally: then the Curse motive (No. 41) makes a sinister gesture in the trombones. It is followed by No. 40 — the motive of Annihilation which had accompanied, in the *Rhinegold*, Alberich's warning of the doom that should for ever cling to the Ring of which he had been robbed; and this by the Servitude motive, that of the Ring once more, and finally No. 132 again.

On the rising of the curtain we see a little knoll in the forest, which descends in the background to the entrance to a cave — Fafner's Neidhöhle. To the left, through the trees, a fissured cliff is visible. It is night, the gloom being thickest in the background, where at first nothing is clearly distinguishable by the eye. Crouched by the cliff is Alberich, brooding darkly, to the accompaniment of No. 40. We learn from his monologue that he is at his unresting watch with straining eye and ear upon the cave, in which his hope of world-mastership is buried. Sooner or later, he is convinced, the fateful day will dawn: will it be today? he asks. As a combination of the Valkyries' motive (No. 74) and that of the Need of the Gods (No. 81) is heard in the orchestra he becomes aware of a stormwind blowing towards him through the forest, and the approach of a bluish light. Is the Dragon-slayer coming, the one who shall rid him of Fafner? But the wind dies down and the light fades away, and darkness and a sinister quiet descend upon the scene again. Out of the shadow, however, he sees someone approaching him; and by the light of the moon, suddenly breaking through the clouds, he recognises the Wanderer. For a moment he recoils in terror; then he breaks out in wrathful reproaches. What does this treacherous trickster want here? he asks. Is he bent on more evil? Let him go his way, work new woe elsewhere, and leave him in peace. Alberich's vehemence contrasts with the composure of the Wanderer, who tells him quietly that on this occasion he comes not to do but to witness ("Zu schauen kam ich, nicht zu schaffen").

As has been pointed out on a previous page, the dramatist in Wagner always makes him range himself, for the time being, on the side of whatever character happens to be speaking, get inside the skin of the character and see the matter of the moment from his point of view. He now puts into Alberich's mouth an unanswerable indictment of the God. He is not so dull now, says the Nibelung, as on that day of his sorrow when Wotan ravished the Ring from him by guile and force and gave it to the Giants to redeem his debt to them, a debt engraved in solemn runes on the shaft of his Spear. Now the God is caught in his own net; another crime like his first, and the Spear that is the source and the symbol of his power will crumble into dust.

The Wanderer's rejoinder has truth in it and yet is sophistical:

> *Not by treaties writ upon it*
> *bound art thou,*
> *base one, to me:*
> *it mastered thee by its own strength:*
> *for strength then ward I it well.*

In half-a-dozen words Alberich pierces through the sophistry to the facts:

> *In pride of power*
> *how boldly thou threat'nest,*
> *yet dark is thy heart with dismay.*

For the Wanderer knows that the Nibelung's curse will bring death to whoever holds the treasure; and the God's consuming fear is that it will come back again into Alberich's hands:

> *That gnaws thee with care unending!*
> *For let it but come*
> *again to my hand,*
> *not like the foolish Giants*
> *I'll use the Ring's great might:*
> *then tremble, thou holy*
> *guardian of heroes!*
> *Walhall's towers*
> *I storm with Hella's hosts:*
> *the world then will be mine!*

The Wanderer replies calmly that all this troubles him not, for the Ring's destined master will deal with it in a way of his own. To this the Nibelung has an effective answer: this hero whom Wotan hopes will gain possession of the Ring has been born of a race that the God himself has bred for his own ends, for that sole purpose. The Wanderer breaks off the argument: "Curse me not", he says, "but wrangle with Mime, who is bringing with him a stripling who will slay Fafner. Nought knows the boy of me: it is the Nibelung who is goading him on for his own ends. Be on thy guard: the boy knows nothing of the Ring, but Mime will tell him all. As for myself, I have no longer any part in the matter. Him whom I love I will leave to work unaided, to stand or fall as he may. He is his own lord: heroes alone avail me." Here a new motive appears:

No. 134
Moderato

that will in future characterise certain aspects of Siegfried.

11

The news that the God will not intervene rejoices Alberich, for with both his despised brother and the unsophisticated boy he is confident he can cope. His direct questions, put eagerly to the Wanderer — "Then with Mime I fight alone for the Ring? Will it fall into my hands again?" — are composedly waved aside: all the Wanderer will tell him is that a hero is drawing near to rescue the Hoard. Two Nibelungs lust for the Gold; Fafner will fall, and then the Ring will be his who can seize it. Would Alberich know more, let him enquire of Fafner himself. The orchestral texture during the whole scene is as a matter of course woven out of motives already familiar to us.

"If thou warn'st him of death", continues the Wanderer, "haply he'll give thee the toy: myself will wake him for thee." He mounts the knoll in front of the cave and calls out, "Fafner! Dragon! Awake!", to the great astonishment of Alberich, who now almost believes, yet hardly dares do so, that the Ring and the Hoard will soon come to him again. Accompanied by the lumbering No. 132 Fafner's deep voice is heard booming through a speaking-trumpet from the dark recesses of the cave. "Who wakes me from sleep?" it asks. "Here is a friend", the Wanderer replies ironically, "with a warning for thee; thy life he will grant thee if only thou wilt yield him the Hoard thou guardest." "What would he?" says the voice from the cave. "Waken, Fafner, and listen", says Alberich urgently; "a hero comes to measure his strength with thine." "I hunger for him", is the reply. The Wanderer and Alberich, the one ironically, the other eagerly, exhort the Dragon to take the prudent course. The stripling is brave, says the former, and sharp is his sword: the golden Ring alone the boy covets, adds Alberich, and if Fafner will yield it to *him* he will stay the fight, and the Hoard shall remain the Dragon's own, for him to sleep upon in peace. "What I have I hold", growls Fafner; and then, with a great yawn, "Let me slumber!"

His joke played out to the end he had foreseen, the Wanderer turns with a hearty laugh to Alberich: "Well, Alberich", he says, "that stroke failed!" Then he approaches him confidentially with some good advice. "All things are as needs they must be", he says, to the accompaniment of the motive which, in the *Rhinegold*, had first of all (in the prelude) symbolised primeval nature (No. 4), and later had accompanied Erda's solemn words to Wotan when she counselled him to give up the Ring, — "Whatever was, know I; whatever is, whatever shall be see I too" (No. 43):

> *all things go as needs they must:*
> *no whit may they be altered.*
> *And now do I leave thee;*
> *look to thyself:*
> *contend with Mime, thy brother;*
> *for truly thou knowest him better.*
> *But stranger things*
> *full soon shalt thou learn!*

and the new motive (No. 134) associated with the free Siegfried, followed by that of the Sword, hints at what that knowledge will be.

The Wanderer disappears into the forest, the same wind blowing and the same light flickering that had accompanied his coming. Alberich gazes after him, ill at ease. "There rides he away", he says, "leaving me to care and scorn. But laugh as ye will, ye light-spirited, lust-covetous race of the Gods! Your downfall yet shall I see; for while the Gold gleams in the sunlight the wise one will keep his watch — and Alberich will win at the last!" He slips into the cleft at the side of the stage, which for a little while remains empty, with only the Dragon motive, heaving in the depths of the orchestra, disturbing the silence.

12

Slowly day dawns, and Siegfried and Mime enter, the former wearing the Sword in a girdle of bast-rope. Mime, reconnoitring warily, at last recognises the cave, which now lies in a deep shadow, while the knoll is becoming gradually lighter. "Now we have reached it", says Mime; "we go no further"; and for some reason or other known only to Wagner the Slumber motive (No. 98) is played upon by the orchestra for a few bars. Siegfried seats himself under a great lime-tree and looks round him. So he has come at last, he says, to the place where, if anywhere, he will learn what fear is; and he bids Mime leave him. Seating himself opposite the boy, so that he may keep his eyes constantly on the cave, the dwarf assures him that if he does not learn fear here and now, no other place, no other time, will teach it him. For there in that cavern lies a grim and grisly Dragon, with vast and horrible jaws that could kill him with one snap: poisoned slaver drips from his mouth, and one drop of it will rot bones and body of him: if the great tail should coil round him, his bones would be crunched like glass.

Siegfried is undisturbed by this catalogue of horrors. Still reclining tranquilly under the tree, he tells Mime that if the monster's jaws are so terrible it will be well to close up his gullet; the poisoned slaver he will evade with a leap; the circling tail he will watch. But has the brute a heart, he asks, and is it where the heart is in men and beasts? Assured by Mime of this, the boy raises himself quickly to a sitting posture. "Nothung straight to his heart I will drive", he says; and he laughs at Mime as an old bungler who can babble of nothing more fear-inspiring than this. The dwarf's next move is to appeal hypocritically to the boy's better feelings: when he sees the Dragon, he tells him, his senses will swoon, his heart will beat madly in his breast, the forest will spin round him — and then, he hopes, he will "thank him who has led thee here, and think on Mime's great love". Siegfried's gorge rises at this as of old; when, he asks, with his usual frank vigour of speech, will he be rid of this slinking, blinking creature who professes to love him but for whom his whole being can feel nothing but loathing and hate?

Mime decides to leave him: he will lay him down by the spring, he says; Siegfried is to wait here until the sun is at its height, for at that time the monster always crawls from his cave to water at the stream. Siegfried amuses himself with the pleasing idea that at the spring the Dragon may come upon Mime and devour him; and he advises him, for his own life's sake, to take at once to his heels as fast as he can and trouble him no more. Once more the dwarf hypocritically urges the boy to call on him should he need counsel, and once more he is roughly repulsed. In the end Siegfried drives him off with a furious gesture, and as Mime slinks away he shows us, in an aside, what is at the back of his treacherous mind:

> *Fafner and Siegfried,*
> *Siegfried and Fafner,*
> *would each the other might slay!*

As the gnome disappears in the forest Siegfried stretches himself out comfortably under the lime-tree, and the lovely episode known as the Forest Murmurs begins. A great pastoral peace descends upon the scene as the woodland becomes slowly astir with morning life:

No. 135

Siegfried falls into a reverie. How fair the forest is, he muses, how it seems to laugh with delight now the loathsome old dwarf has gone, never more, he hopes, to offend his eyes! To have learned that Mime was not his father had filled his heart with joy. But how did his true father look in life — for surely if Mime had a son it would resemble him:

> *grizzled and grey,*
> *cramped and crooked,*
> *hump-backed and halting,*
> *with draggled ears drooping,*

bleary eyes blinking?
Out with the imp!
No more his face I'd see!

The silence seems to become more intense; only the gentle murmur of the forest is heard as the boy goes on with his brooding. Could he but learn what that mother of his was like whom he never saw! surely her eyes were soft and shining and tender like those of the roe-deer, but even more beautiful? She had borne her son in sorrow: must all mothers, then, die that their young may live? Would his eyes could be gladdened by the sight of this mortal mother of his, he sighs, as the 'cellos give out a tender reminiscence of No. 112, which merges into the soft strain (No. 25) to which Loge, in the *Rhinegold,* had told the Gods of the universal power of love.

13

As the boy leans back, lost in dreams, and the forest murmurs grow louder, his attention is attracted by the song of an awakened bird in the branches above him:

and:

and:

and:

As he listens, he muses on what the bird's message to him may be: is it trying to tell him something of his mother? The fretful old dwarf had told him that there was a meaning in the song of birds, could men but understand it. But how to find the way? What if he were to follow the bird's notes on a reed — "If I cannot grasp his words, let me try to pierce to his meaning through his melody". Running joyously to the neighbouring spring:

where there is a clump of reeds, he cuts one with his sword and hastily shapes it into a sort of pipe. He listens once again to the song, then makes an attempt to imitate it; but his clumsy reed either blows false or gives no sound at all. For a moment he is boyishly peevish at his failure; then he smiles and acknowledges the little songster his superior. Perhaps a slender reed is not the fitting instrument for such a dullard as he: why not essay one on which he already has a certain rough skill, and see if it brings him a better companion than the usual wolf or bear?

He puts his silver horn to his lips and blows a vigorous long-sustained call on it that sets the woodland ringing (No. 108, which branches out into the Siegfried motive No. 88 and then into that of the Sword). As the blithe tune rises to its climax something stirs in the background: he has awakened Fafner, who now lurches through the underwood about his cave and drags his monstrous bulk up to the higher ground, on which he rests the front part of his body, the orchestra accompanying him graphically all the time. As he comes to rest he gives out something like a yawn, which makes Siegfried turn round in astonishment and fix his gaze on him with boyish delight. "Oho!" he says jocularly, "at last my song has brought me something! A sweeter comrade could I find than this?"

The Dragon addresses him, his voice being magnified through a speaking-trumpet: who is it, he asks, that has roused him? "One who would learn what fear is", the boy replies; "haply from thee he'll learn it? If not, soon wilt thou be food for my sword." "Drink I came for, and now food I find", bellows Fafner, opening his jaws and showing his teeth. So the dialogue continues, Siegfried goading him with taunts and threats, Fafner growing angrier each moment. At last he roars defiance at the "boastful boy" and bids him come on. He drags his clumsy body further up the knoll, spouting venom from his nostrils and lashing at him with his tail. Angered by a wound he has received he rears up the front part of his body, meaning to throw his whole weight on the boy; he thus lays his breast open, and Siegfried, quickly sensing the place of the heart, plunges his sword into it up to the hilt.

Fafner, groaning with pain, raises himself still higher for a moment and then sinks to the ground. Withdrawing his sword, Siegfried leaps to one side. In a weaker voice Fafner, to the accompaniment of his own motive and that of Annihilation (No. 40), asks the stripling who has pierced him who he is, and who had egged him on to this murderous deed, for his own childish mind would assuredly never have planned it. The answer, for us, is given by the upsurge of the Curse motive in the trombone. But the boy knows nothing, not even who he is; all he can say is that the monster himself had provoked him to combat. Who it is he has slain, says Fafner, he himself will tell him; and he proceeds with the story of the brother Giants — here the augmented fourth of the Dragon motive becomes once more the perfect fourth of the Giants — who long ago won the cursed Gold from the Gods; Fafner had murdered his brother and changed himself into a Dragon the better to guard the Hoard; and now he, the last of his race, has fallen by the hand of a boy:

> *Heed thyself well,*
> *blossoming hero;*
> *he who drove thee blind to this deed*
> *doth plot now for thee also death!*
> *Mark the ending!*
> *Heed my word!*

and again the sinister Curse motive turns our thoughts to both the past and the future. "Wise are thy dying words," replies the boy; "but tell me now, wild one, whence I came: Siegfried I am called". The Dragon merely repeats the name with a sigh, and dies; from him the boy can learn nothing more of what he desires to know.

14

"The dead", he says to himself, "can give no tidings, so be thou, my living sword, my leader." Fafner, in his death agony, had rolled to one side. As the boy draws the sword out of his breast he smears his hand with blood: it burns him, and involuntarily he puts his fingers in his mouth to suck the blood from them. As he does so the song of the birds once more attracts his attention. They seem to be speaking to him, he says; and he realises that by some spell in the Dragon's blood their song has become intelligible to him. One of them is saying, "Now has the Nibelung Hoard been won by Siegfried: it lies awaiting him there in the cave. Could he win him the Tarnhelm too, it would serve him for wonderful deeds; but could he find the Ring it would make him lord of the world!" Thanking the bird, and resolving to follow its counsel, he descends into the cavern and is lost to our view.

The tranquil forest murmurs are suddenly broken in upon by hurried angular figures of this type in clarinet and bassoon:

as Mime slinks in; looking round timidly to make sure that Fafner is dead he goes warily towards the cave. But simultaneously Alberich emerges from the cleft on the other side of the stage, rushes at his brother and bars his way. There follows an episode of consummate musical and dramatic characterisation in which the precious pair volley questions and recriminations at each other. Each sees what the other is after and disputes his claim to the treasure. "What I have earned with bitter bane", screams Mime, "shall not escape me!" "Who was it robbed the Rhine of its Gold and wrought the spell in the Ring?" cries Alberich. "Who made the helm that served so well to hide you in your work?" rejoins Mime. " 'Twas I, not a bungler such as thou, who conceived the Ring that endowed you with the craft to make the helm." "And where is your Ring now? You let it go to the Giants, and what you lost I now have won for myself." "Not yours is the Hoard, but his who won it first." " 'Twas I who brought up the boy and with toil untold made him fit for my work." The more forceful Alberich ends the angry argument with:

> *For the stripling's care*
> *now the beggarly*
> *niggardly knave*
> *coolly claims*
> *forsooth, a king he must be!*
> *To scurviest hound*
> *rather the Ring*
> *should go than to thee:*
> *never, thou marrowless*
> *dolt, shall its might be thine!*

Mime, baffled and cowed, scratches his head and hypocritically suggests a compromise. "Let Alberich be lord of the Ring, but let him call me still his brother. I'll take the Tarnhelm, the pleasant toy: thus shall we both be paid, the booty fairly shared." With a scornful laugh Alberich assures him that he will never let the Tarnhelm pass into Mime's hands, for him to work his cunning will on him in his sleep. "Nothing then is to be mine?" screams Mime, almost inarticulate with rage; "bare must I go, bled to the bone? Not the smallest share of it all come to me?" "Not the smallest; not even a nail-head, knave, shall be thine." "Then no share shall be thine; I will summon Siegfried, whose deadly sword shall avenge me, brother mine!"

15

At that moment Siegfried comes out of the cave. Mime sees, to his astonishment, that the boy has taken nothing of the treasure, only, like a child captivated by a toy, the Tarnhelm. Alberich curses him when he sees he has the Ring too, and Mime adds to his mortification by giving him the malicious advice, "Get him to give it thee, brother, and soon it will be mine!" Mime runs into the forest: Alberich, muttering "Yet back to its lord it soon will come", slips into the cleft on the other side of the stage. Various motives associated with the Ring, the Rhinegold and the Rhinemaidens steal out quietly in the orchestra as Siegfried, coming forward slowly to the knoll, gazes meditatively at the Tarnhelm and the Ring: he has taken these two from the heap, he says, because that was the counsel given him by the wood-bird, but how they may serve him he does not know. To him they are merely baubles, witnesses to his victory over Fafner; yet this has not brought him the one thing he desired — to learn what fear is.

He puts the Ring on his finger and thrusts the Tarnhelm into his girdle. For a while there is dead silence, only the forest throbbing and whispering as before. Then suddenly the wood-bird's voice peals out once more. Siegfried has won him the helm and the Ring, it says; let him not trust Mime, the treacherous dwarf, not be deceived by his lies; he has tasted the Dragon's blood, and through what Mime will say to him next he will be able to pierce to the dwarf's real meaning. A gesture of Siegfried's shows that he has understood the bird; and standing quite motionless, leaning on his sword, observant and self-assured, he faces Mime, who now slinks in from the forest, saying to himself, "He is brooding on what the booty may be worth. Can he have met the Wanderer and been told a crafty tale? I must be doubly sly. I will spread the cunningest snare for him; with friendliest falsest words I will befool the perverse boy."

The scene that follows is another of Wagner's masterpieces of characterisation. Mime comes forward cringing and scraping, welcoming Siegfried with wheedling gestures:

and putting all the honey he can into his creaking voice. He does not know, however, that Siegfried, thanks to his tasting the blood and to the warning of the wood-bird, not merely hears his hypocritical words but reads his mind and realises his treacherous purpose. The wood-bird's constant collaboration with Siegfried is indicated by the occasional recurrence in the orchestra of No. 138. Necessarily what we in the audience hear is not the words actually spoken by the dwarf but the unspoken thought at the back of his mind.

He begins by welcoming Siegfried with effusive deference, complimenting him on his heroic victory over Fafner. "But", replies Siegfried, "he did not teach me fearing; and in truth his death grieves me when I see eviller rascals ranging through the world unpunished. He who egged me on to fight, I hate him more than my foe". So the dialogue goes on, Mime loading him with flatteries and endearments, and astonished that he gets only stern unfriendly words in reply. He tells Siegfried blandly, affectionately, that now he has done the deed desired by the dwarf he will soon close his eyes in endless sleep, and Mime will rob the credulous young fool of all he has won. With each rebuff his tenderness increases, the malignant words become more oily. "Hear me, my treasure! Thee and all thy kind ever I hated. I bore with thee not because I loved thee but because I needed thee to slay the Dragon and win me the Gold." In a cajoling phrase:

No. 143

Sieg-fried, mein Sohn, das siehst du wohl selbst, dein
Sieg-fried, my son, thou seest for thy-self, thy

Le - ben musst du mir las - sen.
life,— my dear one, thou los - est.

he assures him that if he does not yield the booty he will die. He grows peevish at what he takes to be Siegfried's stupid misunderstanding of his words. Taking greater and greater pains to be comprehensible and convincing he shows him the flask containing the broth he has lovingly prepared for the hero's refreshment after the combat: "Drink but one drop, and mine is thy sword, and with it the Tarnhelm and the Hoard." Offering him the draught again, he falls back into the tone of his old whining recital (No. 111) of his unselfish care of him when a child: in those days the boy, petulant and froward as he was, took refreshing drinks from him without demur. "What herb is in it?" asks Siegfried quietly. Merrily Mime assures him that if he tastes it he will soon lie stiff and stark in sleep, and then "with the Sword thou hast made so sharp I'll hack off thy head, and win me rest and the Ring": and he chuckles with delight at the prospect.

"So thou wouldst slay me in my sleep?" says Siegfried. At this, Mime gets vexed and furious: "Not at all! I said not that! Nought will I do but hack off thy head!":

No. 144

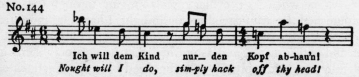

He continues in the most honeyed tones he can assume, while the orchestra gives out the lovely strain of No. 113: "Were not my heart so full of hate for thee, did not thy past jibes and the shame of my labour for thee goad me on to vengeance, I would delay no longer to sweep thee from my path!" He pours the liquor into a drinking-horn and offers it coaxingly to Siegfried: "Now, my Volsung, thou wolf's son! Drink and choke thee to death; it is the last draught thou wilt drain!", and he breaks into a hysterical laugh.

16

Siegfried, who has maintained a dignified quiet until now, is suddenly filled with a violent loathing for the treacherous gnome: with a swift blow from his sword he lays him dead. The wood wind give out a telling reminiscence of the Reflection motive (No. 104) — a last ironical comment on the futility of all Mime's scheming,[1] and Alberich's mocking laughter is heard from the cleft. As Siegfried picks up the body and carries it to the entrance to the cave the trombones intone the Curse motive: as always, it carries our thoughts not only back but forward — the Curse on the Ring has claimed yet another victim, but he will not be the last; Siegfried now has the Ring.

Heaving the body into the cave, Siegfried, with a great loathing in his heart, tells the wretched gnome to sate himself now on what he has so long desired: "with endless guile thou soughtest the Gold; now thou art lord of the lustrous thing. And a goodly guardian I will leave thee, so that thou mayst have no fear of thieves."

[1] The reader will no doubt have observed that the motive of Mime's false cajolement (the first two bars of No. 142) is simply another aspect of No. 104.

With a great effort he pushes the Dragon's huge body to the cave, so that it blocks up the entrance completely: "There lie thou too, Dragon grim! guard thou alike thy glittering Gold and the foe that was so fain to make it his; so find ye both your rest at last!"

He gazes thoughtfully into the cave for a while, then turns slowly to the front of the scene, as if tired. He passes a weary hand over his brow; the sun is now high in the heavens, his blood is afire, and he longs for shelter and shade. He stretches himself out under the lime-tree and evokes again the wood-bird which he sees in the branches above him, twittering and chattering with its brothers and sisters, all delighting in love. In his own heart, too, is a great longing for love:

> *But I — am so alone,*
> *have nor brother nor sister:*
> *and my mother died,*
> *my father fell:*
> *ne'er saw they their son.*
> *The one comrade I had*
> *was a hateful old dwarf:*
> *nought to love*
> *did e'er allure us:*
> *craftiest toils*
> *he laid to entrap me,*
> *until I was forced to slay him!*

A new motive, expressive of the boy's ardent desire for love, is heard in the orchestra:

No. 145
Animato

"Find me a faithful friend", he says to the bird, "give me clear counsel. Oft for a friend have I called, yet none ever came to me. Thou, my dear one, perhaps canst help me, for truth thou hast spoken to me until now."

The bird's voice rings out with the melody of No. 138 and No. 139. Siegfried has slain the evil dwarf, it says, and now there awaits him the most glorious of brides. She lies asleep on a fire-girt rock; let him waken her, and Brynhilde he will win for wife.

To a great orchestral upsurge of No. 145, which will dominate most of the remainder of the scene, Siegfried springs impetuously to his feet, his heart aflame with love: "Forth I fly, then, full of rejoicing, forth from the wood to the fell. But tell me, dear songster, shall I break through the fire and awaken the bride?" The Slumber motive comes out softly in the orchestra as the bird assures him that the deed will be accomplished by one alone — one who has never known fear. "That is I, the foolish boy", he cries in delight. "Today I strove in vain to learn fearing from a Dragon: my heart is afire to learn it from Brynhilde. Where lies the way to the fell?"

The bird hovers for a while teasingly above him, then takes a straight course to the background and is lost to sight. Siegfried follows it, and with the orchestra executing a joyous fantasia on Nos. 145 and 139 the curtain falls.

17

Wotan has set in motion, out of sheer necessity, a chain of events over which he has no ultimate control; and in the first part of the third act we see him, still as the Wanderer, anxiously trying to discover what the future has in store for himself, the Gods, the Ring and Siegfried. One alone, he feels, can raise at any rate a corner of the veil of the mystery that enshrouds and tortures him — Erda; and it is to her that, after leaving Alberich, he has hastened.

His unrest of soul is depicted in the prelude to the third act, which begins with a contrapuntal combination of the motive of the Need of the Gods (No. 81, which is virtually identical with that of Erda, No. 42) and that of the Valkyries; these are followed by the Treaty motive (No. 13), that of Erda, that of the Twilight of the Gods (No. 44), and the moaning figure expressive of grief in general but more specifically associated at times with the idea of Servitude. All these are woven into one compact fabric.

At last the vehement music dies down into a broad statement of the Magic Sleep motive (No. 96) and a hint of the motive of Fate (No. 83); and when the curtain rises we see the Wanderer arriving at a wild spot at the foot of a rocky mountain. It is night: a stormwind is raging, accompanied by flashes of lightning and peals of thunder. The Wanderer strides resolutely towards a vault-like opening in a rock in the foreground, pauses there, leaning on his Spear, and summons Erda (the Wala) to waken from her immemorial sleep in the depths of darkness. The Sleep motive is breathed by the wood wind in soft mysterious tones as she responds to the call: the cavern begins to glow with a bluish light, in which she is seen rising slowly from the depths, covered with hoar-frost, her hair and garments emitting a shimmering light. Who is he, she asks, whose magic power has broken her dream and driven sleep from her? To a constant orchestral interplay of the various appropriate motives he tells who he is and why he has sought her out. Superficially regarded, the long episode merely takes us afresh over ground familiar to us. But, as is the case with all these "narrations" and quasi-narrations of Wagner, it takes us over it in a new way. We do not see the events of old happening under our eyes as before, but as they now shape themselves in retrospect in the mind of this character or that, coloured by his present mood. To achieve this psychological transformation is the business even more of the musician than of the dramatist; and thanks to Wagner's music it is really a new Wotan and a new Erda who play out the following scene before our eyes.

The Wanderer begins by telling her how he had roamed the world in quest of wisdom, seeking it from the wisest of women, the Wala, who knows all that stirs and breathes on earth, in the waters or in the air. "My sleep", she says, in slow grave tones, "is dreaming, my dreaming brooding, my brooding weaving of wisdom. But while I sleep the Norns are ever awake, sitting and spinning what Erda knows: for wisdom, then, seek out the Norns." The Wanderer becomes more urgent: the Norns, he says, weave what they must according to the inexorable law of the world, without power to make or to mar. It is not theirs but Erda's wisdom he needs, counsel "how to hold back a rolling wheel". Again she evades him: in her own mind, she tells him, the deeds of men move as in a mist since she had bowed to a conqueror's will. To Wotan she had borne a Wish-maiden: brave is she and wise; let the God not awaken Erda but go for wisdom to Brynhilde, Erda's and Wotan's child.

Brynhilde had flouted her father's will, replies the God, and for that had been chastised: deep she lies in sleep on the fell, no more to awaken until a hero comes and wins her for wife. Erda broods

for a while on this: "Dazed am I since I awoke; strange and confused seems the world to me. So the Valkyrie, the Wala's child,
does penance of sleep while her all-knowing mother slept?

> *Doth then pride's teacher*
> *punish pride?*
> *Is the deed's enkindler*
> *wroth with the deed?*
> *He who wardeth right,*
> *he, the truth's upholder,*
> *tramples on right,*
> *reigns by untruth?*
> Let the dreamer depart!
> Sleep again seal my wisdom!"

But the anxious God still will not let her go. Once, he tells her,
she had buried care's bitter barb in his venturous heart, warned
him of woe to come, filled him with fear of a shameful ending:
"tell me now how the God may conquer his care". He becomes
more and more urgent, and at last discloses what it is he now
wills. The thought of the Gods' downfall grieves him no more
now he himself wills it so. Of old he had resolved on it in anguish
and despair; now he faces it freely and gladly; and the orchestra
gives out a new motive:

No.146

which is generally referred to as the World Inheritance motive,
because it is associated later with the coming of the new and better world symbolised by Brynhilde and Siegfried.

Once in his rage and loathing, says the Wanderer, he had flung
the world to the Nibelung as his prey; now he leaves his heritage
to the winsome young Volsung. "He, though chosen by me, knows
nought of me; free of my counsel he has won him the Nibelung's
Ring. Over him Alberich's curse has no power, for he is warm and
joyous, free from envy, knowing not fear. Brynhilde, the child of
thy wisdom, will awake to his call and do a deed that will redeem
the world. Slumber thou on, then; close thine eyes, and in dreams

witness my ending. To the ever-young the God yields in joy. Away then, Erda, mother of fear! Primal sorrow, away! Away to endless sleep!" During these last words of his she has already closed her eyes; now she slowly descends and disappears, thick darkness spreading once more over the entrance to the cavern. The storm has wholly ceased; the moon comes out, and by its faint light we see Wotan striding towards the cavern; he leans with his back against it, his face turned towards the stage, awaiting a final turn of events which he dares not control and has now no desire to control, yet to which he must somehow yield not assentingly but under compulsion.

18

Siegfried enters, led by the bird, which flutters towards the foreground singing its heart-free little melody. Siegfried, resolved to follow the course it has indicated to him, makes towards the background, but is halted by a voice asking him whither he is going. The boy turns round, sees the Wanderer, and replies that he is seeking, by the counsel of a wood-bird, a flame-bound rock where sleeps a maid who must awaken to him. Wood-birds sometimes chatter without sense, says the stranger: who taught him to read the meaning of the bird's singing? Thereupon Siegfried tells him how he had been brought by a treacherous dwarf named Mime to Neidhöhle, where he had slain a Dragon that had threatened his life, tasted its blood, and so learned to read the song of birds; his own sword he had wielded in the fight, forged by himself out of splinters that had baffled the skill of Mime the smith himself. "Who made the sword from which the fragments came?" asks the stranger. That the boy does not know — only that unless the sword were new-made the splinters had been useless.

At this naïve reply the Wanderer breaks out into a good-humoured laugh. This makes the boy look more closely at him; he asks why he laughs, and why he delays him there, plaguing him with questions. If the stranger knows the way to the rock let him show it; if not, a truce to his talk! The Wanderer reproves him for his petulance; he is old, he says, and youth should honour age. This is too much for Siegfried's patience: all his life, he bursts out, his path had been barred by an ancient whom at last he had had to sweep away; let the stranger have a care lest he share Mime's fate. Then, looking closer at him, he asks why his face is overhung by a great hat. "That is Wanderer's way", he is told, "when against the wind he goes". And one eye is lacking, the boy continues; no doubt it was struck out by someone whose path he had tried to bar: let him now take himself off, or he may lose the other. The Wanderer replies gravely:

> *I see, my son,*
> *where nought thou know'st*
> *yet well thou know'st how to help thee.*
> *With the one eye*
> *that for long I have lost*
> *thou lookest thyself on the other*
> *that still is left me for sight.*

The subtlety of this is lost on Siegfried: he laughs irreverently and demands to be shown the way to the fell.

Gravely and quietly and lovingly the Wanderer reproves the impetuous boy. "Didst thou but know me, child, thy scoff thou wouldst have spared me. Love I bore to thy race of old, yet in my wrath I scourged it sorely. Thou whom I love, wake not wrath in me now, to the ruin of thee and of me!" Siegfried impatiently orders him to step aside and let him pass to the fell; the bird had shown him the way, though now it had fled from his sight. It fled, says the Wanderer with a touch of anger, to save its life: it saw here the lord of the ravens; woe to it if these fall on it! The way it had pointed out the boy must not take. "It was by my might that the maid was cast into slumber: he who can wake and win her makes me mightless for ever." He points to a glow now visible on the heights, and bids the "foolhardy boy" go back if he would not be consumed by fire.

Siegfried having declared that the fire has no terrors for him, and that he means to go straight to Brynhilde, the Wanderer makes his last effort to assert himself. "At least my Spear shall bar thy path", he says, holding it out. "The haft of it is hallowed; it was on this that the Sword thou bearest was shattered once; now again be it broken on my Spear!". Siegfried draws his sword. "So at last I have found my father's foe?" he cries. "Vengeance lies in my grasp! I shatter thy Spear with my Sword." With one blow he hews it in two; there is a peal of thunder, and a flash of lightning darts from the Spear towards the rocky heights, where the former dull glow now becomes bright flame. The fragments of the Spear have fallen at the Wanderer's feet: he quietly picks them up, recedes, and saying "Advance! I can no more withhold thee!" he disappears in complete darkness.

The drama of the Nibelung's Ring will see Wotan no more. Siegfried's sword-stroke was the symbol of the annulment of his power over events: what has happened he had willed, for the accomplishment of the Gods' purpose, the ultimate righting of a primal wrong. The wheel, to adopt his simile in his colloquy with Erda, has been set rolling by Fate, and by the compulsion of Fate it must now roll to the appointed end. All the God could do, his power to shape the external drama any further having ceased, was to play out his own internal drama. This he had done by barring Siegfried's path with the Spear on which were engraved the runes that bound the world by law: the Spear has been shattered, the writ of that primal order no longer runs. With Siegfried and Brynhilde a new moral world-order will come into being, even though they both perish in creating it. Siegfried himself will remain all-unknowing to the last; but to Brynhilde will come, as Erda seemed to have hinted, the all-wisdom that redeems.

19

When the Wanderer has gone, Siegfried's attention is attracted by the growing brightness of the fire-clouds; and with the bird's song ringing in his ears once more he realises that here, on the fell, is his goal — his promised comrade and bride. He places his horn to his lips, and his vigorous call (No. 108 A) tears again and again through the excited orchestral tissue surrounding it. Fire is in the orchestra as well as on the fell when he disappears from our sight, making his way towards the rock. The blaze rises to a climax and then dies down slowly as the Sleep motives go through one transformation after another. Then the fire-clouds dissolve into a finer and finer mist, through which the rosy light of dawn pierces gradually; and when the mist finally disperses we see once more the setting of the closing scene of the *Valkyrie*. Overhead the sky is bright blue; but over the edge of the rocky height there still hangs a veil of reddish morning mist, suggesting the fire that rages without ceasing at the foot of the fell. In the foreground, under the great tree, Brynhilde is sleeping in her armour, with her helmet on her head and her long shield covering her.

The orchestra dies down to almost complete quietude, the Slumber motive yielding place to the melody (No. 25) to which, in the *Rhinegold*, Loge had sung of the universal enchantment of love, as Siegfried becomes visible on the summit of the cliff at the back. He pauses and surveys the scene in wonder, then advances a little as he sees first a horse, then a sleeping figure in armour. Raising the shield, he is rejoiced to find what he imagines will be a noble companion for him. The helmet seems to be pressing on the recumbent warrior's head; the boy raises it, whereupon a great mass of hair falls down. Startled but pleased, he bends over the sleeper to loosen his breastplate, which he does by cutting through the rings on either side. Seeing a woman's drapery he starts back in alarm, crying "That is no man!". No. 145 and a new motive, that of Love's Confusion:

No. 147 Animato

become the dominant strands in the orchestral fabric as his whole being seems to burst into flame at this new and strange experience; and in his perturbation he invokes the mother whom he has never seen, but who incarnates for him all the love for which he has longed. Can this, at last, be fearing? he asks himself. At last he masters himself sufficiently to waken the lovely sleeper, which he does with a long kiss.

Brynhilde opens her eyes, rises slowly to a sitting position, and raises her arms in silent greeting to the earth and the sky she sees once more, the orchestra painting the return of life to her in phrases that seem to ascend in spirals to the ether and finally break into a motive of her Greeting to the World:

No. 148

Solemnly she hails the light she now sees with joy again after her long sleep. But who is the hero who has wakened her? she asks.

The orchestra gives out the brave Siegfried motive (No. 108) as he tells her it was he, Siegfried, who fought his way through the flames and loosened her helm and roused her from sleep. The Valkyrie's mind goes back to her parting cry to Sieglinde, when she bade her preserve the fragments of Siegmund's sword for the boy who should be born to her in the forest — "His name from me let him take; Siegfried, joyful in victory". She breaks into a rapturous cry at the thought that this Siegfried is her deliverer, and the pair of them bless the mother who gave him birth:

No. 149

O Heil der Mut - ter, die mich ge - bar!
O hail to her who gave me my birth!

To this exultant outburst succeeds a new motive, that of the Rapture of Love:

No. 150

as Brynhilde sings a paean to Siegfried, the awakener to life, the most blessed of heroes, whom she had loved and fostered before ever he was formed. His mother, she tells him, is dead, but in Brynhilde he now has one who is both herself and him, her wisdom to be his. She had been inspired to flout the decree of Wotan because she had read the inmost secret of the God's heart; and now she sees that her disobedience came from the obscure prompting of her love for this hero as yet unborn.

20

They lose themselves in blissful contemplation of what each has won through the other. Then sadness steals over Brynhilde as she recalls what she has lost in ceasing to be a Valkyrie and becoming a mortal woman; and when he embraces her she flies from him in terror:

> *No God's touch have I known!*
> *Before the maiden*
> *low bent the heroes;*
> *holy came she from Walhall! —*

Woe's me! Woe's me!
Woe for the shame,
the pain and disgrace!
For he who wakes me
deals me this wound!
He has broken birny and helm:
Brynhilde am I no more!

For a while she will not be comforted. She doubts her own wisdom; round her is a darkness peopled with shapes that terrify her; and she covers her eyes with her hands. Gently he removes them and exhorts her to rise from the darkness and see the radiant day that is dawning for them both. "It is the day of my shame," she laments: "O Siegfried! Siegfried! look on my dread!"

Then her look softens, as if, according to the stage directions, "a sweet thought had arisen in her mind". "Ever was I, ever am I", she says, "ever in rapture of longing, yet ever to make thee blest!" To these words she takes up, in the minor, a gracious melody that had just been given out by the strings:

No. 151

It is a theme familiar to concert-goers as the main subject of the *Siegfried Idyll;* and it is to the second chief theme of that work:

No. 152

that she continues with a greeting of Siegfried as "highest hero, wealth of the world, life of the life of things, laughter and joy".[1] She begs him to leave her in peace:

[1] No 151 has been dubbed by some commentators the motive of Peace, and No. 152 that of the World Hoard. Both labels are meaningless. It was formerly believed that both these motives were originally conceived for the present episode in *Siegfried* and taken from there later to constitute the basis of the orchestral *Idyll*. We know now, however, that they were first of all imported into the opera, and then taken later into the *Idyll,* from a string quartet which Wagner had sketched in 1864. At this point in the opera, and again for a moment in the *Twilight of the Gods,* Wagner abandoned his ob-

Come to me not
with thy madness of longing,
master me not
with thy ruinous might;
thy loved one oh do not destroy!

Has he ever beheld his own face, she asks him, in the crystal brook, and seen how the fair image was shattered when the waters were disturbed? Even so will his image be destroyed for her by the disturbing mastery of his love. To passionate enunciations of No. 147 and No. 146 (the World Inheritance motive) he beats her protests down. What though the swirling waters deface his image: into them he will plunge, quenching his fire in them, stilling his longing in the flood.

He takes her in his arms, and her own ardent spirit goes out to meet his. When her blood surges like a sea of fire towards him does he not feel fear? she asks. No, he replies: his old courage has come back to him; the fear that his heart could never learn, the fear that she herself could hardly teach him, has fled from Siegfried for ever. She breaks out into joyous laughter, becoming, to the accompaniment of No. 74, almost the wild Valkyrie once more:

Thou foolish marvel
of mightiest deeds!
Laughing must I love thee,
laughing bear my blindness,
laughing leap to destruction,
laughing go down to death!

A last new motive, that of Love's Resolution:

No. 153
Marcato

jective attitude towards his drama and allowed his Siegfried-Brynhilde music to become a record of his own and Cosima's personal emotions. Why he did so was a domestic secret to which, at that time, only he and she had the clue, though it is possible for us now to reconstruct, from one scrap of biographical evidence and another, the situation as it was in Triebschen in the summer of 1869. The subject is far too complex to be dealt with here: I can only refer the reader to four articles of mine in the *Sunday Times* of February 1946 for a summary of the evidence.

is given out in the horn [1] and combined contrapuntally with No. 149 as the pair blend their voices in a final ecstasy of life and love. Brynhilde bids a glad farewell to the splendours of Walhall and the glory and pomp of the Gods. Let the eternals end in bliss; let the Norns sever their rope of runes; let the night of destruction fall; over her shines Siegfried's star:

> *He is for ever.*
> *is for aye,*
> *my wealth and world,*
> *my one and all:*
> *light of all loving,*
> *laughing death!*

In virtually the same words Siegfried sings of the new day that has dawned for him with her; and as she throws herself into his arms the curtain falls to exultant reiterations of No. 150, No. 108 B and No. 146.

[1] The evidence suggests that this theme also was taken by Wagner from a chamber music work of about 1864.

The Twilight of the Gods

1

N the *Twilight of the Gods* we arrive, in reverse, at Wagner's original design for a Nibelungen drama as it was in the *Siegfried's Death* of 1848.

The new work opens, as the old one had done, with a scene for the three Norns, the weavers of destiny. After two harsh chords in the wind instruments the arpeggio-like theme that has taken so many forms in the earlier operas of the *Ring*, expressing now, as in No. 2, primal nature and the Rhine, now, as in No. 42, Erda, appears once more in the strings. Repetition of this sequence is followed by the solemn Annunciation of Death motive (No. 83 B) in the brass, and this again by a new motive symbolical of the weaving of the Norns:

No. 154

etc.

After some twenty bars of this kind the curtain rises, showing the same rock setting as that at the end of the *Valkyrie*. It is night, but fire gleams in the valley at the back. On the right, in the foreground, is a great pine-tree. Three tall women in long, sombre draperies are seen: the first reclines under the tree, the second is stretched out on a rock in front of the cave, the third sits in the centre background, on a rock beneath a peak. The gloomy silence is broken by the voice of the first Norn, asking "What light shineth there?" "Dawns the day already?" asks the second; and the third says "Loge's host licks the fell with tongues of fire: why spin and sing we not?" The first — the eldest of the three — unwinds a golden rope and fastens one end of it to a branch of the tree; later in the scene she throws it to the second Norn, who winds it round the projecting rock at the entrance to the cave; later still the third Norn catches it and throws the end back to the second; and this procedure is repeated in the course of their colloquy.

The first Norn tells how long ago, sitting by a spring that whispered wisdom at the foot of the great world-ash-tree, she had sung of holiest things. A God, Wotan, came to drink at the spring, leaving an eye as tribute;[1] from the tree he broke a great branch and fashioned from it a mighty Spear. But the wound cankered the heart of the tree, which became dry and leafless; the water, too, sank in the spring. So the songs she sang were of dark meaning; and now she weaves no more by the world-ash-tree but fastens the rope to the pine.

The second Norn tells how Wotan engraved runes of treaties on the shaft of his Spear, and by them ruled the world. A hero bold had shattered the Spear. Then Wotan had summoned Walhall's heroes to hew the ash-tree stem and branches in pieces. The tree fell; the spring became for ever dry; and only round the jagged rock can she now bind the rope.

The third tells how Giants built the great fortress in which Wotan sits in state with his hallowed heroes: round it rises a mighty wall of riven boughs that were once the world-ash-tree. When that wood takes fire Walhall will go down in flames:

> the doom of the Gods then dawneth;
> down in dusk do they go.

The first Norn takes up the tale again. Is yonder gleam that of the dawn or of fire? she asks. Clouds deceive her eyes now; but dim within her is the memory of a time when Loge ran swift and free, a ravening flame. But Wotan subdued him, says the second Norn. Loge had gnawed at the runes on the Spear-shaft to gain his freedom; but by the power of the Spear-point the God had bound him to flame round Brynhilde's rock. Then, continues the third Norn, Wotan had pierced Loge's breast with the splinters of the broken shaft; fire had flamed from that blow, and this the God had hurled at the pile of the world-ash-tree's boughs encircling Walhall.

[1] It has often been pointed out that in the second scene of the *Rhinegold* Wotan had told Fricka that when wooing her he had forfeited one eye as pledge of his love. Wagner is following different legends in the two instances.

And after that? The Norns do not know; they can see nothing in the waning night about them. The first of them can feel no more the strands of the rope, which is broken, the warp entangled. The second says it is being cut through by the jagged edge of the rock:

> *from grief and greed*
> *rises the Nibelung's Ring:*
> *a vengeful curse*
> *gnaws at the sundering threads.*
> *Know'st thou what comes from this?*

Too slack is the rope, says the third Norn: if she is to throw it to the north it must be more tightly strained. She pulls strongly at the rope, which breaks in the middle. The three start up in terror, go to the centre of the stage, take hold of the pieces of the broken rope, and bind their bodies together with them, saying:

> *The end this of our wisdom!*
> *The world hears us*
> *wise ones no more.*
> *Descend! To Erda! Descend!*

They disappear. The old order is nearing its end, thanks to the chain of events set in motion first by Alberich, then by Wotan. What will the new order be?

This prelude is a continuous symphonic weaving of various motives already associated with the characters, events, objects or forces referred to by the Norns, with the motive of weaving (No. 154) running through the whole tissue and consolidating it, though of course a motive is often transformed in some subtle harmonic way or other in concordance with a change in its terms of reference, as when the Loge Fire motive assumes this form:

No. 155

and later this:

No. 156

As the rope of destiny breaks, the Curse motive rings out in the bass trumpet, and the Norns' last words ("The end this of our wisdom", etc.) are accompanied by the motive of Renunciation (No. 9), that of the Curse, that of Magic Sleep, and finally the fate-laden Annunciation of Death (No. 83 B).[1]

2

After the disappearance of the Norns a long melodic line uncoils itself slowly in the 'cellos, broken by the Siegfried motive (No. 108) in a broader form befitting the new Siegfried:

No. 157

and by a new motive characterising a new Brynhilde:

No. 158

The red glow of the dawn increases, while down in the valley the fire grows fainter. No. 158 ascends in mountainous waves in one reiteration after another; at the mighty climax of its development No. 157 rings out with the full force of the brass, and Brynhilde and Siegfried enter, he fully armed, she leading her horse by the bridle; and the joyous fanfare that had formerly characterised the simple boy (No. 108) receives a rhythmical transformation that shows him as the man he has now become:

[1] Wagner was agreeable to the prelude being played at concerts as a purely orchestral piece.

No.159 Pesante

To the caressing strain of No. 158 and a new motive, that of Heroic Love:

No.160 Moderato

Brynhilde addresses the hero whom she is now sending forth to fresh deeds of glory. The runes the Gods had taught her she has given to him, she says, while she herself has been bereft of maidenhood by the man who is now her master; weak in wisdom is she now, though strong in love; and she implores him not to forget the poor heart that has given him all it had to give. One thing alone he knows, he replies, — that Brynhilde lives — and this he will always remember. He will leave with her, as token of his love, the Ring. In return she gives him her horse Grane; no more will he carry her on winged feet through the air, but Siegfried he will follow wherever he may lead; thus even in absence each will be present to the other. The long duet ends with their both taking up the Siegfried motive of Freedom (No. 134) in an extended form:

No.161 Animato

Siegfried leads the horse down the rock, Brynhilde accompanying him, and the orchestral episode known in the concert room as Siegfried's Rhine Journey begins. It opens with a lively version of No. 157, followed by No. 161. By the time No. 168 appears Siegfried has disappeared from our sight; but his further course can be followed in the orchestra, and, for a while, with the aid of

Brynhilde's gestures. No. 108, intoned by a horn behind the scenes, indicates that he has reached the valley. Brynhilde descends the rock, catches sight of him once more, and makes rapturous signs to him. A vigorous mutation of No. 153:

No. 162

peals out, at which point he is lost to Brynhilde's view and the curtain falls. A joyous contrapuntal combination of No. 108 and No. 23 (Loge) in a new form suggests that he and Grane are making their way through the wall of fire round the fell. Then a mighty surge of No. 2 combined with No. 3, followed by the song of the Rhinemaidens (No. 7) shows us that he has reached and is passing down the Rhine. Gradually a shadow steals across the exuberant music: the Ring motive appears, followed by that of Renunciation (No. 9), then No. 36 (the groans of the enslaved Nibelungs and Alberich's imperious orders to them), till at last the tone and temper of the music change completely as a first hint of the milieu and the atmosphere of the next scene is given out:

No. 163

The management of the long picture is one of the best examples of Wagner's art of transformation by means of music from one pictorial or psychological plane to another.

3

At this point the tragedy of the *Twilight of the Gods* begins. When the curtain rises we see the great hall of the Gibichungs' stronghold on the Rhine; it is open at the back, where we have a view of the shore running down to the river, with rocky heights enclosing it. On a throne sits Gunther, the King of the Gibichungs, with his sister Gutrune at his side: before them is a table with drinking vessels, and in front of this sits the grim, dour Hagen. He is Gunther's half-brother, the son of Alberich. At the rising of the curtain the music carries on from our No. 163 to a motive representative of Hagen:

No. 164

the continuation of which:

No. 165

will afterwards refer more particularly to the Gibichung race.

Gunther addresses Hagen, asking him how his name and that of the Gibichungs now stand on the Rhine. Gunther's fame fills him with envy, Hagen replies; but his glory had been foretold by her who had borne them both, Queen Grimhilde. Gunther in turn envies this half-brother of his for his superior wisdom. Hagen goes on to say that great as is the Gibichung renown he is not yet content with it, for there are things Gunther might have done but has not yet set himself to do: he has no wife, and Gutrune is still unwedded. Hagen knows of a wife for his brother, the noblest in the world: she dwells on a rock engirdled with fire, through which only a stronger and braver than Gunther could force his way —

Siegfried, the son of Siegmund and Sieglinde, who had earned imperishable fame by slaying the Dragon that brooded upon the Nibelung Gold. What is this Nibelung Hoard of which he has often heard? asks Gunther. "The man who could wield its might", Hagen replies, "could make himself lord of the world: Siegfried has won it, and now the Nibelungs are thralls to him.[1] None but he can penetrate the fire."

Gunther rises angrily from his seat and strides agitatedly about the hall. Why raise this discord and doubt? he asks; why spur him on to long for something he cannot accomplish? Hagen, without ever moving from his place at the table, stops him with a mysterious sign as the wood wind gives out softly a suggestion of the Tarnhelm motive:

What if Siegfried could be induced by magic arts to bring the bride to them, he asks; would she not then be Gunther's? And would not the hero do it at the King's request — if he himself loved their sister? The orchestra gives out the motive of Enticement:

[1] Wagner took this line over unthinkingly from *Siegfried's Death*. It has no point in the present *Ring*, where nothing is said of any connection of Siegfried with the Nibelungs.

as the gentle Gutrune asks what charm she could have for a hero who would have the world's noblest women at his feet. "Remember the drink in the chest, and trust to me who brought it there", answers Hagen; "the hero whom thou desirest shall be afire with love for thee. Let Siegfried but taste of that magic draught, and it will fade from his memory that he has ever seen any woman but thee"; and the orchestra projects the subtle, insidious motive of Magic Deceit:

No. 168

to which is appended (bar 3) the falling figure always associated with Hagen.

4

"Would that Siegfried I might see!" sighs Gutrune: but Gunther praises the mother who bore so wise a son as Hagen. But how to find the hero? Just then, from a distance, but loudly, comes a horn call, and the orchestra takes up the joyous motive of the young Siegfried (No. 108). The hero is roaming the earth, questing for fresh deeds of renown, Hagen tells the others, and no doubt in time he will come to Gibich's hall on the Rhine. The horn call sounds again, a little nearer. Hagen goes to the shore, and to an accompaniment that embodies both his characteristic interval and a phrase that will form part of the chorus of Gibichung vassals in the second act:

No. 169

he tells them that on the river he sees a boat with a man and a horse; with the strongest and easiest of strokes the man drives the boat against the stream; nobody can it be but Siegfried himself.

Hagen hails him through his hollowed hands, welcoming him to the hall of the son of Gibich, and soon the hero fastens the boat to the land and springs ashore with his horse; and as Hagen greets him with feigned cordiality the Curse motive rings out with terrific power in the orchestra, followed by the motive of Enticement (No. 167). Gunther announces himself as the Gibichung King, and Siegfried, in the approved fashion of the sagas, offers him his choice of combat or amity. Gunther gives him warm welcome as friend. Looking fixedly at Hagen, Siegfried asks how he came to address him by name; and to a fresh enunciation of the Curse motive the sinister Hagen explains that he knew him by his strength. The Curse motive flows without a break into that of the hero Siegfried (No. 108 B), in a way that illustrates, on a small scale, Wagner's technique, in the *Ring,* of thematic interlocking: as so many of the motives are variants of the simplest suggestions of tonic and dominant they can join up to or combine with each other in the most natural way:

No. 170

Throughout the *Twilight of the Gods* the orchestral tissue is composed of a constant succession, combination and interplay of motives, in a way that makes detailed specification of them an impossibility.

Siegfried commends Grane to the care of Hagen, who leads him away. Gutrune, at a gesture from her half-brother, has already retired into her inner chamber, as yet unobserved by Siegfried. In courteous fashion Gunther, to the accompaniment of a new motive, that of Friendship:

No. 171

makes Siegfried free of the hall of his fathers. The hero has nothing to offer in return but his sword; but Hagen, who has now returned, says it is rumoured that he is master of the Nibelung Hoard. "That poor treasure I so despised", replies Siegfried, "that I left it lying there with a Dragon to guard it, taking away only this" — he points to a piece of mail-work hanging from his belt — "the worth of which I do not know." "The Tarnhelm it is", Hagen tells him, "the cunningest Nibelung work; with this on thy head thou canst change thy shape as thou wilt, or fly in a trice to lands afar. Nought else hast thou of the Hoard?" "Only a Ring", says Siegfried, "and that is held by a noble woman." "Brynhilde!" mutters Hagen.

5

Just then Gutrune re-enters, accompanied by her sweet and gracious motive:

No. 172

There is no evil in her, nor even strength; she is merely a gentle creature caught in Hagen's web and used by him for his own evil purpose. As the daughter of Gibich's house she welcomes the newcomer and offers him a drinking-horn. He takes it from her courteously, and with the motive of Enticement (No. 167) and that of Love's Greeting to the World (No. 148) interlocking in the orchestra, he drinks to Brynhilde. In the softest of tones and colours the orchestra breathes the mysterious motive of Magic Deceit, which is followed by that of Gutrune. While she lowers her eyes before him in shame and confusion Siegfried declares himself aflame with love for her. Her name, he learns from Gunther, is Gutrune; "and good", he says, "are the runes I read in her eyes." Overwhelmed by the passion of his speech she humbly bows her head, and with a gesture indicating her feeling that she is unworthy of so great a hero she leaves the hall with faltering steps: he follows her with his eyes as if bewitched, while Gunther and Hagen keep their gaze steadily fixed on him.

Has Gunther a wife? he asks. Not yet, replies the Gibichung King, nor is the woman on whom his heart is set to be lightly won, for her home is on a rock protected by a fire through which he could never break: her name is Brynhilde. Siegfried's demeanour all this while shows him trying to capture some definite outline in the mist of things forgotten, but even the word Brynhilde does not restore his memory. At the mention of the fire he turns gaily to Gunther and offers to bring him Brynhilde if he may have Gutrune for wife, for by the magic craft of the Tarnhelm he will change himself into the semblance of the Gibichung. On this they swear blood-brotherhood in saga fashion. Hagen fills a drinking-horn with wine and holds it out to Siegfried and Gunther, each of whom cuts an arm with his sword and lets the blood run into the horn, on which he then places two fingers. Siegfried begins the oath:

No.173

Blü - hen-den Le - bens la - bendes Blut ___
Flow - er-ing life's all - fresh - en-ing blood ___

träu - felt'___ ich in den Trank.
here I ___ drop in the draught.

Gunther answering him with "Brothers' love in bravest blend bloom from our blood in the cup!":

> *Troth I drink to my friend!*
> *Glad and free*
> *let bloom from our bond*
> *blood-brotherhood here!*

They continue:

> *Breaks a brother the bond,*
> *false if friend be to friend,*
> *what in drops today*
> *we two have drunken,*
> *in streams unceasing shall flow,*
> *so shall traitor atone!*

But the Hagen motive in the orchestra gives a sinister turn to the oath, and at the supreme moment of the pledge the ominous Curse motive is heard once more. When each of them has drunk from the horn the orchestra clinches the oath with a decisive octave drop, followed by the Treaty motive in the brass, with, as will be seen (in the third bar) tuba and trombone ejaculating "Hagen!":

No. 174

Siegfried, after drinking, has held out the horn to Hagen, who, however, still standing behind the pair, instead of draining it hews it in two with his sword. Siegfried, looking hard at him, asks why he had taken no part in the oath. His blood would poison the draught, the grim one replies, for it flows not pure and noble like theirs; so sluggish and cold is it that nothing would redden his cheeks; hence he holds himself aloof from bonds of fire. Gunther bids Siegfried give no heed to the gloomy man, and the hero dons his shield and summons the Gibichung to follow him to his boat: in it he will leave him for a night, and in the morning the bride shall be his. So the pair set out down the Rhine, Hagen being left to guard the hall during Gunther's absence. Gutrune returns for a moment, to learn that the pair have gone in quest of Brynhilde; and she goes back to her chamber with an innocently happy cry of "Siegfried — mine!"

Then comes the great interlude of Hagen's Watch. Holding shield and spear he sits down with his back against a post at the entrance to the hall, and his sombre monologue begins, against an orchestral background that incorporates his own characteristic falling diminished fifth with the rhythm of the Annihilation motive previously associated with Alberich (No. 40). The unseen presence of his Nibelung father seems to brood over the scene in an harmonically darkened version of the Motive (No. 36) of the power given to Alberich by the Ring over the Nibelung host:

No.175

Molto moderato

Gibich's son, Hagen muses, will bring back with him, thanks to Siegfried, the bride of brides; but he will bring also a prize for Hagen — the Ring; and with that Hagen will bring down in ruin all these beings, better than himself, whom, because of the Alberich blood in him, he hates:

> *Ye sons of freedom,*
> *lusty companions,*
> *laugh as ye sail on your way!*
> *base though ye deem him,*
> *ye both shall serve*
> *the Niblung's son!*

6

During the sombre orchestral interlude that follows the monologue the curtain in front of the hall is drawn, hiding the stage from the spectator. The psychological purport of the music is still Hagen's dark plotting; but gradually, by means of one of those slow transitions of which Wagner had the secret, the mood changes, the colour lightens, till finally the clarinet gives out the happy Brynhilde motive shown in No. 158, across which, however, there soon creeps the shadow of the Curse. This kind of apposition is maintained in what follows: Brynhilde is about to look out once more upon the world (No. 148), but, we realise, not with the same prospect of happiness as at the end of *Siegfried,* for beneath these tranquil strains there throbs persistently the broken rhythm of the Annihilation motive (No. 40).

When the curtain is drawn aside again we see the rocky heights once more, with Brynhilde sitting at the entrance to the cave, silently and thoughtfully contemplating Siegfried's Ring. "Overcome by happy memories", say the stage directions in the score, "she covers it with kisses." [1] Twice the orchestra breathes tenderly the motive (No. 152) to which, in the final scene of *Siegfried*, she had greeted the hero as the "wealth of the world, life of the life of things"; but thrice the mysterious motive of Magic Deceit (No. 168) hints at the evil that will soon ensnare her as it had already ensnared Siegfried. She has just heard, for the first time since Wotan laid her in slumber, a sound now almost forgotten but as the breath of her nostrils to her of old, that of a Valkyrie galloping through the air: who can it be, she asks, that is coming to visit the solitary one? She is hailed from afar by Waltraute, who, after leaving her horse in the nearby wood, enters and is greeted joyously by Brynhilde, who at first does not perceive that her sister is agitated and anxious. Brynhilde's first ecstatic thought is that she comes from War-father with a message that his heart has turned in forgiveness and love again to his child — though her punishment she does not regret, since it had brought her the love of the noblest of heroes; and she breaks into a cry of delight and embraces her sister Valkyrie, whom she imagines to have come to share her happiness.

Waltraute's agitation soon makes her look for another explanation. Has Wotan, after all, not pardoned her? she asks: has Waltraute come to her racked with fear of his wrath? Were that all, the Valkyrie replies, her anguish would soon be at an end; and she tells in detail what had brought her in haste to the rock. Since he had lost Brynhilde, Wotan had sent out his Maidens no more to the battlefield: for a while even his warriors had seen him no more, for he had ranged restlessly through the world as Wanderer. At last he had come back to Walhall, holding in his hand the splinters of his Spear, shattered by the Sword of a hero. Silently he had sent the warriors to hew the world-ash-tree in pieces. (Here the Walhall motive, in a graver form, links up with the motive of the Need of the Gods (No. 81) in a new aspect in the bass):

[1] Nothing of all this was in the original poem: Wagner, when he came to write the music, saw fit, as he had done in the final duet of *Siegfried*, to incorporate in it certain emotional experiences of his own and Cosima's. Hence his employment here of No. 152, which, as we have seen, came into the *Siegfried* score from the string quartet of 1864 and was used again in the *Siegfried Idyll*. It is only here that Wagner employs No. 152 in connection with the Ring.

No.176

To this majestic accompaniment Waltraute tells how Wotan had ordered a towering wall to be built with these pieces round Walhall. Then he had called all the Gods and heroes to council: tortured with fear they had stood in ring beyond ring round him while he sat silent on his throne, still holding the fragments of the Spear in his hand, of Holda's apples eating no more. Awestruck and spellbound the Gods saw him send out his messengers the ravens:

> *when to the hall*
> *with tidings good they return,*
> *then shall Wotan his grief forget,*
> *smiling his fate will he face.*

The trembling Valkyries had clung to his knees, but he turned a blind eye to their imploring:

> *upon his breast*
> *weeping I flung me;*
> *then soft grew his look;*
> *he remembered, Brynhilde, thee!*

and the motive formerly associated with Wotan's Dejection (No. 79) now merges, in an extended form:

No.177

into one of the most melting passages in all music as the weary God muses on his parting from Brynhilde, when he had pressed his last kiss on her lips:

No.178

With closed eyes, Waltraute continues, he sighed, and whispered, as if sunk in dreams:

> *if e'er the river maidens*
> *win back the Ring from Brynhilde again,*
> *from the Curse's load*
> *released were God and world!*

Then Waltraute, stealing softly from among the silent heroes, had mounted her horse and hastened to her sister, to implore her to put an end to the grief of the Gods.

7

Brynhilde replies tranquilly that all this has no meaning for her now, for it is long since she left the great hall in the cloudy heavens. But what is it that Waltraute would have her do? "Give back the Ring to the Rhinemaidens", says Waltraute vehemently: "from it comes all the world's woe; fling the accursed thing back into the waters, and end Walhall's grief for ever!" But Brynhilde is immovable: the Ring was given her by Siegfried as pledge of his love, and she prizes it more than all the raptures of Walhall, all the fame of the Gods; and she loses herself in happy memories of her awakening on the fell. She refuses to grant the Valkyrie's prayer:

> *Then home to the holy*
> *council of Gods;*
> *and of my Ring*
> *this rede bear thou for me:*
> *while life doth last I will love,*

from love they never will win me;
fall first in ruins
Walhall's splendour and pride!

With a great cry of "Woe's me! Woe to thee, sister! Woe to Walhall!" Waltraute leaves her, in a tempest that suddenly sweeps over the wood.

Brynhilde follows her sister's course in thought. By now evening has fallen, and down in the valley she sees the fire rising furiously to the very heights of the mountain. It must be Siegfried returning to her, she says; and she springs up in delight as the familiar horn call resounds from below. Suddenly he becomes visible on a high rock: the flames leap out fiercely at him, but recede as he slowly advances. He is in Gunther's form, with the Tarnhelm concealing the upper part of his face, leaving only the eyes free. Brynhilde recoils in terror before this sinister apparition, with a cry of "Betrayed! Who forced my fire?"

A sombre enunciation of the Tarnhelm motive is followed by a long silence, broken at last by a murmuring of the motive of Magic Deceit (No. 168) and a fateful suggestion of the Gibichung motive (No. 165). After another spell of silence, Siegfried, in a feigned voice, deeper than his own, answers her question: a wooer has come, one whom her fire could not affright: he wins her for his wife, a hero who, if nought but force will serve, by force will tame her: let her follow him now where he leads. What is this shape of dread? she asks again in terror — a mortal? an eagle that has swooped on her to rend her? one of Hella's night-born host? "A Gibichung", is the reply; "Gunther is my name, and thou must follow me." No. 177 becomes definitely a motive of her own calamity:

No. 179

col 8va

as she breaks into a wild lament: this, then, is Wotan's vengeful way of punishing her? Now, she thinks, she divines the God's pitiless purpose. In a frenzy of despair she holds out the Ring, to which she trusts to guard her. "Husband's right gives it to Gunther", Siegfried tells her, and he will have it by force.

They struggle together for a while, and at last he seizes her by the hand and tears the Ring from her finger. As she sinks brokenly into his arms her unconscious look meets his; and the orchestra gives out a pathetic reminiscence of No. 152, followed by the motive of the Tarnhelm and that of Magic Deceit as he lets her fainting body sink on to the stone bench at the entrance to the cave, tells her that now she is Gunther's bride, and bids her show him the way to her cave. The sinister rhythm of the Annihilation motive (No. 40) pulsates in the orchestra as he drives her before him into the cave with an imperious gesture. Then comes an astonishing musical-psychological stroke, of a kind of which only music among the arts is capable. Three times we hear the decisive octave drop of the motive of the Troth sworn with Gunther, followed by three bars of a contrapuntal combination of the Sword motive in the upper part, the Treaty motive in the middle part, and that of Hagen in the lowest:

No. 180

Siegfried draws his sword and says, in his natural voice:

> Now, Nothung, witness thou
> that pure my wooing was;
> that troth I keep with my brother,
> bar me from Gunther's bride.

There is a bitterly ironic upsurge of the happy Brynhilde motive (No. 158), succeeded by a final triumphant statement of the Troth motive (the octave drop) and a sinister reminder of Hagen in the depths of the orchestra, and as Siegfried follows Brynhilde into the cave the curtain falls.

8

The tremendous second act, which is in some ways Wagner's supreme achievement in music drama, shows us not only Siegfried and Brynhilde but Gunther and Gutrune becoming inescapably entangled in Hagen's net. The drama is tense, the action swift and compact; and the musical fabric consists for the most part of incessant interweavings of the motives now familiar to us.

An orchestral introduction depicts the sombre brooding of Alberich and Hagen on the problem that obsesses them: prominent in it are the sinister rhythmic throb of the Annihilation motive, the Hagen motive, and an harmonic intensification of what we have sometimes called, for convenience' sake, the motive of Servitude (Nos. 33 and 36), but which is freely used by Wagner to express now this aspect of woe, now that:

No. 181

This harmonic subtilisation of earlier motives is a leading feature of the opera from now onward; as the tragedy deepens, the darker become the meanings with which the themes are seen to be charged.

When the curtain rises we see an open space on the shore in front of the hall of the Gibichungs. The open entrance to the hall is now on our right; on the left stretches a bank of the Rhine. Running across the background towards the right of the stage is a series of rocky heights, on which stand three altar-stones, one for Wotan, one for Fricka, and one for Donner. It is night: Hagen is still where we left him when Siegfried and Gunther set out on their journey down the Rhine — apparently asleep, leaning against one of the posts of the hall, with his arm round his spear and his shield by his side. As the moon suddenly pierces through the clouds we catch sight of Alberich, crouching before Hagen and leaning his arms on the latter's knees. He asks his son softly if he is sleeping and unable to hear him whom rest and sleep have long forsaken. Hagen, who throughout the scene remains motionless and speaks as if in sleep, though his eyes are open, replies that he hears him well: what message has the Nibelung for him? Is he as bold, Alberich asks him, as the mother who bore him? "Stout heart my mother gave me", is the reply, "yet may her son not thank her that she was caught by thy craft: old too soon am I, pale and wan: I hate the happy! Joy I know not." "Hate the happy!" says Alberich eagerly; "so wilt thou love thy joyless, woe-weighted father as thou shouldst. Be crafty, strong and bold. Those whom we fight with the forces of darkness are stricken to the heart by our hate; for the ruthless robber Wotan has been vanquished by one whom he begat, and now he sits in dread, awaiting his downfall." It is not that he fears Wotan, continues Alberich, for the God is doomed to go down with the rest. It is his lost power that Alberich covets, and down to ruin he will go if he and Hagen are true to themselves and each other, linked by a common rage and hate; and a new motive, that of Murder, is heard in the orchestra:

No. 182

The Ring has passed into the hands of a fearless stripling over whom Alberich has no power, for he does not know the worth of it and makes no use of its might; he is warm with life and lives only for love. One aim alone, says the Nibelung, he and Hagen should have — the ruin of the God. The Ring has been given by the boy in love to a woman; if on her prompting it should return to the Rhinemaidens, all the Nibelung's wiles will be in vain for ever. Alberich himself had lacked the strength to slay the Dragon; but he had begotten a grim son and bred hatred and the passion for vengeance in him. "Win me the Ring, in Wotan's and Volsung's despite! Swear it to me, Hagen, my son!"

"The Ring I will win thee", Hagen replies; "rest thou and wait!" Alberich is gradually lost in the shadows as the morning twilight slowly steals in, but out of the darkness comes the reiterated hoarse appeal, "Swear to me, Hagen, my son! Be true to me! Be true!" "To myself I swear", says Hagen; "be silent and have no care!" Alberich disappears completely; Hagen, still without moving, looks with fixed eyes towards the Rhine, over which the light of dawn is now spreading:

No.183

The phrase shows Wagner once more practising his art of almost imperceptible transition. (The fragment marked B is a foreshadowing of a motive that will afterwards be associated with the barbaric merriment of Hagen and the Gibichung vassals).

9

The Rhine becomes more and more clearly visible in the red light of dawn, but the warm glow of the music is flecked for a moment by a reminder of the Tarnhelm motive as Hagen gives a slight start. Suddenly, to the accompaniment of his horn call, Siegfried emerges from a bush near the shore: he is now in his own form, but the Tarnhelm is still on his head. Taking it off and hanging it at his girdle he gives Hagen a cheery greeting. Hagen rises to hear the news that Gunther and Brynhilde are following down the river. The hero calls gaily to Gutrune, who comes out from the hall: they shall hear, he says, how he subdued Brynhilde and is now come to claim Gutrune for wife. She hails him joyously in the name of Freia, to the accompaniment of a modification of her own motive (No. 172), to which is now added (at A) a theme that will later be associated with the Gibichung greeting to herself and Siegfried:

No.184

Gunther, she learns, had passed unscathed through the fire, which Siegfried had braved for him, singing, as he clove the flames, for love of Gutrune: the Tarnhelm had disguised him, as Hagen had said it would, and it was to Gunther that the Valkyrie thought she had yielded. To her new lord she had submitted all the bridal

night till the dawn; but, he assures Gutrune, between Siegfried
and Brynhilde had been his sword, "as between east and west is
north; so near was Brynhilde to him, so far": and once more we
hear the combination of motives shewn in No. 179. In the morning
mist, he continues, she had accompanied him to the valley; when
near the strand, swift as thought Gunther stood there in his stead.
The Tarnhelm had carried Siegfried in a trice to the hall, and
Gunther and his bride were following in the boat. Gutrune hails
him with a glad cry of "Siegfried! Mightiest of men! I faint for
fear of thee!"

Hagen, looking down from the height in the foreground, sees a
sail in the distance on the river. "Give the bride a joyous greeting",
cries the happy Gutrune, to the strain of No. 184 A, "that glad and
blithe she bide among us"; and she bids Hagen call the men of
Gibich to the hall for the wedding. She herself, taking Siegfried
with her by the hand, goes out to summon the women to share
her own happiness with her.

Ascending a rock in the background, Hagen blows on his hoarse
cow-horn a boisterous, uncouth melody:

No. 185

as he calls to the Gibichung vassals to assemble with their weapons — "goodly weapons, strong weapons, sharp for strife, for Need
is here"; and the orchestra comments on these last words with the
motive of the Doom of the Gods (No. 44) plunging downward in
great waves. Cow-horns behind the scenes answer his rough call,
and a wild crew of armed vassals rushes in from all quarters and
gathers on the shore in front of the hall. There follows the first
chorus to be heard in the whole *Ring*, an affair of wild ejacula-
tions to the accompaniment first of all of the motive of the
vassals:

No. 186

They ask why they have been summoned: Hagen tells them that Gunther is returning to them, bringing with him a wife. But no vassals will she have in her train: she comes alone: the King had been shielded from harm by the hero Siegfried, the slayer of the Dragon. What need then has the King of them? they ask: what work have they to do? They are told to slaughter great steers on Wotan's altar, with a boar for Froh, a lusty goat for Donner, and "sheep in plenty for Fricka, that she may smile on the marriage" — and Hagen breaks into an ironic melodic phrase with rough shakes in it. After the sacrifices they must fill the horns deep with mead and wine and drink with their women, carousing till they fall like logs.

They have listened to his rough jocularity with growing merriment; now they burst into ringing laughter, and to strains built up of No. 183 A, the Wedding motive already associated with Gutrune (No. 172), and the pendant to this shown in No. 184 A, they sing a barbaric paean to this grim Hagen of theirs, who has now become a bridal herald! For all his savage jocularity, Hagen's demeanour all the while has been grave: now he comes down among the vassals and bids them cease their laughter and prepare to receive Gunther and his bride: let them serve their lady loyally, and if she be wronged let their vengeance be swift.

10

The boat with Gunther and Brynhilde comes into sight and gradually reaches the shore: taking her ceremoniously by the hand he presents her to the vassals, who, clashing their weapons together, acclaim them in a massive chorus founded on the Gibichung theme (No. 165):

No. 187

Brynhilde stands with lowered eyes as Gunther presents her as his wife, who shall be the crowning glory of the Gibichung name. A hint of what is passing in her mind is given us by a recurrence in the bassoons of No. 179, which we now begin to associate with Brynhilde's desire for vengeance on Siegfried. But she does not

speak or raise her eyes even when Siegfried and Gutrune, accompanied by the latter's women, come in from the hall: the happy
Gutrune is now accompanied by a still sweeter form of her characteristic theme:

No. 188

Gunther greets them: "two happy bridals", he says "we celebrate
together — Brynhilde and Gunther, Gutrune and Siegfried".

At this last word Brynhilde starts out of her torpor and perceives Siegfried. Her eyes remain rivetted on him in amazement
while No. 179 raises its ominous head in the orchestra, joined with
a suggestion of the Hagen motive and that of Death (No. 83).
She trembles violently; Gunther releases her hand, perplexed, like
the vassals, by her behaviour. Siegfried asks calmly what it is that
troubles her: she can only ejaculate incredulously "Siegfried —
here? Gutrune?" "Gunther's gentle sister", says Siegfried, "won
by me, as thou by him." She gives him the lie, then staggers and
appears about to fall. Siegfried, who is nearest to her, supports
her in his arms; she looks up at him and says feebly, "Siegfried
knows me not!" He calls to Gunther to come to his bride, and as
she does so she sees the Ring on Siegfried's finger and breaks into
a wild cry as something of the truth begins to dawn on her.

Hagen, recognising that the decisive moment has arrived, turns
to the vassals, bidding them hearken to this woman's words. Mastering herself with difficulty Brynhilde says:

> *On thy hand there*
> *I beheld a Ring;*
> *not thine to wear it:*
> *he who won it*
> (pointing to Gunther)
> *standeth there!*

How came then to thee
the Ring from his hand?

Siegfried, quietly contemplating the Ring, assures her that it did not come to him from Gunther. Then Brynhilde turns to the latter: "Thou who didst win from me the Ring with which I wedded thee, teach this man thy right: demand back the pledge!" The embarrassed Gibichung disclaims all knowledge of the Ring, and is finally reduced to bewildered silence. Then all becomes clear to Brynhilde: in a passionate outburst she denounces Siegfried — who is still lost in musing on the Ring — as a "treacherous thief" who stole it from her. All eyes are turned enquiringly on him. No woman gave him the Ring, he says; he won it by his sword at Neidhöhle, where he had slain the Dragon who guarded it.

Hagen steps between them: if this is indeed Brynhilde's Ring, he says, the one that Gunther wrested from her, then it is his by right, and Siegfried took it by craft; and for that the traitor should atone. With frenzied cries of "Betrayed! Shamefully betrayed! Deceit, vile beyond all vengeance!" Brynhilde calls on the Gods above to say if all this was part of their decree — to inflict on her a shame past bearing. If so, then

teach me a vengeance
too dire to be told!
Stir me to wrath
that may never be stilled!
Break in pieces
the heart of Brynhilde,
may but this traitor
taste bitter death!

Gunther tries in vain to calm her: she calls on them all to witness that she is Siegfried's wife. The unknowing Siegfried in his turn accuses her of falsehood. He had sworn blood-brotherhood with Gunther, and he had been true to his bond, for his good sword Nothung had lain between himself and Gunther's wife. By now Brynhilde has reached the breaking-point: no longer mistress of herself, possessed by only one idea, that of vengeance, she swears that it is Siegfried who is lying — that on the bridal night the sword had lain in its sheath on the wall while its owner forced her love.

11

This is the explosive spark of the drama. Gunther reproaches Siegfried with having betrayed him: Gutrune implores him to swear that Brynhilde is not speaking truth: the vassals demand that he shall confirm his word with an oath. He accepts the challenge: on whose weapon shall he swear? "On mine", replies Hagen. The vassals form a ring round the pair, and Hagen holds out his spear, on the point of which Siegfried lays two fingers of his right hand, the orchestra thundering out No. 179. Solemnly he swears that he has spoken the truth:

No. 189

Hel - le Wehr, hei - li - ge Waf - fe!
Shin - ing spear, hal - low-ed wea - pon!

hilf mei - nem e - wi - gen Ei - de!
hold thou____ my oath__ for ev - er!

when his hour comes to die, may it be this very spear that deals him his death-stroke if in anything he had betrayed his brother Gunther. Forcing her way through the vassals, the maddened Brynhilde tears his hand away from the spear, seizing the point of it with her own. To the melody of No. 189 she swears an oath like Siegfried's: may the spear-point deal this man death, for he had been false to Gunther and now he has sworn falsehood. The excited vassals call on Donner to break this knot with his thunder. Siegfried, turning to Gunther, bids him take this wild mountain maid — in whose breast some demon or other has instilled his evil craft, so that she now slanders and shames the man who had won her for wife — and lead her back to peace of mind with time and rest. He himself, he thinks, must have played his part ill on the fell, the Tarnhelm having perhaps hidden only half of his face: "but woman's spite is soon at an end, and ere long she will thank thee for having won her through me". The vassals and the women he tells to come to the wedding feast with him and be gay. Lightheartedly he throws his arm round Gutrune and takes her with him into the hall, whither they follow him, carried away by his gaiety.

Only Brynhilde, Gunther and Hagen remain on the stage while the orchestra pours out motive after motive in comment on the situation. The silence is at last broken by Brynhilde, who, speaking more to herself than to the others, asks sombrely what may be the meaning of this mystery. What wizard has stirred up this storm by his craft? Her wisdom fails her: she had parted with all her runes to Siegfried, and now he gaily casts her, sorrowing in her shame, to his friend. "Who now will bring me the sword wherewith I may sever my bonds?" She turns a dull look on Hagen as he approaches her and says, "Trust in me; vengeance I'll wreak on him who betrayed thee!" "On whom?" she asks vacantly. "On Siegfried, the traitor to thee!" She smiles bitterly as she replies:

> *one single flash*
> *of the eye of the hero,*
> *one glance such as gleamed through the helm,*
> *shedding glory on me,*
> *and in fear*
> *thy hand would falter!*

Truth or falsehood, oaths or spears, what will all these avail against the strongest of heroes? Hard indeed will it be to slay Siegfried in combat, Hagen admits; let Brynhilde's wisdom, then, tell him how the hero may fall to his spear. Accompanied by one of the most expressive strains in the whole *Ring*, which Wagner, however, has no occasion to employ later as a regular motive:

No. 190

Brynhilde laments that every art she knew she had bestowed on him to guard him in battle; and the orchestra gives out sad reminders of the bliss associated with No. 150. But, she recalls, there is one place in which he is vulnerable; knowing he would never

turn his back on a foe she had set no spell there. "And there strik
eth my sword!" says Hagen grimly.

12

Turning quickly to Gunther he urges him to rouse himself to
action. For only reply the Gibichung King passionately bewails
the deceit that had been practised on him, and calls on his
stronger and more crafty brother to help him. Brynhilde taunts
him with weakness and cowardice: Hagen insists that

> *no help from brain,*
> *no help from hand,*
> *nought helps but Siegfried's death!*

Gunther recoils in horror: "Blood-brotherhood I swore with him",
he cries, to the accompaniment of No. 173 in the hoarse tones of
the horns. The others goad him on relentlessly to the deed from
which he shrinks, and at last Hagen plays the decisive card. Brynhilde's insistence that Siegfried's death alone will glut her vengeance or blot out the guilt of the Gibichung pair who had plot-
ted against her does not move the weak but honourable man; but
Hagen wins him over by hinting softly to him that when Siegfried
falls the Ring will be his, and with it power beyond his dreams.
(The reader will recall that at Gunther's first appearance in the
opera he had put to Hagen the question that was evidently always
uppermost in his thoughts — "How stands it with my fame? Is the
name of Gibich glorious on the Rhine?"; and it was to win the
greater fame hinted at by Hagen that he had consented then to
the plot for duping Siegfried and beguiling Brynhilde). Sighing
deeply, he agrees at last to Siegfried's murder, though he feels he
will not be able to face his gentle sister again with her husband's
blood on his hands.

At the mention of Gutrune Brynhilde breaks out angrily once
more:

> *from depths of despair*
> *it dawns on me now:*
> *Gutrune is the spell*
> *that won my hero from my side.*
> *Woe be to her!*

The cynical Hagen has an answer for Gunther: if Siegfried's death will grieve their sister, she need not be told of the plot; on the morrow they will go hunting, and when they return to the hall their story to her will be that the hero has been slain by a boar. "So shall it be", they decide in a final great trio, in which Brynhilde and Gunther invoke the aid of Wotan, as "oath-witness and ward of vows", in the accomplishment of their vengeance on the traitor, while Hagen exultantly invokes his father Alberich: "So let him die, this hero fair; mine shall be the Hoard and the Ring. Alberich, my father, fallen prince! Warder of darkness! Nibelung lord! Soon shalt thou summon the Nibelung host again to bow down before thee, the Ring's master and theirs!"

As Gunther and Brynhilde turn vehemently to the hall they are greeted by a bridal procession, with boys and maidens waving flower-staves and Siegfried borne by the men on a shield and Gutrune by the women on a chair. Siegfried and the vassals blow a wedding summons on their horns. Vassals and maids are seen on the heights in the background, making their way with sacrificial beasts to the altar stones of the Gods, which they deck with flowers. The innocent Gutrune beckons with a friendly smile to Brynhilde, who at first stares at her blankly and then makes as if to step back; but at a sign from Hagen Gunther seizes her, whereupon he himself is raised by the men on a shield; and to a combination of motives in the orchestra, in which that of Gutrune predominates, only to be ousted at the end by that of Hagen, the procession moves towards the heights, and the curtain falls.

13

To the tension of the tremendous second act succeeds a gracious woodland idyll.

In the orchestral prelude to the third act we hear first of all, from behind the scenes, the horn call of Siegfried, which is answered by the cow-horns of the hunting Gibichungs in the further distance. Next there is a hint of the gently flowing Rhine (No. 2) and a suggestion of the song of the Rhinemaidens (No. 7), with once more a reminder that Siegfried is not far away. Then the orchestra settles down to the elaboration of two new motives to be associated with the Rhinemaidens:

No. 191

and

No. 192

The curtain rises on a wild, wooded, rocky valley by the Rhine, which flows past a steep cliff in the background. Woglinde, Wellgunde and Flosshilde rise to the surface of the water and swim around as if circling in a dance, singing, to the strains of Nos. 191 and 192, a song the sweetness of which is tinged with sadness: no longer, they say, does the Rhine's lustre match that of the sunlight playing on the waves, as it did in the days when the glittering Gold was safe in their keeping. They pause and listen to another horn call in the distance, and their hearts revive a little: will the hero come soon who shall restore the Gold to the waters? Once more Siegfried's call peals out. "The hero nighs", they say; and they dive swiftly to take counsel with each other.

Siegfried appears on the cliff, fully armed, wondering how he came to lose the track of his fellow-hunters and of the game. The Rhinedaughters rise to the surface again and greet him, tease him over his mishap, and exhort him to tell them all. If it was they, he answers good-humouredly, who had lured to their lair the shaggy brute he was pursuing he wishes them joy of their lover. They laugh loudly. What will he give them, they ask, if they yield him his quarry? Hands so empty as his are today will grant them anything, he replies. They ask for the golden Ring that gleams on his finger, but this he refuses: to win it he had slain a Dragon grim, and shall he now part with it for a paltry bear-skin? Besides, he adds gaily,

> *if my goods in the water I fling,*
> *I fear me my wife will scold.*

They banter him on his miserliness and his fear of his wife. "She beats thee, then, perchance?" says Wellgunde. "The hero feels the weight of her hand!" adds Woglinde. Let them deride him to their hearts' content, says Siegfried, but the Ring shall never be theirs. Still laughing at him — "So fair! so strong! So meet for love! Alas, that he's so niggard!" — they dive below the waters again.

Stung by their gibes he descends from the cliff, calls to them to come back, and offers to give them the Ring, which he draws from his finger and holds aloft. When they reappear they are changed beings, grave and solemn. Let him keep the Ring, they say, until he has learned what ill-fate clings to it: fain enough will he be then to be freed by them from the curse on it. Replacing the Ring on his finger he quietly asks them to tell him what they know.

Three times they address him warningly by his name:

Then they tell him the history of the Ring and the doom of death that lies, through the Curse, upon all who acquire it. As he slew the Dragon so he himself shall be slain that very day unless he gives it back to the waters that alone can wash out the Curse. He replies that as he was not tricked by their fawning, so now he is not frightened by their threats. To a repetition of No. 193 they warn him once more: there is no escape from the Curse, which is woven by the Norns into the rope of time and fate. With the Sword that had once shattered a Spear, Siegfried answers, he will cut through even that rope, for fear he has never learned. In the Ring, he knows, lies all the world's wealth: he would give it for the grace and joy of love, but not under the threat of his life; this he values no more than the clod of earth which he picks up and throws behind him.

Swimming in wide circles close to the shore the Rhinemaidens excitedly urge each other to leave this madman, who, deeming himself strong and wise, is bound and blind. Oaths, they say, he had plighted and heeded them not; runes he sees and reads them not; a glorious gift [Brynhilde] had been his, and in his ignorance he had spurned it; but the Ring that will deal him death he will not surrender! This very day a woman proud will inherit his treasure and work their will better than they themselves can do; let him go now to her. They swim away to the background, singing their "Weialala, leia" to the strain of No. 191 and No. 192. As they disappear from his sight he philosophises on them after his fashion: women's ways, on land and sea, he has learned; the man who is deaf to their fawning they seek to frighten with threats, and if he smiles at these they give him the sharp edge of their tongue. And yet he had liked these three, and had not Gutrune his troth he would have sought the love of one of them.

14

As the music of the Rhinedaughters dies away in the distance horns are heard, and Siegfried, starting out of the reverie into which he has fallen, answers them with his own horn call. The off-stage voices of the vassals hail him, and soon Hagen and Gunther enter, followed gradually by the vassals: here, says Hagen, they will rest and make a meal. The game is piled in a heap, wine-skins and drinking-horns are produced, and all lie down. Hagen asks Siegfried how it had fared with his hunting since they had lost sight of him, and laughingly he tells them that his luck had been out: no wood-game had he brought down, and only three young water-fowl had he seen who had sung to him from the Rhine a warning that that day he would be slain. Gunther starts at this and looks darkly at Hagen, and the sinister outline of the Covenant of Vengeance motive unwinds its dark coils in the depths of the orchestra:

No.194

"A grievous chase that would be", says the grim Hagen, with a double meaning that only Gunther understands, "for the lurking beast he hunts to slay the hapless hunter!" Siegfried says he is thirsty, and as Hagen hands him a drinking-horn he has filled for him he asks him if there is any truth in the tale that he understands the song of birds. It is long since he listened to their chatter, Siegfried replies, and he offers the drinking-horn to Gunther, who looks thoughtfully and sadly into it and mutters gloomily:

> *the draught is dull and blanched:*
> *thy blood alone is there!*

while once more the orchestra gives out a mutation of the ominous No. 194. Siegfried's generous heart overflows with tenderness for this unhappy blood-brother of his; and while Gunther can only ejaculate mournfully, "Thou over-joyous hero!" he pours the wine from Gunther's horn into his own, and asks Hagen if perchance the King is still grieving over the hurt dealt him by Brynhilde. Step by artful step Hagen brings Siegfried to sing them, for the heartening of Gunther, tales of his boyhood and its wonders; and sitting upright while the others recline around him he begins his story.

To the appropriate motives at each stage he tells of his being brought up and taught by Mime for the dwarf's own ends, how he had forged the sword Nothung and slain the Dragon, learned from the taste of its blood how to understand the song of the birds, taken from the cave the Tarnhelm and the Ring, and killed the treacherous Mime. As Siegfried pauses for a while Hagen fills another horn with wine, into which he drops the juice of a herb; then he hands it to Siegfried, saying that the spiced draught will revive his memories of things forgotten. The hero looks thoughtfully into the horn, drinks slowly, and takes up his story again. He tells how the wood-bird had sung to him of the bride awaiting him on the fell; and Gunther listens with growing astonishment as he goes on to tell how he had broken through the fire and found the sleeping Brynhilde, wakened her with a kiss, and been folded in her arms. Gunther, enlightened at last, springs up in horror. Two ravens, Wotan's messengers of death, fly up out of a bush, circle over Siegfried, and then take their course to the Rhine. "Canst thou read me those ravens' runes?" Hagen asks Siegfried; and as the hero rises to his feet and gazes after them, thus facing away from Hagen, the latter drives his spear into his back, saying, "Vengeance they cry to me!"

Gunther strikes Hagen — too late — on the arm. With a last mighty effort Siegfried swings his shield aloft with both hands to crush his murderer; but his strength fails him, the shield drops behind him, and he himself falls on it with a crash, while the orchestra throws its full weight into a motive that will shortly become the binding element of Siegfried's Funeral March (No. 195). The horrified Gunther and some of the vassals ask, "Hagen, what deed is this?" "Vengeance for a false oath!" he replies. He turns away and goes out alone, slowly striding away in the twilight that had begun to fall at the appearance of the ravens. The vassals, filled with sympathy, stand round the dying man: Gunther, grief-stricken, bends down over him.

Supported in a sitting position by two of the vassals, Siegfried opens his eyes. His memory now fully restored, he hails "Brynhilde, holiest bride!" to the strains that had accompanied her awakening in the final scene of *Siegfried* (No. 148). He remembers every episode of that slow ecstatic wakening, and the orchestra recreates them all for us with reminiscences of Nos. 149 and 150. But the Death motive (No. 83) throws its shadow over his darkening mind: he sinks back, dead. By now night has fallen. At a silent command from Gunther the sorrowing vassals raise the body and carry it in solemn procession over the rocky height, Gunther walking by its side.

15

There follows the impressive Funeral March, during which the mourning train slowly passes out of sight, the moon breaking through the clouds and for a moment illuminating it as it reaches the summit of the height; then mists come up from the Rhine and gradually wrap the scene in complete darkness. The March begins with the solemn theme of the mourning cortège:

and then passes in slow review a number of motives associated with the hero — that of the Volsung race (No. 58), those of Sieglinde's compassion and love for Siegmund (Nos. 51 and 52), that of the Sword (No. 48), that of Siegfried (No. 88), that of the horn call that had symbolised him in the lustiness of his youth (No. 108, now in broad heroic form), and that of Brynhilde as we saw her at the opening of the *Twilight of the Gods* (No. 158) — all woven into one great threnody, through which No. 195 runs at this point or that like a dark connecting thread.

As the last echo of No. 108 dies away and the minor second familiar to us since its first definite appearance in No. 33 wails out once more, the curtain rises again, revealing the hall of the Gibichungs as in the first act. It is night, with the moonlight reflected in the Rhine. To a melancholy re-statement of her motive Gutrune appears, coming out from her chamber into the hall. Dreams of evil, in which she had heard the neighing of Siegfried's horse and the laughter of Brynhilde, had driven sleep from her; now she believes she hears Siegfried's horn, and she listens intently. She has seen a woman go silently towards the Rhine: was it Brynhilde? "I dread this Brynhilde", she says to herself. She goes to the inner room on the right, looks into it timidly, and calls to Brynhilde; but the room is empty. "Were my Siegfried but here!" she sighs. She turns to go to her own room again, but hearing Hagen's voice without she stands petrified with fear.

As the orchestra gives out again the figures shown in No. 194 Hagen is heard outside, hailing the sleeping household with his hoarse "Hoiho!", and bidding it waken and come with torches, for he brings home a fine booty. Entering the hall he greets Gutrune with boisterous jocularity: "Up, Gutrune, to greet thy Siegfried! The hero strong has come home again." "I heard not his horn", says Gutrune in terror. The savage Hagen replies:

> *his bloodless mouth*
> *will blow it no more;*
> *to hunt or to fight*
> *no more will he fare,*
> *nor woo winsome women to love him.*

A crowd of men and women with lights and firebrands enters confusedly, together with a procession bearing the body of Siegfried on a bier: Gunther is among them. The body is set down on a hastily raised mound in the centre of the hall; and Hagen tells the distracted crowd that Siegfried has been slain by a wild boar. Amid the general agitation Gutrune falls on the body with a shriek, and Gunther tries to comfort her. Recovering herself she repulses him violently, crying out that he has treacherously murdered her husband. "Not I, but Hagen", he tells her; "he was the accursed boar who dealt the hero his death"; and he pours out reproaches on him.

Hagen steps forward defiantly. Yes, it was he, he tells them all, who sent Siegfried to his doom with the very spear on which he had sworn a false oath: hunter's right is now his, and for his spoil he claims the Ring. A quarrel ensues between him and Gunther: claiming "the Nibelung dower for the Nibelung's son", Hagen rushes at his brother and strikes him dead with his sword. Then he grasps at Siegfried's hand, which raises itself threateningly. Gutrune and the women shriek with horror: the vassals draw back, appalled.[1]

16

The clamour subsides to a pianissimo as the motive (No. 44) of that Doom of the Gods that had been foretold by Erda in the *Rhinegold* makes its way downwards in the orchestra and Brynhilde comes forward from the background, slowly and solemnly. The remainder of the great drama now passes entirely into her hands. Sternly, to the accompaniment of Nos. 2 and 44 — the antithetical ascent and descent of which seem to hold together and epitomise the two great opposing principles of the *Ring*, the birth of things and the end of things — she bids them all cease their wailing of woe, for the woman they had all betrayed had come for the vengeance due to her — a different vengeance, however, from the one she had had in her heart in the second act, for now illumination has come to her. She hears them crying, she tells them, like children for their mother when sweet milk has been spilled; but not a sound of lament has she heard befitting the noblest of heroes. Gutrune, raising herself from the ground, cries out on her passionately:

[1] This was the greatest difficulty of all that confronted Wagner in the construction of his drama: as Siegfried is now dead, what is to stop Hagen from taking the Ring? Wagner probably took a hint for the solution of his problem from a passage in the *Deutsche Mythologie* of the brothers Grimm, which tells of a figure of one Thorgeror höhgabrûor, which had rings of gold round its arm, before which the people knelt: when anyone tried to snatch a ring from the arm and the goddess was not disposed to let him have it, the figure bent its hand upward. The man would then bring a lot of money, lay it at the figure's feet, fall on his knees and shed tears, then rise and grasp again at the ring, which the figure would now allow him to take.

> *Brynhilde! Black with envy!*
> *Thou broughtest this bane on us all:*
> *thy tongue did goad the men against him:*
> *woe the day when here thou cam'st!*

Calmly Brynhilde waves her aside: *she* was not Siegfried's true
wife, only his light-o'-love: "his troth he had plighted to me ere
ever thy face he saw". The poor gentle Gutrune, who has unconsciously helped to weave the net in which she and all of them had
been caught by Hagen, turns with curses on him:

> *Ah, sorrow!*
> *The truth I see now!*
> *Brynhild' was his true love*
> *whom through the draught he forgot!*

In grief and shame she turns away from Siegfried and bends over
Gunther's body; from now to near the end of the opera she remains motionless. Hagen, standing defiantly apart from the others, leaning on his spear and shield, is sunk in sombre brooding.

Disregarding alike the lamentations of Gutrune and the trucu-
lence of Hagen, Brynhilde stands alone in the centre of the stage
while the orchestra begins a paean to the dead hero, into which,
as will be seen, is inwrought a reference to the majesty of the
Gods:

No.196

Lost in sorrowful memories she gazes for a moment at the body of
Siegfried, then turns in solemn exaltation to the vassals and the
women. They are to pile up mighty logs by the river side for a
pyre for the hero and kindle a fire to consume him; her horse
Grane they are to bring to her that he may share her reunion with
his master. They build up the pyre in front of the hall, close to
the Rhine, and the women are to strew it with flowers.

A great sweetness transfigures Brynhilde's face as she sings the last praises of the hero she had lost. He was like glorious sunshine, she says: he betrayed, yet he was true: his wife he beguiled, but between them lay his sword. How came the truest of men to play the traitor? She herself gives the answer: the Gods it was, and Wotan foremost among them, who had brought on him and her this woe. "Turn now your eyes on my grievous distress", she adjures them, "and on your own eternal guilt!" The wish of Wotan's heart he had laid on Siegfried, to escape the Curse that was consuming him; and all-unwitting the hero had done the God's will, "that wise a woman might grow". Now her eyes see clear to the heart of it all. The ravens rustle about her; she sends them to Walhall with the tidings Wotan fears yet hopes for; and with a great pity in her great heart she murmurs "Rest thou, rest thou, o God!"

17

At a sign from her the vassals lift the body on to the pyre, to the strains of No. 196. She takes the Ring from Siegfried's finger and gazes at it meditatively. Her heritage has come to her again, she says: the terrible Ring, the accursed Gold, had come to her once, and now from her they shall go. Apostrophising the Rhinedaughters, she promises them the Ring again that had been stolen from them:

> *what ye desire*
> *I give you now:*
> *win from my ashes*
> *all ye have wept for!*
> *The fire that burns me with him*
> *cleanses the Ring from its curse!*
> *Ye in the flood*
> *wash it away,*
> *and ever the gleaming*
> *Gold keep pure,*
> *that once ye lost to your bane!*

She puts the Ring on her own finger, turns to the pyre, and takes a firebrand from one of the men. "Fly home, ye ravens", she cries: "take to Wotan the tale of what ye have heard here on the Rhine.

629

But go first to Brynhilde's rock, where Loge flames: bid him haste to Walhall, for the end of the Gods is nigh. So — cast I the brand on Walhall's glittering towers!"

She hurls the firebrand into the pile, which breaks into bright flames, while two ravens fly up from the rock by the shore and disappear in the background. Brynhilde turns to greet her horse, which two of the younger men have now led forward. Quickly unbridling him, she addresses him in loving, intimate words. Does he know whither they two are faring? she asks him, as the motive of Redemption by Love (No. 89) steals in softly in the orchestra:

(The Siegfried motive combines with it in the second and third bars). Motive succeeds motive as she tells Grane that there, in the heart of the fire, lies his master and her lord, Siegfried the hero; does he not chafe to join him? No. 197 grows into a richer and richer tissue as she sings of her own rapture as already she feels the flames leaping about her heart:

> *Siegfried enfolding,*
> *held fast in his arms,*
> *in love unending*
> *made one with mine own!*
> *Heiajaho! Grane!*
> *Go we to greet him!*
> *Siegfried! Siegfried! See!*
> *Brynhilde greets thee in bliss!*

Mounting the horse, she urges him with a single leap into the burning pile, round which Loge's fire is now raging fiercely.

The horrified vassals and women recoil to the foreground of the stage, the whole space of which now seems filled with fire. But suddenly the glow dies down, leaving only a cloud of smoke which drifts off slowly towards the background, where it overhangs the horizon like a dark cloud-bank; at the same time the Rhine swells mightily, rolling in a flood over the fire; and where the flames had been we now see the three Rhinemaidens swimming. Hagen, who all this while has been watching Brynhilde with growing anxiety, is filled with terror at the sight of them: hastily ridding himself of spear, shield and helmet he plunges madly into the flood in pursuit of the Ring; Woglinde and Wellgunde throw their arms around his neck and drag him into the depths as they swim away, while Flosshilde, leading her sisters, holds the recovered Ring exultantly aloft.

Their gracious song is heard in the orchestra, followed by a broad statement of the Walhall motive as a red glow breaks through the cloud-bank, while in the now calmer waters of the Rhine, which has gradually fallen to its normal level, the Rhinemaidens are seen swimming in joyous circles, sporting with the Ring; and now their song blends contrapuntally with No. 197 as the men and women gaze, from the ruins of the fallen hall, at a fire-glow that slowly spreads over the sky. The Walhall motive combines in great masses of tone with that of the majesty of the Gods (No. 196) as the interior of Walhall comes into view, as Waltraute had described it to Brynhilde in the first act, with Wotan sitting mute and grave among the Gods and heroes with his shattered Spear in his hand, all of them waiting in resignation for the end that had been foretold. Flames seize upon Walhall and hide the Gods from our sight as the motive of the Downfall of the Gods (No. 44) comes crashing down in the orchestra. Then comes one of Wagner's most magical strokes: after all this racking turmoil the last word is given to the great theme of Redemption by Love (No. 197), which seems to spread consoling wings over not merely the present scene but the whole stupendous drama:

No.198   Sostenuto

etc.

18

We have seen, in our preliminary study of Wagner's Prose Sketches and poems, the changes the original plan for the ending of the *Ring* drama underwent; from a dénouement in which Siegfried's death and the redeeming deed of Brynhilde's self-sacrifice had effected the firm establishment of the beneficent rule of the Gods, he gradually arrived at an ending in which the Gods pass away in the flames that consume Walhall — "the Gods' great ending dawneth at last".

His conception of the inner meaning of his drama had undergone a drastic change as early as the spring of 1851, when he put the following final words into Brynhilde's mouth: "Powerless depart, ye whose guilt is forgone. From your guilt sprang the joyfullest of heroes, whose free deed has redeemed it: spared are ye the anxious conflict for your ending power: pass away in bliss before the human hero whom ye begat. I proclaim to you blessed death-redemption from your anxious fear."

But the actual verbal conclusion of the tetralogy and the previous motivation of it remained a perpetual problem for him. One evidence of his confusion is plainly visible in the present *Rhinegold* poem, where Erda warns Wotan to yield the Ring, because if he keeps it

> *Nought but ruin*
> *and disaster*
> *will it bring to thee!*
>
> . . . . .
>
> *A day of gloom*
> *dawns for your godhood;*
> *I charge thee, give up the Ring!*

This implies, surely, that *if* Wotan surrenders it he will avert the doom; yet in the end he and all the Gods of the old order go down in doom in spite of the renunciation! Wagner's friend August Röckel, to whom he had sent a copy of the imprint of 1853, struck at once to the heart of the matter with the commonsense query, "Why, seeing that the Gold is returned to the Rhine, is it necessary for the Gods to perish?" Wagner's involved reply suggests that he himself could not logically justify that dénouement in words but hoped that it would all explain itself to the listener through the medium of his *feeling* — through the intervention of the music.

In 1856 he made a sketch (published for the first time in 1933) for yet another ending; and shortly afterwards we find him telling a correspondent that he had decided not to bring out a public edition of the poem until after he had set it all to music: "not un-anticipated changes in the concluding parts are impending", for "it has become clear to me that the poem has travelled far beyond its original schematic tendency, as still retained in the present ending. . . Of course the result remains essentially the same; only the explanation put into the mouth of the all-knowing Bryn-hilde becomes something different, wider-reaching, more deci-sive. . ."

He cast this new "explanation" into verse but never set it to music. In the 1872 definitive edition of the poem, however, he printed it all in a footnote to the present text for the scene, with a curious commentary: "Before the musical working-out of the poem the following lines were given to Brynhilde" at the point where she turns towards the background and takes a torch from one of the bystanders. Wagner quotes thirty lines of verse, the last ten of which run thus in Alfred Forman's translation:

> *Not goods, nor gold,*
> *nor greatness of Gods;*
> *not house, nor land,*
> *nor lordly life;*
> *not burdensome bargains'*
> *treacherous bands,*
> *nor wont with the lying*
> *weight of its law;*
> *happy, in luck or need,*
> *holds you nothing but love.*

Then Wagner continues thus: "In these lines the poet had tried to express the musical effect of the drama anticipatorily, in a sen-tentious sense; but in the course of the long interruptions that held him up in the composition of his music he was impelled to-wards another version of the final words of farewell that corresponded still better to this idea: these lines ran as follows ". . . and he goes on to quote a further twenty lines of explanation by Brynhilde, ending thus: "Know ye how I won to the blessed end of all things eternal? Deepest distress of grieving love opened my eyes; I saw the world-end." To them he appended the following remark: "The musician had in the end, in the act of composition, to sacrifice these lines, as the sense of them is fully expressed by the agency of the *musical drama.*"

Wagner's words are difficult to translate, but in the light of all we now know of the matter his general meaning is clear: he relied on his music, as he had said to Röckel, to convey to the *feeling* of the listener what the poet in him had found it almost impossible to express in words. His dilemma is the most curious phenomenon of its kind in the whole history of art. As we have seen, it is unnecessary to drag in the political events of the early 1850's to account for his veering round, about that time, from an "optimistic" to a "pessimistic" interpretation of the fundamental meaning of his *Ring* drama. The cause of it all was internal, and, strange to say, *musical.* The poet in him was pulling him one way, the musician another. The man of feeling in him, as distinct from the man of intellect, was being quietly, subconsciously, but irresistibly drawn towards a dénouement in which the world should go down in outer ruin yet somehow be taken up into the arms of a redeeming love. This he could convey, and has conveyed magnificently, in his music to the closing scene; but how to express it in words was a problem that always baffled and finally defeated him.[1]

[1] For a more detailed statement of the vicissitudes of his thought during those many years, together with quotations of the relevant texts, I must refer the reader to my *Life of Wagner,* Vol. II, chapter 17.

Parsifal

CHARACTERS

AMFORTAS	*Baritone*
TITUREL	*Bass*
GURNEMANZ	*Bass*
PARSIFAL	*Tenor*
KLINGSOR	*Bass*
KUNDRY	*Soprano*

Wagner's description of the Scene of the Action:
In the territory and the castle of the Knights of the Grail,
Monsalvat. The scenery is in the style of the northern mountain ranges of Gothic Spain. Klingsor's magic castle is on the
southern slope of this range, fronting Arabic Spain.

1

F at any performance of *Parsifal* we were to ask the first man
we ran into during an interval what the Grail was, he would
almost certainly reply in much the same words as those of
Wagner when, in 1865, he was giving King Ludwig II of Bavaria the ground plan of the opera he hoped some day to write:
"The Grail is the crystal Cup from which the Redeemer and His
disciples drank at the Last Supper; Joseph of Arimathea caught in
it the blood that flowed from the spear-wound in His side when
He was on the Cross. For a long time it was mysteriously withdrawn from the sinful world and preserved as the holiest of relics.
Then, at a time when the world was harsh and hostile and the
faithful were hard pressed by the unbelieving and were in great
distress, there sprang up in certain divinely inspired heroes, filled
with holy love-longing, the desire to seek out this strengthening

relic of which tradition spoke, in which the blood of the Saviour (*sangue réale,* whence San Greal, Sanct Gral, the Holy Grail) had been preserved and was divinely potent for a humanity in dire need of salvation. The relic was supernaturally revealed to Titurel and his faithful band and given over into their keeping. He gathered about him a holy company of knights for the service of the Grail, and in a wild inaccessible forest in the mountains he built the castle of Monsalvat, which no man could discover unless he had proved himself worthy to have care of the Grail." And so on, with certain other details which we shall consider in due time.

If our interlocutor were a scholar versed in mediaeval literature, however, he would tell us a great deal more than this, and something very different from it here and there. He would outline for us first of all the story of Parsifal and the Grail as it is told by the old German poet, Wolfram von Eschenbach, from whom Wagner primarily derived his inspiration; and we would then discover that there was nothing whatever in that story associating the Grail with the traditional Cup of the Last Supper, or with the blood of the Saviour on the Cross, or with Joseph of Arimathea, or, indeed, any conception even of the Grail as a chalice.

But this would not be all. Our first mentor, in reply to our request for information about the spear that plays so large a part in the opera, would tell us that it was the weapon with which the Roman soldier Longinus had pierced the side of the Saviour on the Cross. But the scholar would assure us that not only had Wolfram no such notion as this of the spear that figures in his story of Parsifal and the Grail, but a sacred spear was not even a feature of Wagner's original plan for an opera on the Parsifal subject. He had been brooding on the theme at least as early as 1857, but it is clear from his letters of that period to Mathilde Wesendonk that as yet he had no notion of introducing what may be called, for convenience' sake, the Longinus motive; Wagner's Amfortas has indeed been grievously wounded by a spear; but it is not yet, for Wagner, *that* spear. Even when he sat down to write the above-mentioned Sketch for King Ludwig in 1865 he appears to have had no thought of making the spear identical with that of Calvary. In his account of the tragic adventure of Amfortas in Klingsor's garden he merely says that, "turning to flee, he [Amfortas] received the spear-wound in his side from which he now suffers

and for which no healing can be found". A little later in the
Sketch, at the point in the first act where Amfortas is bewailing
his sin and its consequences for not only himself but the brethren
of the Grail, Wagner says that once more the wound begins to
bleed, "the selfsame wound received by the Redeemer on the
Cross and through which He poured out His blood in love and
compassion for wretched sinful man". Even in this, however,
there is still no hint of any conception on Wagner's part of the
wound having been inflicted on Amfortas by the very spear that
had pierced the Saviour. In the opera poem as we now have it the
words which Wagner puts into Amfortas's mouth at this point are
these:

> *In maddest tumult, by sin defiled,*
> *my blood back on itself*
> *doth turn and rage within me;*
> *to the world where sin is lord*
> *in frenzied fear is it surging:*
> *again it forces the door,*
> *in torrents it poureth forth,*
> *here through the spear-wound, alike to His,*
> *and dealt me by the selfsame deadly spear*
> *that once the Redeemer pierced with pain,*
> *and, tears of blood outpouring,*
> *the Holy One wept for the shame of man,*
> *in pity's godlike yearning.*

This agrees with the corresponding passage in the Sketch of 1865
in every respect [1] but one: there is nothing in the Sketch answering to the line in the poem "and dealt me by the selfsame spear".

2

Is it likely, we ask ourselves, that Wagner would have omitted
so vital a motive from his very detailed epitome of 1865 of the
first act had it been present in his mind at that time? It was

[1] Even down to verbal parallelisms: for instance, the "sprengt die Wunde
von Neuem und ergiesst sich in die Welt der Sünde" of the Sketch links up
with the "in die Welt der Sündensucht mit wilder Scheu sich ergiessen" of
the poem; and the "durch dieselbe Wunde, wie sie einst der Erlöser am
Kreuze empfing" of the former with the "hier durch die Wunde, der seinem
gleich . . . der dort dem Erlöser die Wunde stach" of the latter.

probably on the 29th August that he put the plan for the second act on paper. He outlined the final episode of that act thus: "Klingsor appears on the tower of his castle. Armed men rush in. Parsifal recognises the spear with which Amfortas had been wounded and wrests it from the Knight [Klingsor]. 'With this sign I exorcise you all! As the wound once dealt by this spear-point closes, so let everything here pass away, and its splendour crash in ruins'. He swings the spear: the castle collapses with a frightful crash: the garden withers to a desert." But between "the spear with which Amfortas had been wounded" and "wrests it from the Knight" there is added (in parenthesis in the printed version), "it is the spear with which Longinus had once wounded the Redeemer in the side, and of which, as a very valuable means to magic, Klingsor had possessed himself". Apparently, then, Wagner had had no intention, until he inserted that parenthesis, of identifying the spear that had once wounded Amfortas, the spear now launched by Klingsor at Parsifal and seized by the boy in mid-air, with the very Spear that had been thrust in the Saviour's side.

And that even yet he had no clear perception of the bearing this new interpretation would have on his future drama is shown by a little phrase near the end of the Sketch. When Parsifal, returned from his wanderings, encounters Gurnemanz and is reproached by him for bearing arms on Good Friday, he stands silent for a moment: "then he opens his helmet, removes it from his head, strikes the spear into the ground, lays down his shield and his sword before it, sinks to his knees, and prays earnestly with his eyes fixed fervently on the bleeding spearpoint". Why "bleeding"? we naturally ask ourselves. In Wolfram von Eschenbach, as we shall see shortly, the spear that is carried into the hall of the Grail has indeed a trickle of blood running down the shaft, but in Wolfram neither is the Grail the Cup of the Last Supper and the Cross, nor is there the smallest identification of the spear with that of the Crucifixion. Clearly by the time Wagner had arrived at the final stage of his Sketch of 1865 he had had an intuition that he must combine Wolfram's account of the ceremonial in the hall of the Grail with the story, stemming from another source, of the spear of the legendary Longinus. The possible significance of the "bleeding" lance was beginning to dawn upon him, and so possessed is he with it that he now describes the spear as "bleeding" when Parsifal thrusts it into the ground, though there has been no suggestion of any such property in it in his preceding references to it in the scene in Klingsor's garden. In his final poem — written years later — the spear does not bleed at any point of the drama; Wagner, indeed, conscious later that there would be no sense in characterising it in that way, omits the "bleeding" of the passage just quoted from the Sketch from the stage directions for the Good Friday scene with Gurnemanz in the opera: Parsifal now simply "thrusts the spear into the ground before him" and "kneels before it in silent prayer". Nor in the crucial moment in the final scene, in which Parsifal heals Amfortas with a touch of the spear, is there any suggestion, either in the text or in the stage directions, that it is "bleeding".

Wagner's difficulty apparently came from his having felt that the bleeding lance of the scene in the hall of the Grail in Wolfram's poem (to which we shall come shortly) must necessarily have some sort of connection with the lance of the Longinus legend, whereas there is no connection at all between the two. His perplexity over the matter is shown by a jotting of the 2nd September 1865 in his diary:

"How am I to deal with the bleeding lance? The poem [i.e. Wolfram's] says that the lance was carried [into the hall] at the same time as the Grail, and that there was a drop of blood on the point of it. Moreover, Amfortas's wound has been dealt by this lance-point. But how does this hang together? There is great confusion here: the lance is a relic that accompanies the vessel in which is preserved the blood drawn by the lance-point from the Saviour's side.[1] The two are complementary. Therefore, one of two alternatives:

"The lance was given into the charge of the brotherhood at the same time as the Grail, and in times of great distress was borne in combat by the guardian of the Grail. Amfortas, in order to overcome the magic of Klingsor, which is so ruinous to the brotherhood, has taken it from the altar and gone out with it to fight the arch-enemy. When he succumbed to seduction, and shield and spear fell from his hands, the holy weapon was used against him,

[1] The "confusion", however, was Wagner's own; it came from his reading into the Wolfram epic something that was never in the poet's mind.

and he was wounded by it as he turned to flee. (Perhaps Klingsor, because he wants to have Amfortas in his power alive, orders him to be wounded by the lance, as he knows that this wounds but does not kill. — Why?). Consequently the healing and redemption of Amfortas are possible only when the lance is rescued from unholy hands and placed with the Grail again. — Or,

"When the Grail was given to the knights the lance also was promised them; but it must first be won in hard fights. Were it once lodged with the Grail the knights could no more be assailed by temptation. Klingsor has found the lance, and preserves it partly because of its great magical virtue — for it is capable of wounding even the holiest if there is a trace of a failing in him, — partly to deprive the Grail brotherhood of it, as the possession of it would make them invincible. Amfortas has sallied forth to take the lance from Klingsor; succumbing to the seduction of love he is wounded by it when Klingsor hurls it at him. — The outcome remains the same: it must come back into the possession of the knights. — Klingsor hurls the spear at Parsifal, who grasps it; he has heard of it and knows its magic, its significance."

As we know, the first of these alternatives was the one ultimately adopted by Wagner.

But this was only one of the many difficulties he had to overcome before he could shape Wolfram's poem into the opera as we now have it. Let us follow him step by step over the years of the creation of *Parsifal;* and first of all we must survey the story as he found it in the old poets.

3

We must begin our investigation of the story of Parsifal and the Grail with a poem by a French author, Crestien de Troyes, entitled *Li Contes del Graal,* which was written about 1180. (It is impossible to say to what extent Crestien constructed his poem out of legends or written sources already current: scholars are not agreed on this point). In one episode of the poem the young knight Perceval [1] arrives at a castle in which is an old king, who,

---

[1] The spelling of proper names in the following pages — Parzival, Perceval, Parsifal; Cundrie, Kundry; Klingsor, Clinschor; Anfortas, Amfortas; Gornemans, Gurnemanz; Graal, Grail, etc. — conforms in general to that of the mediaeval work under discussion at the moment. Wagner himself hesitated

by reason of sickness, cannot rise from his couch. Four hundred knights are with him in the hall. The boy has previously been schooled in courtesy by a certain old knight named Gornemans, who has warned him against asking unnecessary questions: accordingly, though lost in wonder, he remains silent when a strange scene is enacted before his eyes. A squire passes through the hall in front of the couch, from one side-room to another, bearing a lance down the shaft of which runs a trickle of blood.[1] Two other squires follow with lighted candles and take the same course as the first; after them comes a maiden carrying a "graal" of pure gold, set with precious stones, which emits a dazzling light. Supper is served, and at each course the graal is borne across the room. Curious as he is about it all, Perceval refrains from asking the meaning of what he sees, but resolves to do so on the morrow.

When he rises the next morning, however, he finds his horse and armour placed ready for him but no sign of life in the castle. He rides away in sore perplexity. Soon he meets with a lady who learns from him that he has been in the castle and seen the lance and the graal but has asked no question concerning them. For this she upbraids him: had he thought to do so, she tells him, the sick king would have been healed and misfortune averted from the land. Later he encounters another woman, hideous of aspect and riding on a grotesque yellow mule — the "Loathly Damsel" of some versions of the tale: she too reproaches him violently for his failure to ask the question, as a consequence of which the sick king will continue to suffer, wars will break out, many knights will be slain, and the land will be laid waste; and the guilt for it all will be on Perceval's head.

The boy, oppressed with a vague wonder, goes on his way in deepest sorrow, vowing never to rest until he has solved this fateful mystery of graal and lance. After years of wandering he finds himself in the company of some penitents who chide him for bearing arms on that day of all days: does he not know, they ask him, that it is Good Friday morning? They direct him to a hermit who

---

for many years between "Parzival", "Percival" and "Parsifal", and only decided on this last in 1877.

[1] There is also a mysterious sword which plays a considerable part in the story. We need not concern ourselves with this, however, as that particular motive was not utilised by Wagner.

turns out to be his uncle on his mother's side: the sick king, it appears, is also his uncle, and his grandfather — the father of the hermit and the king — has sustained life for the last twenty years by virtue solely of the Host contained in the graal. Perceval learns also that he lies under the sin of having unwittingly caused his loving mother's death; it was for that reason that it had not been given to him to ask concerning the spear and the graal. The hermit shrives him, and the twain partake of the eucharist. Crestien's tale ends, so far as the adventures of the hero concern us here, at this point; he died leaving his work unfinished.

Passing over, as irrelevant to our enquiry, two or three later re-tellings of part of Crestien's story, with several new inventions, we arrive at the actual main source of Wagner's drama, the masterpiece of German mediaeval poetry, the *Parzival* of Wolfram von Eschenbach, written in the early years of the thirteenth century. Crestien had told his readers that he derived his story from a certain book belonging to Count Philip of Flanders. Of this book nothing is now known. Wolfram, in his turn, seems anxious not to come under the suspicion that he derives from Crestien. He names as his source one "Kyot the Provençal", who, according to him, has alone told "the true story"; Crestien had told it wrongly, for which Kyot "would have been wrathful with him". Of this Kyot, however, we know nothing. (Attempts were made at one time to identify him with the poet Guiot de Provins, but this theory has been abandoned). In the main Wolfram agrees with Crestien so far as the latter's tale of Perceval and the graal extends; but whether he derived his incidents and took over his motives from his French predecessor, or both of them built upon a common foundation that has now disappeared, is a problem which presumably will never be solved. It is not until the final stage of his poem (Book XVI) that Wolfram describes how Parzival found the Grail again and asked the question he ought to have asked in Book V. Perhaps Crestien too had been reserving this telling climax for the end of his poem.

As Wagner derived his first impulse to write an opera on the Parsifal theme from Wolfram, we must now examine in some detail the latter's treatment of the story. A very large literature has developed during the last hundred years around the legend of

Parsifal and the Grail, which bristles with problems that still defy solution. Here, however, we must confine ourselves to the features of it that bear on the genesis and evolution of the Wagnerian work.[1]

4

Wolfram's hero is from the beginning the "pure fool" with whom Wagner has familiarised the world. A brave and essentially good man "becoming slowly wise" is how the poet describes his Parzival in his opening pages; this links up with Wagner's well-known:

> *made wise through pity,*
> *the blameless fool,*
> *wait for him,*
> *my chosen is he.*

Parzival's father, Gahmuret of Anjou, has been slain in one of his knightly adventures, leaving a widow, Queen Herzeloyde (Heart's Sorrow), to whom is born, fourteen days after Gahmuret's death, a comely boy. That the son may not meet with the father's fate the grieving mother withdraws with him and a few of her people into a wood, where she brings him up in ignorance of the mad world in which men fight and slay each other, — ignorant, indeed, of his own name. The child makes for himself a bow and arrow with which he brings down birds in the wood, only to break his heart afterwards with grief for the tiny beings that had sung to him so sweetly. Bigger game he kills with his javelot, for he is strong and daring beyond his years. One day he comes upon a splendid company of knights riding through the wood, whom in his innocence he takes for gods. He learns from their leader what knighthood is, and is bidden, if he wishes to know more, to betake himself to the court of King Arthur. All his desire now is for a horse and armour and adventures; but his mother, anxious to save him for herself and preserve him from his father's fate, sends him

---

[1] Wolfram's great poem is written in mediaeval German. It has been admirably rendered into modern German verse, with a few omissions, by Wilhelm Hertz. Those who know no German can acquaint themselves with it in the English verse translation of Miss Jessie L. Weston (1894), which gives an excellent idea of the original, though its long hexameter lines lack the directness and concision of Wolfram's pithy couplets.

forth into the world in a "fool's garb" of sackcloth, with a fool's cap and coarse boots of untanned leather, and mounted on the sorriest of steeds. Her hope is that, humbled and disillusioned by contact with the rough realities of the world, he will be glad to return to her.

But the boy will not be denied. Grotesquely garbed as he is he sets out in blind quest of Arthur's court, in the unconscious cruelty of his ignorance leaving his mother to die of grief. He meets with a maiden, — his cousin Sigune, as it turns out — sorrowing over the body of her slain lover. She tells him much he had not known — that his name is Parzival, and that one day he shall be what his father was, King of Norgals and Waleis. The simple boy, whose beauty and frankness win him the hearts of all except the wicked, finds at last the company of the Round Table, and, having killed the Red Knight Ither in single combat, takes his horse and armour and sets out in quest of adventures. One day he meets with a certain Gornemans, lord of Graharz, who instructs him in knightly honour and courtesy: one of his precepts — which becomes of the greatest significance in the sequel, both in Wolfram and in Wagner — is to "ask few questions but give well-considered answers". Thus schooled, Parzival, in his wanderings near and far, does many knightly deeds and marries the Lady Condwiramurs, the queen of a city hard pressed by its enemies.

5

It is in his fifth and sixth Books that Wolfram describes that first strange experience of Parzival's in the castle of the Grail that was later to constitute the core of Wagner's opera. One evening the boy comes to a lake where some men are fishing from a boat; of one of them, who is richly dressed,[1] he asks where he may obtain lodging for the night. The "earnest, sorrowful man", as the old poet describes the Fisher, assures him that within thirty miles of them there is no habitation but one: Parzival is to ride on to where the rock ends, turn to the right, ascend the hill, and, having arrived at a castle, bid them lower the drawbridge and let him enter. "If you do not lose your way", says the Fisher, "I myself will be your host there tonight, and you can thank me then. But have a care! There are many wrong roads and you might easily go

[1] The "Rich Fisher" of some of the legends, the "Maimed King" of others.

astray, and for that I should be sorry." Already we have a hint, though of the slightest, that much, for himself and others, depends on Parzival finding that castle and its lord.

Arrived at the moat he tells the warden of the drawbridge that he has been sent there by the Fisher as his guest. He is courteously received and royally tended; his armour is taken away, and the Queen of the castle, Repanse de Schoye, clothes him with her own mantel of fine Arabian silk. He is ushered into a great hall, lit by the tapers of a hundred chandeliers: a hundred couches, each with a carpet before it, are set out; on each of them is room for four men. The lord of the castle — the Fisher — is carried in on a couch and laid before the centre one of three great fireplaces: "he and joy had long been parted; a painful dying was his life"; his sick body cries out for great fires and many furs.

Suddenly a cry of anguish breaks from the assembled knights as a squire comes running into the hall, holding aloft a spear from the point of which blood runs down the shaft and into his sleeve: at the sight of it all break into tears and lamentations. The squire traverses each of the four walls before returning to, and disappearing through, the door by which he had entered; whereupon the wailing ceases.

Maidens enter who place ivory trestles before the lord of the castle, while others bring in a precious stone of lustrous red jacinth, cut long and broad and thin so that it may be used as a table: this they lay on the trestles. Next come two damsels bearing two bright and sharp silver knives on napkins, which they place on the jacinth table. The maidens are followed by the Queen, clothed in a robe of the finest Arabian tissue, and carrying, on a cloth of emerald silk, "the glory of Paradise, the root, stem and shoot of salvation, a thing called the Grail, a treasury of marvels beyond number"; it is borne by the Queen herself because in virtue of its noble nature only the pure of heart are worthy to tend it. She bows and sets the Grail before the lord of the castle. Then a hundred tables, covered with a cloth of white linen, are brought in, and one of them is set in front of each four of the knights. Parzival, seated by the silent, melancholy lord, washes his hands, like him, in water. Bread, in white napkins, is laid before the Grail by a hundred serving squires and set before the knights. The nature of the Grail was such that whatever food a man desired, cold or warm, new or old, it would yield him in abundance. "For I tell you the story", says the poet to the reader, "as I have received it"; and a little later, "If anyone thinks this too wonderful and unexampled, let him not blame the tale." (This suggests that Wolfram himself had no definite conception of the meaning of the "Grail"). "Blessings streamed from it, a rain of earthly felicity; it was equal almost to what we are told of heaven". And as with food, so with drink: with whatever a man desired the Grail filled his cup: all were the guests of the Grail.

6

Parzival watches it all in great astonishment, but out of courtesy he will not ask the meaning of it: "within himself he thought, 'The good Gornemans enjoined me to refrain from asking many questions. I will wait courteously until they tell me everything unasked, as Gornemans did'". While he is thus communing with himself a squire approaches him with a splendid sword, the gift of the lord of the castle. (This sword seems to be an element that has filtered into the Parzival story from another saga, dealing with the obligation of the hero to revenge a murder. Neither Crestien nor Wolfram appears to understand precisely what he should do with it). "Alas", Wolfram comments, "that he did not ask the question then! For his own sake that was a pity, for the sword was a hint to him to speak. Grieved am I also for his host, for the question would have rid him of his unnamed torment."

The meal comes to an end: the Queen approaches the Grail and bows low to the lord and his guest: then all pass out by the door by which they had entered. As they go, Parzival has a glimpse into the room beyond; there, on a couch, lies the most beautiful old man he had ever seen, whiter than hoar-frost. "Who he was", says the poet, "you shall learn later; at the right time, too, I will tell you who and what were the lord, the castle and the land."

Parzival retires to rest, tended with great courtesy. He sleeps uneasily, beset by troubled dreams. When he wakes next morning he finds no squires or pages to do him service, though on the carpet lie his armour, his own sword, and the one given him by the lord of the castle: he dons his mail unaided and goes to the outer door, where he finds his horse, his shield and his spear awaiting him. Perturbed and a little angry at what he takes to be discourteous treatment of a guest he goes through room after room, but nowhere is there a sign of life. He returns to the courtyard, where he sees that the grass has been trodden down and the dewdrops scattered. Mounting his horse he makes for the great outer gates: they stand wide open, and beyond them, stretching away into the fields, he sees the tracks of many horses. He spurs his own steed across the drawbridge, which is raised by an unseen hand almost before he has cleared it, and he hears the voice of the warder saying, "Away with you, and may the sun never shine on you! A goose you are! Could you not have opened your mouth? Would that you had not been so sparing of your speech but had asked your host a question! A great prize have you forfeited!" Parzival asks the meaning of these bitter words but receives no answer; the gates close with a crash behind him. Assuming that the knights have ridden forth to fight in some cause of their lord's he decides to follow them, which he does until the tracks grow fainter and at last he loses the ever-narrowing trail.

He rides on until he comes to a woman lamenting over a dead knight who lies clasped in her arms, and he offers her his knightly service. It is Crestien's Sigune once more. Where did he lodge last night? she asks him. In a lordly castle, he replies. "Only one castle is there in this wood", she says. "In it does every wish find its fulfilment. But whoso seeks for it can never find it: he who is to discover it must come upon it unawares. Its name is Munsalvaesche,[1] and Terresalvaesche is the land in which it lies. The old King Titurel bequeathed his realm to his son Frimutel, a brave knight who died in combat, slain in the cause of love. He left four children: three are rich but full of sorrow; the fourth, Trevrizent by name, has chosen poverty for his portion and does penance for past sin. His brother Anfortas [2] is now lord of Munsalvaesche; he is a stricken man who can neither walk nor ride nor stand nor lie, but only recline. If indeed you came to that castle where all is sorrow, then surely must its lord have been healed of the pain he has borne so long . . . Did you see the Grail and its joyless lord?

[1] Not Monsalvat (the mountain of salvation), it will be observed. Salvaesche means wild: (French *sauvage,* Italian *selvaggio,* Spanish *salvaje.*)

[2] Wolfram spells the name in this fashion and accents it on the first syllable.

Give me the tidings I fain would hear. If his woes are at an end, then of good omen was your journey, for you shall be praised and served by all things living, and every wish of yours shall be fulfilled if you have asked the question you should have done."

Parzival confesses sorrowfully that he had asked no question. "Alas!" cries Sigune, "that ever I set eyes on you, that were too faint of heart to ask the question. You beheld all the wonders of the Grail, and the silver knives, and the bleeding spear. Why came you to me here? You are dishonoured and accursed; the venomous tooth of the wolf is yours, gall has poisoned troth and love in you. Were you not touched with pity for him? You asked not what ailed the sore-afflicted man? You live, but you are dead to blessing." "Be not angry with me", Parzival replies humbly; "I will atone." But she drives him from her, cursing him for a blot on the fair name of knighthood.

7

So Parzival, sick of soul for that he has somehow failed in kindliness and pity, and with the thought of his beloved Condwiramurs always tugging at his heart, passes on to a series of fresh adventures at the court of King Arthur and elsewhere. At the court a new shame is put upon the ignorant boy. There rides in one day a hideous woman, the sorceress Cundrie, who curses him and denounces him as a disgrace to knighthood. He is more loathsome than even she, she cries, for his heart is false: he had been to Munsalvaesche, he had seen the suffering King, the Grail, the silver knives, the bleeding lance, and had failed in the duty laid on him. "Ah, Munsalvaesche!", she cries as she rides away on her ugly mule, "home of grief, woe to thee, for no man comes to thee with pity and with help". And Parzival stands mute under her revilings, suffering he knows not why. He had always been brave and loyal and generous; there was no will to evil in his simple young heart; yet somehow in his ignorance he has done a monstrous, unforgivable wrong.

With his further adventures as a knight, and with those of Gawain, who now plays for a while the more prominent part in the poet's tale, we are not concerned here. It is upon Gawain that, by a new turn in the story, is laid, for a time, the task of going in search of the Grail. But the one predestined to find it is not Gawain but Parzival, who comes into the foreground once more in Wolfram's ninth Book.

After years of wandering through many lands and over the seas he has come to a forest where once again he encounters Sigune, still mourning her dead lover; her own life, it appears, is sustained by the Grail, provision from which is brought to her each week by Cundrie. She recognises him as the Parzival who had gone long ago in search of the Grail, and asks how it had fared with him in his quest. Mournfully he confesses that neither Munsalvaesche nor the Grail has he yet found, and he asks counsel of her in his distress of soul. She bids him follow the track of Cundrie's mule. But the forest is wild and soon he loses his way: once more he has missed the Grail and the opportunity to ask the question from which, he tells himself, he would not shrink a second time. At last he comes upon an old grey knight who chides him gently for bearing arms on that holiest of days, Good Friday, when all creation should be at once mourning and rejoicing. Parzival again rides on. He has been at bitter strife with God all the years since first he saw Munsalvaesche, for God seems to have deserted him and been his enemy. But what if God after all can help him in his torturing need? He lets the reins fall loosely on his horse's neck. The animal takes him straight to the Fontaine la Salvaesche; and there, from the lips of a good old hermit, Trevrizent the pure, he learns the story of the Grail.

No one can ever find it, says Trevrizent, save the Grail's own chosen. It is kept at Munsalvaesche, guarded by knights, who are nourished and kept for ever young by a certain pure and precious stone. Its name is *lapis exilis* [1]; it is the stone that brings the phoenix to life again from its own ashes, and preserves a sick man from death for a week after he has gazed on it; "its other name is the Grail". Each Good Friday its powers are renewed by a white dove which descends upon it from heaven, bearing in its beak a wafer; and thus the stone yields daily to the brotherhood all the meats and fruits they need for their sustenance. The elect of the Grail are chosen when children by the Grail itself, for the name of anyone destined for its service, man or maid, appears in mystic letters

[1] Or iaspis, lapsit; exilix, erillis; etc., in this manuscript or that. It looks as if the mediaeval scribes had no definite idea of the meaning of the word they were copying.

on the stone; these letters remain until they have been read, and then fade away. Long ago, when Lucifer contended with God, many of the angels took no side in the strife, for which offence they were cast out of heaven and sent down to earth to tend the stone, which they have guarded ever since: "this, Sir, is how it standeth with the Grail".

Hearing this, Parzival thinks that God should choose him to be one of the shining brotherhood, for he has been a knight honourable and brave. But Trevrizent reproves him: "You must beware of pride and insolence of will; your youth may mislead you, for always pride has its fall". And with tears in his eyes the old man tells Parzival the story of King Anfortas, whose undoing had been wrought by pride, for he had pursued an unchaste love. That is not the way of the Grail, says Trevrizent, which demands of its servants not pride but humility and purity of spirit. As for Munsalvaesche and the Grail, none know where they are to be found but those called to their service. "One alone came there unsummoned — a young fool who went away again with the burden of sin on him, for he saw his host's anguish and spoke no word of pity". "I will reproach no man", continues Trevrizent; "yet for that sin, that he asked not the question of the host on whom God's hand lay so heavy, he must pay dear."

8

As they talk, he and Parzival learn more of each other. Titurel, the boy learns, had bequeathed his holy heritage to his son Frimutel, whom Parzival resembles in looks. Herzeloyde was Trevrizent's sister; Trevrizent is the son of Frimutel, and the Queen Repanse de Schoye is sister to Trevrizent and to Anfortas, the present lord of the Grail. He, in the pride and ardour of his youth, had fought many a fight in the service of love, "for *Amor* was his battle-cry". But one day, having ridden out alone on an adventure, he fell a victim to love and was pierced in the groin by the envenomed spear of a heathen who had come over the sea from his own land — "in Ethnisé, where the Tigris flows out of Paradise", — burning to win, if he might, possession of the Grail: "his name was graven on the spear". He was slain, and Anfortas rode home, sick and weary, to his lamenting people. The physician, groping in the wound, found in it the spear-head and part of the shaft, and drew them out. Then Trevrizent, in horror, put away his weapons and foreswore henceforth bread and wine and the flesh of animals.

Trevrizent tells Parzival more about the Grail and the trouble of the brethren by reason of Anfortas's fall. The Grail, it appears, chooses for its service young children of noble birth, maidens as well as boys. It will send in secret, if prayed to do so, one of its knights to rule over a lordless land; but the men of that land must pledge themselves to unquestioning allegiance to him [1]. The maidens of the Grail can be openly sent out to wedlock in other lands: Herzeloyde had been such a one. Whoever has been dedicated to the Grail must forswear the love of women; only the King and those sent to foreign lands are allowed a wife, and they must not seek love outside the marriage bond.

To heal the wound of Anfortas every remedy has been sought and tried — the mystic waters of the four streams of Paradise (Fison, Geon, Tigris and Euphrates), the golden bough which the Cumæan Sibyl promised should protect Aeneas against the perils of Hades, the blood of the pelican's breast on which she nourishes her young; the heart of the unicorn and the potent carbuncle that lies beneath its horn; the magic herb that springs from the ground bedewed by a dying dragon's blood. All had been in vain. The knights had prayed for help, and seen it written on the Grail that one should come who would ask the King the question that would lift the burden of suffering from him, the deliverer who should then reign in his stead. But he would have to come unbidden and ask the question without prompting, and that on his first night in the castle. One knight indeed had come, says Trevrizent, but he had failed to ask, and thereby lost his chance of being blessed and plunged the King back into his intolerable woe. Always when Saturn has run his course Anfortas's sufferings increase: the frost enters the wound, and there is no remedy but to cure one maddening pain by another, by thrusting the burning spear into the wound; its heat draws out the frost and turns it to crystals of ice, which can be cut away from the spear only by two sharp silver knives. At the change of the moon the King is carried to the lake called Brumbane, where the pure air cleanses the

---

[1] The legend of Lohengrin is foreshadowed here.

wound: there he fishes, and so the story goes that he is a Fisherman.

Hearing all this, Parzival discloses that he was the peccant knight who had arrived at the castle and failed in what was expected of him. Trevrizent gives him wise and loving counsel, but urges him to cleanse his soul and atone for the wrongs he had done. For twice the unschooled boy had unwittingly wrought evil: in the thoughtless lustihood of youth he had left his loving mother and broken her heart, and, in his first passion to become a knight, he had slain the Red Knight Ither and possessed himself of his armour. God has not forgotten these misdeeds, and will requite him for them. But the peak of his offending against heaven had been his failure in the castle of the Grail. For his coming, Trevrizent now tells him, had filled them all with hope: it was because they saw in him the healer of Anfortas and the chosen successor to the kingdom of the Grail that the Queen had covered him with her own mantle and the King had given him a sword. The fair old man of whom Parzival had caught sight through the open door was his mother's grandsire, Titurel, the first custodian of the Grail, now old and bedridden, but kept alive by the sight of the Grail. And so, after fifteen days, Parzival rides away from Trevrizent, with the counsel in his ears to be steadfast and true and leave his sins in the old hermit's keeping, who will render account for them in the sight of God.

9

This was the strange story which Wolfram had refrained from telling earlier, leaving it to reach us at this stage through the mouth of Trevrizent. And now his poem takes a curious turn: Parzival becomes for a while a subsidiary character, only to come back in the end, however, as the true hero of the long tale. And much of what now follows is of prime importance to us because of the part it plays in Wagner's drama.

The action shifts to another land of marvels — Terre Merveille, which is not only as wonderful in its own different way as Terre Munsalvaesche but curiously connected with it.

A certain Cidegast, the lover of the queen Orgeluse (who in Wolfram's poem is one of the greatest figures in mediaeval literature), having been slain by a rival suitor for the lady's hand, King

Gramovlanz, Orgeluse's one passion henceforth is to avenge his death. To this end she had accepted in days gone by the services of Anfortas, who had failed, however, in the combat with Gramovlanz and received a grievous wound. Thereupon Orgeluse, still thirsting for vengeance, had concluded a pact with one Clinschor, a mighty magician, the lord of the enchanted Terre Merveille and its castle, the Schastel Merveille. He had once loved the wife of King Ibert of Sicily, who found them together and by a stroke of his knife unmanned the knight. Thereafter, in a mad hatred of humanity, Clinschor had devoted himself to the study of magic. High up on a mountain he had created a palace and a garden the like of which the earth did not contain. There he held in thrall the knights and ladies who fell into his power, the victims of his malignant hate of all mankind. Orgeluse bribes him with the gift of a pavilion, full of costly merchandise, which she had received from Anfortas, to whom it had been presented by the Indian queen Secundille. Along with it she had sent two messengers to the lord of the Grail. (At this point it becomes tolerably clear that Wolfram was drawing for his material upon more than one oral or written source, and making an attempt to combine certain characters and milieux either in a way of his own or in some way sanctioned by usage. Cundrie, for instance, brings remedies and salves for the healing of Gawain's wounds, just as, in the other story, she brings them for Anfortas).

It was Cundrie who, making one of her mysterious appearances at the court of King Arthur, had persuaded Gawain and other knights to go to the rescue of four queens and four hundred maidens who had been made captive by Clinschor; and it is with the adventures of Gawain that a great deal of Wolfram's space is taken up at this point. It is to Gawain that Orgeluse finally trusts for the avenging of the death of Cidegast. She had indeed met the mysterious Red Knight (Parzival), and after he had overthrown her men in combat she offered him her hand and her kingdom. But he had passed on his way with a touch of anger and scorn: two desires alone possessed him, to be joined again to his Condwiramurs and to find the Grail. In the end, however, it is Parzival, not Gawain, who overcomes Gramovlanz in combat and so works the will of Orgeluse.

We next find Parzival, in the course of his wanderings, encoun-

tering his half-brother Fierefiz, the son of Gahmuret by a dusky
queen of the east, and in face half-black, half-white. After he and
Parzival have fought to the equal honour of each of them they discover their blood-relationship; and the pair ride on to King Arthur's court, whither, one day, a changed Cundrie comes. She falls
at the feet of the Parzival whom she had once so cruelly derided
and cursed, and begs his forgiveness; she tells him that the in-
scription on the Grail has been read and that he is the destined
new lord of the Grail; he has only to ask the question and Anfortas
will be made free of his pain; Condwiramurs and one of Parzival's
twin sons, Loherangrin, have also been chosen to be of the company of the Grail. So Parzival, Cundrie and Fierefiz set out together for Munsalvaesche. They are well received by the knights.
The weary Anfortas implores Parzival to deny him the sight of the
Grail for seven nights and eight days and so bring his burdensome
life to an end. But Parzival weeps and prays for him, rises to his
feet, and asks the simple question, "Uncle, what aileth thee?"; and
instantly Anfortas becomes well and young again. Parzival is made
King in his stead; and soon he has the joy of being re-united to his
Condwiramurs after so many years. Loherangrin he keeps with
him; the later story of the boy is enshrined in the anonymous epic
of *Lohengrin*. The other son, Kardeiz, is sent to rule over his father's earthly kingdom of Brobarz.

10

The story as told by Crestien and Wolfram differs in many fundamental respects from that of Wagner's *Parsifal*. For neither of
the old writers does the Grail mean what it did for Wagner and
does for most people today. Crestien, indeed, does not even speak
of "*the* Grail"; it is "*a* graal" that the maiden carries into the hall.
There is no hint of it containing the blood of the Saviour, and it is
plainly, for Crestien, not a cup but a dish. That, indeed, seems to
be the true primal meaning of the word itself. All the popular deri-
vations of it are fanciful, whether from the Latin "gradalis", signifying a dish in which the various foods were arranged in rows
(gradatim), or from "Sang réal" (royal blood). It comes from an
old Latin word "garalis", meaning a dish (old French "graal" or
"gréal", Provençal "grazal"). In the will of a certain Count Eber-
hard (A.D. 873) a bequest is made of several "garales," including

"two of silver with two spoons each" ("garales argenteos cum binis cochleariis duos"); and under the rules and regulations of the courts of the Kings of Jerusalem "all dishes and graals" from which the food was served on feast days were placed in the custody of the seneschal.

For Wolfram, as we have seen, the Grail is not even a dish but some kind of talismanic stone. The denizens of Munsalvaesche, Trevrizent tells Parsifal, are miraculously fed by "a stone of pure and sublime nature, called *lapis exillix*. It is this stone that enables the phoenix to rise renewed from its ashes. Be a man ever so sick, a sight of the stone preserves his life and his colour for the space of a whole week. A man might look at it for two hundred years and show no sign of age except a greying of his hair. The other name of the stone is the Grail." Such a stone would presumably be meteoric; and to precious stones in general the ancient and the mediaeval world attributed magic powers. Wolfram is very vague as to the provenance of the stone that is the Grail, but he christianises it to the extent of making it have its powers renewed each Good Friday by a dove that descends from heaven, bearing a sacramental wafer in its beak: this it lays on the stone, which thereafter yields the brotherhood everything it desires in the way of food and drink "in paradisiac profusion". Thus it is no longer the merely talismanic qualities of the stone itself but the sacred Host deposited on it that endows it with its supernatural powers.

It is tolerably clear that neither Crestien nor Wolfram was working upon any clear-cut conception of the nature and origin of the Grail. The complete christianisation of it had gradually come about as the result of the infiltration into the basic Perceval-Grail story of another legend, that of the transmission, through Joseph of Arimathea, of the sacred Blood in a dish or cup: one form of the story even presents us with two holy relics — "li saintisme graals", meaning the dish with the Blood, and "li saintisme vaissaus", the dish from which Christ and His disciples ate at the Last Supper. What is certain is that for Wolfram a "graal" is not a dish or a cup. He probably took over the word, without understanding it, from the French version he had before him; as a German scholar has put it, he imagined "graal" to be a proper name, and so did not translate it into German but changed Crestien's "a graal" into "The Grail".

Of the bleeding lance neither Crestien nor Wolfram gives us any explanation; but certainly for neither of them was it the legendary spear of "Longinus". Manifestly it had great significance in Crestien's eyes, but he died before reaching the point in his poem at which, presumably, he would have told us more about it, as Wolfram has done at a later stage of *his* story, when he makes the bleeding lance of the scene in the hall of the Grail the same poisoned weapon that had dealt Anfortas his wound. (In the old Celtic legends, from which a good deal of the Perceval-Grail story sprang, a bleeding lance was the traditional symbol of the desire of the Celts for revenge upon the Saxon invaders who had driven them from their homes. Crestien seems to have been aware of this aspect of it).

11

The story of Perceval and the quest for the Grail has come down to us in various forms in poetry and prose: it seems to have excited the liveliest interest in Western Europe and Britain for a half-century or so between 1170 and 1220, and then to have faded out as suddenly and inexplicably as it had come in. As we have it now it must represent the gradual interfusion and proliferation of several legends. Crestien and Wolfram, it seems evident, worked upon a common source or sources, though either they inserted features of their own in it or the two versions that lay before them already differed from each other in some respects. Crestien's unfinished poem was continued by three writers, Wauchier (or Gautier) de Denain, Manessier, and Gerbert de Montreuil. Each of these seems to have drawn upon sources anterior to Crestien and in some ways different from his. Wauchier's romance perhaps presents us with the story in its earliest form. In his version the hero of the Quest for the Grail is Gawain, and the Grail is not a "holy" but merely a "rich" object which in some mysterious fashion provides food. Wauchier knows also of a bleeding lance which is that of Longinus. Gawain asks the King of the castle what the lance is, and by so doing makes the rivers flow and brings verdure back to the wasted land again. But he does not enquire also about the Grail; by his failing to do so the land is not wholly restored to life, and so the people of it mingle curses with their blessings of him.

The legend, or complex of legends, seems to have been in a

state of constant inner flux and of amalgamation with others. The widespread primitive folk-tale of a brave, simple boy coming slowly to strength and wisdom becomes gradually inwrought with the conception of a Grail, which mysterious object is now one thing, now another, until finally it and the lance become ecclesiasticised as the Dish (or Cup) and the spear of Longinus. Perceval gradually supplants Gawain in the legends as the quester for the Grail and is in turn supplanted by Lancelot, who is later replaced by Galahad: it is in this last form that the story comes to us in Malory's *Morte d'Arthur* (first printed in 1485) and in Tennyson's *Idylls of the King*.

But so far as the brave and simple hero and his quest of the Grail is concerned the best telling of the tale, and, indeed, the finest flower of northern mediaeval literature, is undoubtedly Wolfram's *Parzival*. For Wolfram's genius has fused the romantic and the ethical into one in a way beyond the powers of any of his contemporaries. He alone sees Parzival steadily and whole as a character developing in humanity under the stress of bitter circumstance — the "brave man becoming slowly wise". Here alone in all the Perceval-Grail stories of the Middle Ages was something upon which a modern dramatist and musician could build, though necessarily with a good deal of sifting and modification of the material. Here and there a modern specialist in mediaeval literature has seen fit to censure Wagner for not having kept more closely to Wolfram; but in doing so they lose sight of the difference between epic and drama and between mediaeval and modern ethical concepts. Another core than that of the legend has of necessity to be found for a Parsifal drama or opera of today; had Wagner docilely followed Wolfram he would have had to make the dénouement turn upon the restoration of the King to health and the saving of the wasted land by Parsifal's simple asking of a question, which would have been too naïve a climax for the modern mind.[1] Wagner, for his purposes, had to lift the whole action

---

[1] Mr. H. O. Taylor, in his searching study of the mediaeval mind, has pointed out that Wolfram was quite logical, from the standpoint of his epoch, in his implied ethical sequence: "failure to ask the question was a symbol of [Parsifal's] lack of wisdom . . . So the sequence becomes ethical: from error, calamity; from calamity, grief; and from grief, wisdom". (*The Mediaeval Mind*, I, 601, 602).

out of the sphere of folk-story into that of ethics; the simple old tale of a misfortune befalling the rash Anfortas had to be made a symbol of sin in general and its atonement by one made wise and understanding by pity not merely for an individual but for all men.

Wagner's letters of 1859 — the period of his first struggle with the huge and confused material of the legends — show him to have had rather a poor opinion of Wolfram and of the mediaeval poets in general, — which merely means that they saw matters in terms of their own age instead of in those of ours. Wagner could neither do anything himself with the "question" motive nor understand what it signified in the legends. "That business of the 'question'", he wrote to Frau Wesendonk, "is quite absurd and meaningless. Here, therefore, I should just have to invent everything for myself." His problem was *what* to invent that would take the vital place of the "question" motive in Wolfram. It was not until nearly twenty years later that he found the solution of his problem. From Cosima's diary we learn that on the 25th January 1877 he said to her, "I am starting on [the poem of] *Parsifal,* and I shall not lay it aside until it is finished." Three days later he could tell her that he had got over what had been his greatest difficulty: the nodal point of his drama would be not the asking of the question but the recovery of the Spear.

12

It was necessary, too, for Wagner to fuse Wolfram's account of the Grail with the later developments that associated it with the Chalice and the Sacred Blood; Wolfram's Grail — a talismanic stone with magic-working properties — would have stirred no emotion in the modern spectator, besides being too weak to bear the great ethical superstructure Wagner had it in his mind to raise. In general, Wagner's solution of the problems of the handling of the varied material presented to him by the mediaeval legends was to tighten it up everywhere and provide it with one or two central episodes from which the action and its ethical motives could consistently develop. It was a stroke of genius on his part to bring the world of Monsalvat and that of Klingsor into both connection and apposition, to make the magician of evil wound the custodian of the Grail with the very weapon that had pierced the Redeemer's side on the Cross, thus inflicting on Amfortas an agony for which there could never be any healing save by virtue of the sacred Spear itself. By adopting this development Wagner was able to make the essence of Parsifal's long and weary trial not so much the quest for the Grail as that for the Spear; it was the loss of this, through Amfortas's sin against the purity of the Grail, that had brought disaster on the brotherhood, and only the recovery of it, and the second finding of the hall of the Grail, could bring healing to the King and restore to Monsalvat its lost spiritual power.

He had further to compress the meandering action at several points, to eliminate many superfluous characters, to amalgamate others, and to make Kundry not only a more definite personality but a more significant one. As usual, he concentrated on essentials. The numberless picturesque details in which Wolfram, writing an epic, could safely indulge had to be eliminated — for instance, the poet's expansive and richly wrought picture of the procedure in the hall of the Grail had to be condensed into a single impressive ritual act. Wolfram's long preliminary story of Parsifal's origin, of the death of his father Gahmuret and his mother Herzeloyde, and of his upbringing in ignorance of the world, had to be simultaneously communicated to the spectator and made part of the psychology of the drama by means of Kundry's narrative in the second act.

Of the numerous figures that crowd upon each other in Wolfram's vast tapestry Wagner needed, for his purpose, only four for the main action — Parsifal, Amfortas, Kundry, Klingsor, — with a fifth, Gurnemanz, in the second line, to bring the others into connection with each other at vital points of the drama and to make clear sundry things in this that could not be shown on the stage. Gurnemanz himself is an amalgam of Wolfram's Gornemans and his Trevrizent. Klingsor is not simply the traditional magician of mediaeval romance but the incarnation of evil, the force in implacable warfare with the ethical world symbolised by the Grail. Kundry becomes infinitely more than the Loathly Damsel of the mediaeval legends. Her complex nature is difficult to analyse in words — it is defined for us mostly in her music; but we can see

how enormously Wagner increased the significance of the character by making her at once the instrument of Klingsor, the servant
of the Grail, and a spirit in revolt against the evil which Klingsor
compels her to work at times.

13

The basic Gawain-Perceval legends seem to have been Celtic
in origin; but from the moment when the Grail came to be associated with the Last Supper the stories tended to become overlaid
with an ecclesiastical symbolism which at first formed no part of
them. As for the Grail element itself, the truth of the matter seems
to be with the modern scholars who trace it back to some such ancient fertility rite — the primitive meaning of which, however,
had by Wolfram's time been forgotten — as is set forth for us in
the pages of Frazer's *Golden Bough* and similar works. Primitive
man, like backward tribes today, practised at certain times of the
year a ritual designed to encourage the powers of nature to make
the earth and rivers and seas fertile for his needs. In the course of
time the ritual would take on a dramatic form, the winter decline
of earth and the spring reawakening being symbolised in the per-
sons of gods or heroes such as Attis, Adonis, Tammuz or Mithra,
who, like the vegetation, died and after an interval came to life
again. The Mithraic cult in particular, which was the favourite
one of the far-travelled Roman legionaries, had an extensive
vogue in Western Europe and the islands during the early centuries when Christianity was establishing itself; and a good case
has been made out for seeing in the sick king who is afterwards
healed, and in the aversion of evil from the land by virtue of that
healing, a last vague relic of one of the pagan fertility cults. This
view would help to account, again, for the title of "the Fisher
King" or "the Rich Fisherman", borne in the Grail legends by the
king who is mortally sick from a wound in the groin: for the fish
was one of the most widely-spread symbols of fertility in the ancient world. But the whole subject, on not only the literary side
but that of comparative religion, is packed with problems which
will perhaps never be mastered, extensive as the literature dealing
with them already is. And with all this we have on the present occasion nothing to do: all that concerns us is the nature of the poetic material from which Wagner derived his subject, and the

processes within him that gradually developed it into the form it assumes in *Parsifal*.[1]

14

In July 1845 Wagner, having completed the music of *Tannhäuser*, took a holiday and "cure" in Bohemia, taking with him for his reading, as he tells us in *My Life*, "the poems of Wolfram von Eschenbach in the [modern German] versions of Simrock and San-Marte,[2] as well as the anonymous epic of *Lohengrin* with the long introduction by Görres. With the book under my arm I hid myself in the neighbouring woods, and, seated by a brook, feasted myself on Titurel and Parzival in Wolfram's strange yet intimately appealing poem." His imagination was kindled, and he felt a burning desire to cast the rich but diffuse poetic matter into musical-dramatic form. But he had been warned by his doctor against over-excitement during his cure in Marienbad, and so, though with great difficulty, he damped down his passion for the Parzival subject and concentrated on the story of Lohengrin, which had been occupying his thoughts more or less since the Paris days of 1841–2. After that, as a kind of sanitary reaction against the excitement of working out the scheme of his *Lohengrin*, he sketched a text on the subject of Hans Sachs and the Mastersingers of Nuremberg.

He would have been surprised had he been told at that time that a *Parsifal* would be the last of his works for the stage, that it would not be until thirty-seven years after that ardent first reading of Wolfram in the woods at Marienbad that the opera would see the light of day, and that it would show the world a Richard Wagner more remote in every way from the one who had just completed *Tannhäuser* than the Beethoven of the last quartets is from the Beethoven of the Second Symphony. The Parzival sub-

---

[1] About 1930 a German orientalist, Dr. Fridrich von Suhtscheck, made out a strong case for a Persian origin and Persian setting of the Parsifal legend. He contended that "Grail" came from two Persian roots, *gohar* or *ghr*, meaning pearl, and *al*, meaning brilliant colour, the Grail, therefore, signifying the pearl of pearls. Kyot he identified with Giut, an Armenian who rendered a Parsifal story into French about the middle of the twelfth century. His argument is profoundly interesting, but a full statement of it would take us too far afield.

[2] San-Marte was the pseudonym of one Albert Schutz.

ject had to go through a long period of silent gestation within him before he could feel that he was really ripe for it. It was not merely that as dramatic craftsman he did not quite see as yet how to condense Wolfram's long epic into the three-hours' traffic of the operatic stage; and his artistic instinct must have warned him to wait until he was much more developed as poet and musician and man before trying to find the right expression for the strange new world of which the old poet had given him a glimpse. But though we hear nothing more from him about Parzival for several years it is evident that the subject was often in his thoughts, working out its own destiny in the silent and slow but sure way that was habitual with him.

We next hear of it towards the end of 1854, in what seems to us today, however, the strangest connection with the story of Tristan and Isolde. He drew up a broad plan for an opera in three acts on the latter subject; and in the third act, he says, "I introduced an episode which I did not work out later — Parzifal, in his quest for the Grail, coming to the sick-bed of Tristan: for Tristan, ill from his wound and unable to die, had become identified in my mind with Amfortas in the Grail legend." [1] Hans von Wolzogen, drawing upon his recollection of conversations with Wagner, gave us further information on this point in 1886. "Parzival, questing for the Grail, was to come in the course of his pilgrimage to Kareol, and there find Tristan lying on his death-bed, love-racked and despairing. Thus the longing one was brought face to face with the renouncing one, the self-curser with the man atoning for his own guilt, the one suffering unto death from love with the one bringing redemption through pity. Here death, there new life. And it was intended that a melody associated with the wandering Parzival should sound in the ears of the mortally wounded Tristan, as it

[1] It has to be remembered that at some time or other the Perceval saga and that of Tristan had tended to coalesce, as was the way with many of these mediaeval stories. "In the final stage of the evolution of the Arthurian cycle", says Miss Jessie L. Weston, "when its tentacles, stretching far and wide, had laid hold of the originally quite independent *Tristan* theme and drawn it within the meshes of the Arthurian net, the Galahad Quest became enlarged in order to permit of the participation not only of Tristan himself but also of other knights who had become more or less closely connected with him." Wagner must have been aware of this coalescence, but his sense of fitness soon made him turn away from it.

were the mysteriously faint receding answer to his life-destroying question about the 'Why?' of life. Out of this melody, it may be said, grew the stage-festival-drama [*Parsifal*]." The melody referred to is apparently the one written out by Wagner for Mathilde Wesendonk about April 1858; it runs thus:

("Where shall I find thee, holy Grail, for which my yearning heart is searching?").

15

A note-book of 1854–5 that has survived contains Wagner's sketch for the episode in question as originally planned for *Tristan and Isolde*. It runs thus: "Act III. Tristan on his sick-bed in the garden of the castle. At the side of the stage a battlement. Awaking from sleep he calls to his squire, whom he believes to be on the battlement, though he cannot see him. The squire is not there, but in response to Tristan's call he comes at last. Reproaches. Excuses — a pilgrim has arrived and has been entertained. Once and now. Tristan's impatience. The squire can still see nothing [of the expected ship bringing Isolde]. Tristan's reflections. Doubts. A melody from the distance, dying away. What can it be? The squire tells him about the pilgrim — Parzival. Profound impression. Love and torment. My mother died in giving me birth; now I live, dying because I was born. Why this? Parzival's refrain — repeated by the shepherd. The whole world nothing but unsatisfied longing. What can ever allay it? Parzival's refrain again."

As the reader knows, this plan for introducing the questing Parzival into the last act of *Tristan* was never carried out: Wagner's dramatic sense must soon have convinced him that it would constitute an unmotived, alien element there. And the melody he had put into the mouth of Parzival is obviously not in the vein of the *Parsifal* we now know; Wagner's muse had to pass through a long period of deepening and purification before it was ripe for taking imaginative control of the strange world of Parzival and the Grail.[1]

We next find his thoughts turning in the direction of Wolfram again in the April of 1857. According to his story in *My Life*[2] he awoke in the "Asyl" — the little house on the Wesendonk estate at Zürich that had been placed at his disposal — on a marvellously beautiful Good Friday morning; the garden was freshly green, the birds were singing, and over the whole world brooded a divine peace. He was suddenly reminded, he says, of Wolfram's poem — "with which I had never occupied myself since that stay of mine in Marienbad when I had conceived the *Mastersingers* and *Lohengrin*." [This would seem at first sight to conflict with the fact that in 1854–5 he had planned an entry of Parzival in the third act of *Tristan*. But there is no real contradiction. He had perhaps been concerned with Parzival at that time only as a possible figure in an episode of the *Tristan* drama]. "Now its ideal contents took irresistible possession of me, and out of my thoughts about Good Friday I swiftly conceived an entire drama in three acts, of which I put a hasty sketch on paper." His memory was a little at fault as regards the date, for Good Friday in 1857 fell on the 10th April, and Wagner did not take up his residence in the Asyl until the 29th: no doubt he had visited the garden on the 10th, felt the emotions he describes and been reminded of the Good Friday

---

[1] We do not know when the melody quoted above was written. One would be inclined a priori to date it from long before 1854, perhaps even from the days of the first impact of the Parzival subject on him in the summer of 1845. *The Rhinegold* and *The Valkyrie* had been written between November 1853 and the end of 1854, while 1856 and 1857 saw the completion of the first two acts of *Siegfried* and the first act of *Tristan*. Even by 1854 he had developed so enormously as a musician that it is difficult to believe that for this Parzival theme he had reverted to the *Tannhäuser-Lohengrin* musical idiom of six to ten years earlier.

[2] This section of the autobiography was dictated about 1870.

episode in Wolfram's poem, and then, in later years, assumed the date of this experience to have been Good Friday.

If that sketch of 1857 survives it has not yet been given to the world, so we can only speculate as to its nature. It goes without saying that there must already have been a good deal of conscious or subconscious sifting of the Wolfram material on Wagner's part, for a stage drama on purely Wolframian lines was from the beginning an impossibility. We may be sure also that the conception of the Grail as the Chalice containing the Redeemer's blood was already essential to his drama; for although, as we have seen, there is not the smallest suggestion of either Cup or Sacred Blood in Wolfram's poem, the sources consulted by Wagner in 1845 had familiarised him with other mediaeval handlings of the Grail story in which the legend of Joseph of Arimathea and the Holy Blood plays a vital part.[1] The germ-cell from which Wagner's plan for a three-act drama evolved in 1857 must have been the Good Friday scene, which, indeed, is the emotional focal point of the present *Parsifal*, as Senta's Ballad is that of *The Flying Dutchman*. But apart from a few more or less plausible conjectures of this kind we can throw no light at present on the draft of that year.

16

In the late 1850's Wagner's whole thinking about life and the cosmos took a mystical-metaphysical turn, the result partly of his study of Schopenhauer, partly of his contact with Buddhistic literature, partly of his own tortured broodings upon the nature of the world and the destiny of man and beast, partly of the flood of new emotion set coursing in him by the sorrowful Tristan subject. The centre of his ethic now was pity for everything doomed to carry the burden of existence; and it was from this centre outwards that he had already come to survey the Parzival subject afresh.

The biographical record now shifts to the autumn of 1858, when Wagner began for Frau Wesendonk's benefit that "Venice Diary"

---

[1] We first meet with it in a prose narrative, *Joseph of Arimathea,* by one Robert de Baron, which tells of the adventures and the magic properties of the Dish from which Jesus and His disciples ate at the Last Supper, and which later received the Blood that welled from His wounds on the Cross.

that is of the first importance for our understanding of him at that time. "Nothing touches me seriously", he wrote, "save in so far as it awakes in me fellow-feeling, that is, fellow-suffering. This compassion I recognise as the strongest feature of my moral being, and presumably it is also the fountain-head of my art." Even more with animals than with man, he says, does he feel kinship through suffering, for man by his philosophy can raise himself to a resignation that transcends his pain, whereas the mute unreasoning animal can only suffer without comprehending why. "And so if there is any purpose in all this suffering it can only be the awakening of pity in man, who thus takes up the animal's failed existence into himself, and, by perceiving the error of all existence, becomes the redeemer of the world. This interpretation will become clearer to you some day from the third act of *Parzival*, which takes place on Good Friday morning." Manifestly, then, the Parzival drama had already defined itself within him as the drama of compassion.

17

The dates of composition of *Parsifal* are as follows.

Poem. Act I finished 29 March 1877.
Act II finished 13 April 1877.
Act III finished 19 April 1877.

Music. Begun August 1877.
Prelude Sketch finished 26 September 1877.
Act I Composition Sketch finished 31 January 1878.
Act II Composition Sketch finished 13 October 1878.
Act III Composition Sketch finished 26 April 1879.

Orchestral Score.
Act I Begun 23 August 1879 but soon abandoned; resumed 23 November 1880. Finished 25 April 1881.
Act II Begun 6 June 1881. Finished 19 October 1881.
Act III Begun 5 November 1881. Finished 13 January 1882.

The final page of the manuscript of the orchestral score, however, is dated 25 December 1881. The explanation of the discrepancy is that Wagner had promised Cosima that the work should be complete for presentation to her on Christmas Day, which was also her birthday. Finding himself unable to keep this promise to the letter he scored the final page on the 25th December, inserted the date at the end, and filled in the few pages thus left blank between then and the 13th January 1882.

The work was produced for the first time at the Bayreuth Festival of 1882. Sixteen performances of it were given, running from the 22nd July to the 29th August. Partly to avoid undue strain on the singers, partly to insure against illness or the caprices of the artistic temperament, Wagner employed a double cast. That for the opening performance consisted of (1) Winkelmann (Parsifal), (2) Scaria (Gurnemanz), (3) Hill (Klingsor), (4) Reichmann (Amfortas), (5) Amelia Materna (Kundry). The alternative cast was (1) Gudehus and Jäger, (2) Siehr, (3) Fuchs, (5) Marianne Brandt and Therese Malten. Reichmann sang Amfortas in all sixteen performances. Hermann Levi conducted.

On the afternoon of the 12th November 1880 Wagner, who was in Munich at the time, conducted two performances of the *Parsifal* prelude by the orchestra of the Court Theatre for the private hearing of King Ludwig. To assist the King's comprehension he gave him the following description of it:

"Love — Faith — Hope?

First theme: *Love.*

'Take ye my body, take my blood, in token of our love!' (repeated by angel voices gradually dying away). 'Take ye my blood, take my body, that you may hold me in your remembrance!'

(Again repeated and dying away).

Second theme: *Faith.*

Promise of redemption through Faith. Firmly and stoutly Faith declares itself, exalted, unshakeable even in suffering. — The promise is repeated and answered by Faith from the remote heights — hovering downwards, as it were on the pinions of the white dove — taking more and more complete possession of the breast, the heart of man, filling all nature with the mightiest force, then looking aloft again to heaven's vault in sweet tranquillity. —

But once more, from out the awe of solitude, there throbs the lament of loving pity: fear, dismay, the holy sweat of Olivet, the divine death-throes of Golgotha, — the body pales, the blood wells forth and glows with heavenly blessing in the Chalice, pouring out the grace of redemption on all that lives and suffers. We are made ready for Amfortas, the sinning keeper of the holy relic, who, racked with repentance, quails before the divine chastisement which the sight of the glowing Grail brings with it; will the gnawing anguish of his soul find redemption? — Once more we hear the promise; and — we *hope!*"

18

This, however, is a doctrinal elucidation of the prelude rather than a musical analysis of it. Anything of the latter kind would have been useless to the King, whereas he had always been intensely interested in the emotional and philosophical motives of the poem, which Wagner now drew into one focus for him.

The long prelude [1] begins with an extended theme that is an entity in itself:

No. 1

yet embodies three leading motives that can be used in the course of the work either in conjunction or separately: that marked B is always associated with suffering, particularly that of Amfortas, while C pertains more especially to the Spear. As so often happens in connection with Wagner, it is difficult to attach to our No. 1 a single label that will characterise it in every one of its appearances. It is generally referred to by the commentators as the Love Feast motive, because it forms the basis of the song that accompanies the serving of the Bread and Wine in the Hall of the

[1] As already stated, it was completed by the 26th September 1877, on which date Wagner played it to Cosima; therefore not only some of the central musical motives of the opera but the psychological connotations and interactions of them must have been fully formed in his mind some time before he began regular work at the opera itself.

Grail. It must always be borne in mind, however, that during the opera each of the three limbs of No. 1 has a life and a function of its own, calling, for purposes of analysis, for an individual title.

The seemingly indeterminate rhythm of the unaccompanied melody as a whole, arising from its syncopations, caused much headshaking among some of the musical critics who heard it for the first time in 1882; they were unable to read a shape into a phrase in which the stresses occurred so irregularly, with such small concern for the sacred laws of four-four. But Wagner knew quite well what he was about: the seeming vagueness of the rhythm and the enunciation of the melody without supporting and key-defining chords gives us a feeling of being plunged straight into a world remote from that of everyday reality.

At the end of our quotation No. 1 the orchestra (flutes, clarinets, etc.) builds up in arpeggios a succession of chords that conclusively establish the key as that of A flat major. Wagner is in no hurry: he has a great deal of mystical emotion to evoke from No. 1 before he relinquishes it for his next main theme, the entry of which he deliberately delays. First of all he repeats the motive with arpeggio harmonies an octave higher in the violins, trumpet and oboe, the soft yet urgent trumpet tone giving it a peculiar poignancy; and once more the close is in A flat. Then he shifts the plane of No. 1 to the key of C minor, but follows the same deliberate procedure as before — (a) a quiet unaccompanied statement of the melody in strings and wood wind, followed by (b) a slow building up of the harmony of C minor, (c) a repetition of the theme an octave higher in violins, oboe and trumpet, which involves taking the trumpet up to the extreme height of its compass:

No.2

and so intensifies the sense of poignancy, (d) a long dwelling on the C minor harmony that has now been reached.

The brass then give out a new motive, that of the Grail, in compact soft harmonies:

No. 3

It is repeated immediately an octave higher, pianissimo, in the wood wind. There are still innocents abroad who gleefully inform the world that they have discovered this theme in Mendelssohn's Reformation Symphony, so that this is one more instance of Wagner's shameless "stealing" from other composers. The fact is that the theme is the ancient "Dresden Amen", which Mendelssohn had used in 1830, and Wagner used half-a-century later, because it had for them and for thousands of their hearers a special appropriateness to the solemn matter in hand. Wagner must have heard the "Amen" times without number during his kapellmeistership in Dresden.

So far the markings in general have been piano and pianissimo. Now, for the first time, the orchestra rises to a forte as the horns and trumpets give out the resolute motive of Faith, with the trombones coming in later to clinch the cadential harmonies:

No. 4

The *ff* dies down again to *pp*. A soft repetition of the Grail motive steals in in the strings, followed by a quiet repeat of the Faith theme in a higher register but gradually descending into the depths again. Then comes a dramatic high light. No. 4 is given out once more fortissimo,[1] but this time Wagner guards against any possible impression of monotony by a majestic extension and rhythmical alteration of the theme:

No.5

which afterwards reverts to its original steady 6/4 and dies away into silence.

This concludes the first section of the prelude, which so far has been mainly devoted to establishing the general atmosphere associated with the Grail and stressing the motive of Faith. Now Amfortas and his sufferings become the centre of interest. No. 1 is taken up again and developed, with particular insistence on the agonised No. 1 B and a poignant harmonisation at one point of the motive of the Spear (No. 1 C):

No.6

This is repeated three times at successively higher pitches; then it merges into a figure which is much used later in the opera in connection with the agony of Amfortas:

[1] When he was writing the prelude Wagner told Cosima that "the modulation into D major" in this section "symbolised for him the spreading of the tender revelation throughout the whole world."

(See, for instance, No. 26 below). Out of the opening notes of this phrase Wagner distils for a moment the last drops of human anguish:

after which the music slowly soars aloft and poises itself for a while on a prolonged indecisive harmony as the curtain rises.

19

Nietzsche's ill-bred vituperation of *Parsifal* in public in *Der Fall Wagner* will probably be familiar to the reader. Less well known is a passage in one of his private letters to a musical friend in which he confesses to have been shaken to his depths by the prelude. He had not been present at the production of the opera in Bayreuth in 1882; but he heard the prelude at a concert in Monte-Carlo in January 1887, and wrote thus concerning it to a musical friend: "Putting aside all irrelevant questions (to what end such music *can* or *should* serve?), and speaking from a purely aesthetic point of view, has Wagner ever written anything *better?* The supreme psychological perception and precision as regards what had to be said, expressed, *communicated* here, the extreme of concision and directness of form, every nuance of feeling conveyed epigrammatically; a clarity of musical description that reminds us of a shield of consummate workmanship; and finally an extraordinary sublimity of feeling, something experienced in the very depths of music, that does Wagner the highest honour; a synthesis of conditions which to many people — even 'higher' minds — will seem incompatible, of strict coherence, of 'loftiness' in the most startling sense of the word, of a cognisance and a penetration of vision that cuts through the soul as if with a knife, of sympathy with what is seen and shown forth. We get something comparable to it in Dante, but nowhere else. Has any painter ever depicted so sorrowful a look of love as Wagner has done in the final accents of his prelude?"

And to his sister he wrote a little later: "I cannot think of [the prelude] without feeling violently shaken, so elevated was I by it, so deeply moved." Then follows a passage which those would do well to ponder who rail at *Parsifal*, as Nietzsche did in *Der Fall Wagner*, because it is a "Christian" work, Wagner here, according to Nietzsche — the Wagner who had been a freethinker — having "fallen sobbing at the foot of the Cross". "It is as if someone were speaking to me again after many years", says the philosopher, "about the problems that disturb me — naturally not supplying the answer *I* would give, but the Christian answer, which, after all, has been the answer of stronger souls than the last two centuries of our era have produced. When listening to this music one lays Protestantism aside as a misunderstanding — moreover, I will not deny it, *other really good* music, which I have at other times heard and loved, seems, as against this, a misunderstanding."

The artist in Nietzsche was wiser than the philosopher. The beauty and profundity of the *Parsifal* prelude made him conscious, at any rate for the time being, that in a work of art it is only the art that matters, not the body of knowledge or system of thought with which it happens to be conjoined. The fact that we do not believe in ghosts does not make us shut our ears to *Hamlet;* the fact that the gods of the Greeks are not ours does not make us abuse the Greek dramatists for falling at the feet of Zeus, as we might put it after Nietzsche's fashion. A work of art like *Parsifal* is to be accepted in virtue of the appeal it makes to the artist in us, whether we are Christian or Jew or freethinker. This or that theological or philosophical "answer to the problems that disturb us" — to hark back to Nietzsche's words — is valid for one of us and invalid for his neighbour, but art has no concern with these things; and to fulminate against *Parsifal* for the Christianity of its subject is, even to the freethinker who happens to be also an artist, as absurd as it would be to turn our backs on the *Divina Commedia* because we have no belief in the mediaeval theological system that was accepted as the final truth by Dante. Art of itself has nothing to do with "truths" of the material world that are true for one man, one sect, but false for another. Nietzsche's classical studies should have taught him that more than one ancient critic had pointed out that the "truth" of art and the "truth" of life are entirely different things. Poetic truth, said Aristotle, "should not be confused wih truth historical, logical or moral"; and Philodemus of Gadara, writing in Rome in the first century B.C., laid it down that in poetry anything and everything can be "true", "including themes fabulous and even false, monsters or legendary spirits, provided they are artistically represented, in concrete and vivid fashion."

20

The long-drawn-out chord of the seventh that marked the end of the prelude is still poised, unresolved, in the upper air when the curtain rises, showing a forest, solemn and shady but not gloomy, in the domain of the Grail. On the left a road ascends to the castle: at the back, at a lower level, is a lake. In a glade in the foreground Gurnemanz, an elderly but vigorous man, and two young squires are sleeping under a tree. Day is breaking, and from the left, behind the scenes, comes, as if from the castle, the morning reveille of the trombones (the opening notes of No. 1). At Gurnemanz's call the squires leap to their feet; then the three sink to their knees and, to the soft accompaniment (muted strings) of No. 4 and No. 3, silently offer up the morning prayer.

This done, the old man bids the others look to the bath, for it is the hour when the sick King is wont to bathe in the lake, and his litter is even now approaching. A motive symbolising the sickness and weariness of Amfortas is first heard in the strings at this point:

No. 9

It will appear later in a variety of forms.

Two knights from the castle enter. How fares the King today? Gurnemanz eagerly asks them. Has the wild herb that Gawain [1]

---

[1] This Gawain must not be associated with the famous Gawain who, in some of the legends, shares the quest of the Grail with Parsifal. In the opera "Gawain" is merely the name of one of the knights of the brotherhood of

lately found brought him any relief? No, they reply; the old irremediable pain racks him more grievously than ever. The faithful, anxious Gurnemanz sinks his head sadly: fools are they all, he says, for ordinary human solace seeking, when one thing only, one man only, can bring the King relief: and in the orchestra we hear a first suggestion of the enigmatic motive of the Pure Fool — the core of the mystery of redemption through simple pity. For greater convenience of reference it is quoted here in the fuller form it assumes later in the act:

No.10

"Who then is the one? Name him for us!" says the second knight; but Gurnemanz, who alone among them knows the secret of how the King had received his wound, fends him off with an evasive "See ye to the bath!"

No sooner has he said this than the orchestra breaks into a succession of hurrying figures, announcing the approach of "the wild woman", as the squires call her, sweeping across the moss on her "devil's mare". The motive of her frenzied ride runs thus:

No.11

Monsalvat; he is not included among the *dramatis personae*, nor is he even mentioned by name after the present scene.

Notice the stabbing accentuation of some of the notes, with its suggestion of breathless panting — a vital feature of the theme that is rarely brought out properly in performance.

The excited comment of the squires as they watch the approaching figure is cut short by a tearing dissonance in the orchestra as Kundry makes her entrance on the stage:

No. 12

"She rushes in hurriedly, almost reeling", say the stage directions. "Her garment is wild and looped up high; she wears a girdle of snakeskins the long ends of which hang down: her hair is black and falls in loose locks: her complexion is a deep reddish-brown: her eyes are black and piercing, sometimes flashing wildly, but more often fixed in a stare like that of the dead." Wagner regarded Kundry as the greatest of his female creations; she is certainly the most original and the most enigmatic, and the part is the most difficult of all the Wagnerian characters to play.

She stumbles forward to Gurnemanz and thrusts a small crystal vial into his hand, muttering "Here! Take thou! It is a balsam brought from further hence than thy thought can fly. Should this fail, Arabia holds no other simple for his relief. Ask no further! I am weary!" and she throws herself exhausted on the ground.

21

Gurnemanz turns his attention from her as a train of knights and squires comes upon the stage — to the accompaniment of the weary, dragging No. 9 — bearing the litter in which the King reclines. Gurnemanz's heart goes out to him in a surge of love and pity. "Alas!" he cries,

> *What grief beyond enduring!*
> *The proudest flower of manhood faded,*
> *the master of the conquering race*
> *to his own sickness bound a slave!*

The "conquering race" is of course the Grail brotherhood of knights, leagued to do battle against the heathen; and as Gurnemanz speaks the words the orchestra gives out a theme which will be recognised as a variant of that of Faith (No. 4):

No. 13

At A, it will be observed, to the words "to his own sickness bound a slave", the music melts into the melancholy motive of Amfortas's Suffering that is embedded in the opening theme of the prelude (No. 1 B).

The King, a little refreshed by the anticipation of his bath in the lake, would rest awhile. His night of pain, he says to the accompaniment of No. 9, is over: "earth's light is sweet again": and the orchestra, with the pastoral oboe as soloist, paints a gracious little vignette of the beauty and solace of uncorrupted nature:

No. 14

The phrase will appear again, in essentials, in the ecstatic meadow music of the Good Friday scene in the third act. (See No. 51).

Amfortas calls wearily for Gawain, but is informed that the knight, his search for a healing herb having failed, has set out in quest of another. "Unbidden!" says Amfortas: "the Grail will make him atone for having thus flouted its command" — that is to say, for having looked for the King's healing to any other than the mysterious one chosen by itself: woe to Gawain if he should happen to fall into Klingsor's toils! As for himself, says Amfortas, he can but wait for the promised one, the blameless fool: would that as Death he could greet him! Gurnemanz implores him to essay the balsam brought by "the woman wild" from Araby. The King turns with a gentle word of thanks to the rough repulsive figure crouching on the ground; but Kundry, to a flash of the feverish No. 12 in the orchestra, disclaims the thanks and bids him pass on to the bath. Amfortas gives the signal: the squires raise the litter, and, to the quiet strains of No. 9 and No. 14, the procession moves slowly into the deep background, followed by the grieving eyes of the faithful old Gurnemanz.

22

When the King has disappeared the squires [1] turn savagely on the prostrate Kundry, "lying there like a wounded beast". "Are not even the wild beasts holy in the Grail's domain?" she asks. Doubtless, they reply; but does that tolerance apply to her? Will not "the witch's magic balm" bring bane to the King? Gurnemanz gently intervenes. What harm has she ever done to them? he asks: is it not she who carries messages to the knights in distant lands fighting against the heathen?

> She needs you not — afar she bides:
>   nought common has she with you;
> yet need ye her help when danger threats,
> afire with zeal she flies through the air,
> and never word of thanks will ask.
>   Meseemeth, is this harmful,
>   for nought but your weal it worketh.

[1] Some of the squires of the King's retinue have remained behind after the departure of the litter.

"She hates us though", the squires insist: "her wild eyes flash rancour on us: she is a heathen, a sorceress." "Yea, under a curse she haply lies", Gurnemanz answers quietly:

> *Here lives she now —*
> *perchance her soul*
> *for sins of old is penance paying,*
> *for which in vain she sought forgiveness.*
> *Seeketh she now to make atonement*
> *among our brotherhood by lowly service*
> *good doth she do, as ye all know;*
> *serving us — herself she aids.*

When Gurnemanz speaks of her perchance paying penance for some sin of old the orchestra, with a soft suggestion of No. 1 A in the bass clarinet, followed by No. 12, gives us a hint that that sin was connected with the brotherhood of the Grail.

"It is some unforgiven guilt of hers, then", ask the squires, "that brings on us this bitter dole?" Step by step Gurnemanz tells them what he knows of the mystery surrounding her. He himself has known her long, but Titurel, the father of Amfortas, longer: for he had found her, one day when the castle was building, asleep in a thicket, frozen, lifeless; and the orchestra, projecting in dark wood wind colours the motive of Klingsor's magic:

tells us what even Gurnemanz himself does not know — that Kundry is bound to the service of the sorcerer Klingsor. It had been benumbed in a thicket that Gurnemanz himself had found her, he tells the squires, on the day when ill-hap fell on the brotherhood through "that evil one beyond the mountains". "Where wert thou, wild one", he turns and asks her, "the day when our King lost the Spear? Why was then thy help withheld?" "I ne'er give help", she mutters; but once more the orchestra, by a reiteration of No. 15, tells us something which the old man himself has never fathomed.

If she be so faithful to them all, and so strong and bold, says a third squire, then let her be sent to find the lost Spear. Alas, Gurnemanz replies, that is another matter; the way to the Spear no one knows. And he breaks into a poignant lament as he recalls that drear day when he saw the sacred weapon held aloft in the unhallowed hand of Klingsor. With the Spear to strengthen Amfortas, how had it come about that he could not lay the evil magician low? Gurnemanz knows only that hard by the castle walls the King had been enticed away by a woman of terrible enchantment: the old man had found him lying in her arms, the Spear fallen from his hand. Amfortas had given a cry like that of death: Gurnemanz had rushed to him, but only to see Klingsor mocking him with obscene laughter and brandishing the holy Spear in triumph. The old knight had brought Amfortas back to safety; but in his side was burning a wound so grievous that it will never close again. The orchestral texture throughout this episode is a complex of motives, including that of Klingsor's magic and those pertaining to the Spear and the anguish of Amfortas. All through *Parsifal*, indeed, Wagner's art of the psychological interweaving of motives is at its finest.

The squires who had accompanied the King to the lake now return.[1] The bath and the balsam brought by Kundry had soothed his pain, they say; and we hear in the orchestra the heart-easing No. 14, which, however, merges instantly, by one of those subtle transitions of which Wagner is a master, into the music associated with the King's sufferings as Gurnemanz reiterates mournfully, "This wound it is that ne'er will close again".

23

Wagner's favourite technique of dramatic explanation is a sound one, the product of the musician as well as of the dramatist in him. He himself had pointed out long ago, in connection with *Tristan*, how infinitely richer the musical dramatist's resources are than those of the ordinary playwright or novelist. The latter has to begin with a statement of facts and incidents, material data

[1] These are the two original squires. For some reason or other Wagner had made them leave the stage with the King's litter, while some of those who had accompanied its entry remain, and, according to the stage instructions, "pass to and fro". With the return of the original two there are four in all during the present scene. Wagner's procedure was dictated by the necessity of having that number for the four-part harmony of the Pure Fool motive later.

which he gradually builds up into a complex from which the psychological or emotional essence of the action emerges in due course. The musician has no need to approach the heart of his subject from a remote distance in this slow way: he can pierce at once to the core of *feeling*, leaving the material details to be made manifest later. In the case of *Tristan*, for example, as Wagner says, the artist in prose or verse would have to begin by telling us at great length who and what Tristan and Isolde were, where they lived, what adventures they went through, and how these adventures led them gradually to their dolorous end. But the musician can strike at once, as Wagner does in the first bars of the prelude, into the emotional heart of the story, leaving the factual details to emerge of themselves later.

This is how he proceeds in *Parsifal*. He does not begin, as Wolfram von Eschenbach and the others had had to do, with the ancestry and birth and boyhood of Parsifal, showing how he came to be what he was in himself, how, adventure by adventure, he was drawn into the orbit of the Grail, and so on. Wagner first of all condenses the main emotional motives of the drama into his prelude. In this he does not attempt to tell the full story in the customary overture or symphonic poem form; as the reader will have observed, the prelude contains no reference at all to Parsifal or Klingsor or Kundry. It is sufficient for Wagner's purpose to show us the mystical beauty and solemnity and holiness of the domain of the Grail, the sombre fleck made on all this by the fault and the anguish of Amfortas, and to hint at the end at a possible lifting of the clouds. Then, when the stage action opens, he begins not with a point-by-point exposition of the fundamental incidents of the story — the history of the Grail, the personality of Klingsor, the connection between him and Kundry, the seduction of Amfortas, the rape of the Spear, and so forth — but with the present spiritual consequences of all this. After that, having attuned us by his music to the inner import of all these happenings, he addresses himself to placing us in possession of the facts antedating the emotions — very much as, in the first scene of *Tristan*, he had first of all shown us the scorn and anger of Isolde and the sombre reserve of Tristan, and then, by means of Isolde's "Narration" to Brangaene, unravelled for us the precedent facts that had led up to the strained phase of the action at which the opera had begun.

24

The device he now adopts, in *Parsifal,* to acquaint the audience with everything that had led up to the emotional tension of the opening scene is again a "Narration". It is not a hoary operatic device dragged in willy-nilly, as in *Il Trovatore,* to tell the audience what it needs to know under the pretext of one character telling another on the stage. It is psychologically justified. The squires are young, new to the castle, to the nature of the Grail and the Spear, ignorant of how these came of old to Monsalvat, ignorant of the nature of the magician on the other side of the mountains, of why he desired to win possession of the Spear, how he came to do so, and the dire consequences of the loss of it to the King and the brotherhood. Only when this has been made clear to all is the action ripe for the entry of the hero who is predestined to change the course of events.

How came Gurnemanz to know of Klingsor? the squires ask the old man. They group themselves at his feet under the great tree, and he tells them the whole story. Klingsor had been well known to the pious hero Titurel, who long ago had defended the realm of faith when it was assailed by its enemies. Then had come to him a wonder. One night the Saviour's messengers descended from heaven, bearing with them the sacred cup from which He had drunk at the Last Supper and into which His blood had flowed on the Cross, and the soldier's spear that had pierced His side. The orchestral tissue now becomes a continual linking and interweaving of motives, with some of which we are already familiar. At the mention of the bringing of the Cup and the Lance by the angelic messengers to Titurel we hear what at first sight appears to be a new motive:

No. 16

but is seen, on examination, to be, as No. 13 is, yet another metamorphosis of No. 4 (the Faith motive). It becomes of great importance in the closing moments of the opera. At Gurnemanz's words:

> *Wherein His blood upon the Cross did flow,*
> *therewith the soldier's spear, that dealt the blow,*

we hear the agonised No. 8 in a new form:

No. 17

Obviously, therefore, No. 8 is to be taken as pertaining less specifically to Amfortas than to the agony of the Redeemer on the Cross, which becomes the torture of Amfortas himself after he has been wounded by the self-same Spear.

To house the sacred relics, Gurnemanz continues, Titurel had built a fane wherein he gathered a company of the pure in heart, whose mission it should be to purify the world through the wonder-working power of the Grail. Hence Klingsor, whose sinister motive is now heard in clarinets and bassoons:

No. 18

was excluded from the brotherhood. "Alone dwelt Klingsor in yon distant valley, where all the land is rank with heathendom. Never knew I what sin he had there committed; yet now atone would he — ay, holy make him. No strength had he to slay the raging lusts within him; desperate, he turned against himself his hand. And then the Grail he fain would grasp, but scornfully its guardian drove him forth." But Klingsor's vain mutilation of himself had brought him knowledge of a dark magic (No. 15 in the orchestra, followed by No. 12, indicating Kundry as the instrument of his evil designs). He had turned the desert into "magic gardens, with women rich in all beguilements"; whereupon we hear a foreshadowing:

No. 19

Con moto, grazioso

Komm'! / Come! Komm'! / Come! Hol-der / Gen-tle Kna-be! / lov-er!

of the motive of the Flower Maidens, which is quoted here in the more definite form it assumes in the second act. "There doth he lurk to lure the Grail's pure warders to shameful joys and soul's defilement. Whom once he snares" — and No. 12 again hints at Kundry as the instrument of Klingsor's magic — "no more is saved: full many hath he now enslaved."

When Titurel, old and weary, gave his guardianship of the Grail into the hands of his son, Amfortas turned with holy zeal to rid the earth of this plague. The rest, says Gurnemanz, his hearers already know: the Spear fell into the hands of Klingsor, who thus has won power over the brethren, and hopes ere long to possess himself of the Grail itself. All the while that Gurnemanz has been speaking Kundry has been silent; but she frequently turns towards him, as the stage directions have it, "in angry and passionate disquiet".

One thing, the old man continues, must before all be done — the Spear must be won back again. The maimed Amfortas had prostrated himself in prayer before the deserted sanctuary, imploring a sign from heaven. Thereupon the Grail had flooded him with its radiance, and a voice had given him a mystic token: "Made wise through pity, the Blameless Fool — wait for him, my chosen one"; and the squires repeat the words softly and wistfully in four-part harmony. (No. 10).

25

There is a long contemplative pause after the mysterious words, and then a wild outburst in the orchestra, and cries of "Woe!" from knights and squires behind the scenes, from the direction of the lake. First of all we hear (No. 20 A) the opening notes of the bold motive henceforth employed to characterise Parsifal: for convenience of further reference it is quoted here:

No.20

in the full form it assumes a little later. It is instantly succeeded by an agitated passage:

No.21

which outlines a motive that will shortly define itself as that of the swan:

No.22

which Wagner takes over from his *Lohengrin*. A wounded wild swan flies brokenly across the scene, to the accompaniment of cries of horror from them all: it sinks heavily to the ground, and one of the knights draws an arrow from its breast. The King, says another, had hailed the bird, flying round the lake, as a happy omen; but a wanton shaft had sped through the air and pierced it. Parsifal, a rough boyish figure, is dragged in, carrying his bow and arrows, and he admits it was he who had brought down the swan. The knights and squires clamour for his punishment. Gurnemanz addresses him in sad reproach: he would do murder, then, here in the holy woodland where all is peace, where the dumb creatures are tame and trustful and regard man as their friend? The swan had been circling over the lake looking for his mate, meaning to consecrate the bath for the King; and this brutal boy had no thought but to slay him.

The first dawning of something which afterwards, though slowly, he comes to know as pity rises in Parsifal's heart; he passionately breaks his bow, hurls his arrows away, and passes his hand over his eyes. Does he feel the burden of his guilt? Gurnemanz asks him. What mad impulse had driven him to this deed? "I knew not it was wrong", says the boy humbly. "Whence art thou come?" "That know I not." "Who is thy father?" "That know I not." "Who sent thee here?" "That know I not.". "What is thy name?" "Once I had many, but none of them can I now recall"; and the orchestra breathes softly the tender motive that will later characterise his sorrowing mother Herzeleide (Heart-in-sorrow):

No.23

"So dull a one ne'er have I found", says Gurnemanz despairingly, "save Kundry here." We are brought face to face, indeed, but in an intensified emotional form, with the all-unknowing boy of the early stages of Wolfram's poem.

But a faint light seems to be breaking upon Gurnemanz. He bids the squires leave him and tend the King, and they go off, bearing with them reverently the dead swan on a bier they have made out of fresh branches from the glade. Only the old man, Parsifal and Kundry remain behind. Gurnemanz turns to the boy again. Something, surely, he must know, he says. "I know of my mother", Parsifal replies: "Herzeleide is her name; my home was in trackless meadows. My bow I made myself, to scare the savage eagles from the forest." "Yet thou seem'st of noble birth", says Gurnemanz; "why taught thee not thy mother the use of worthier weapons?" To this the unschooled boy cannot reply; but Kundry, hoarsely breaking her long silence, answers for him. His father Gamuret, she says, was slain in battle; and lest the same fate should come upon him also his mother had brought him up in seclusion, strange to arms, a simple fool — and no less fool she! Parsifal's memories of his childhood revive, and he breaks into eager speech. He remembers now that once, on the fringe of the wood, men in glittering raiment had swept by him, mounted on splendid animals: fain would he have been like them, but they passed on their way with laughter. This story of his is accompanied in the orchestra by a new version of No. 11: evidently for Wagner the motive did not relate specifically to Kundry's ride but, as it were, to riding in general.

The boy had run after the knights but soon lost sight of them. He had wandered long and far, over hill and dale, night following day; and against robbers and giants and wild beasts he had had no defence but his bow. "Ay!" interjects Kundry, "all feared the valorous boy!" "Who fears me?" asks the astonished Parsifal. "The wicked", she replies. "Were those who threatened me wicked? Who then is good?" he asks. Gurnemanz laughs for a moment at his simplicity; then, becoming serious again, he answers the latter part of Parsifal's question: "Thy mother, from whom thou fleddest, and who for thee now doth pine and grieve." "She grieves no more", says Kundry. "She is dead: as I rode by I saw her dying, and to thee, fool, she sent a greeting." "It is false!" cries Parsifal; and he springs at Kundry in a passion and seizes her by the throat. Gurnemanz restrains him, and once more reproaches him for his violence. The boy stands for a while as if turned to stone: then a paroxysm of trembling seizes him, and he seems about to faint; whereupon Kundry hastens to a spring in the wood, brings water in a horn, sprinkles him with it, and gives it him to drink.

Gurnemanz praises her kindness: this is the Grail's own grace, he says, that turns evil aside from one who meets it with good. "Good I do never", she mutters, to a motive that has already been used to symbolise her service:

No. 24 *Andante*

which is followed by that of Klingsor's magic (No. 15); and when Gurnemanz turns kindly to Parsifal again she drags herself, unnoticed by them both, towards a thicket. Oh that she might slumber and never waken! she groans; and yet she hardly dares to sleep, for horrors and terrors hag-ride her. At last she is overcome by weariness; she lets her arms sink to her side, bows her head, staggers convulsively behind the thicket, and is lost to view.

26

Just then the train of knights and squires becomes visible in the background, bearing the King in his litter back from the lake to the castle. Something in what Parsifal has said, and, even more, something in his unconscious bearing has struck deep into Gurnemanz and raised a faint hope there: he resolves to take the boy to the holy meal that is to be partaken of in the castle; "for art thou pure", he tells him, "the Grail will give thee food and drink." "Who is the Grail?" the ignorant boy asks in wonder. Gurnemanz evades the question:

> *I may not say; but art thou to its service bidden,*
> *not long the knowledge shall be hidden.*
> *And lo! methinks I know thee now indeed:*
> *no way doth to its kingdom lead;*
> *no human foot the pathway treadeth*
> *save him whom itself it leadeth.*

"I hardly stir", says the astonished Parsifal, "and yet I move apace." This Gurnemanz explains to him: "Thou seest, my son, here time is one with space."

In this world of mystery and magic, indeed, there is no dividing line between the physical and the metaphysical. For some minutes Gurnemanz and Parsifal remain stationary at the front of the stage, while a curtain that has descended, which depicts various aspects of rock and woodland, moves slowly from left to right, thus creating, in the mind of the imaginative spectator, the illusion that the two figures are moving from right to left.[1] "The wood disappears", run Wagner's stage directions; "a gate opens in the rock, through which the pair pass and are lost to sight; later they become visible once more, apparently ascending a path." Accom-

---

[1] I have pointed out elsewhere that Ludwig Börne, in a letter of 1831 from Paris, described at some length a dramatic-panoramic history of Napoleon I which he had just seen at the Odéon Theatre: in the episode of the escape from Elba, while the man-o'-war carrying the Emperor remained stationary, the coastal scenery kept changing, "so that", as Börne put it, "the spectator gets the impression that the ship itself is in motion." It is possible that this device was popular in Paris in the 1830's, and that Wagner may have seen it in operation during his residence there between 1839 and 1842.

panying the change is the magnificent Transformation Music. First of all we hear the solemn motive, which has been already anticipated a few times, of the bells pealing out from the castle:

This is interwoven with the Grail motive and the Faith motive (Nos. 3 and 4), and with the agonised motive of Amfortas's repentance (No. 6) in the heightened form it generally assumes from now onwards; it is quoted here in the last and most tremendous of its three enunciations during the Transformation Music:

where it is given out fortissimo by the full orchestra.

As the theme rises to its climax and dies away again there pierces through the tissue a commanding statement of the Love Feast motive (the opening bars of No. 1), volleyed from the still invisible castle by six trombones behind the scenes:

and then a second time, with the addition of six trumpets; at the same time the solemn chime of the bells comes nearer (No. 25).

This tonal picture of the journey from the glade to the castle is one of unrivalled splendour.

27

The curtain having risen again, we see that Gurnemanz and Parsifal have by now come to a vast hall, which is surmounted by a great vaulted cupola through which alone the light enters. From the heights we hear the tolling of the bells, becoming ever louder and louder. "Now," says Gurnemanz to Parsifal, "give good heed, and let me see, if thou art a fool and pure, what wisdom may come to thee." From this point until the end of the act the boy stands immobile at the side-front of the stage, with his back to the audience, lost in wonder at the marvellous pageant that unfolds itself before his eyes.

What he sees first is the great pillared hall, with two doors opening into it from the back. To the pealing of the bells the knights of the Grail enter through the door on the right and proceed in grave procession to their places at two long covered tables, which run in parallel lines from back to front of the stage, leaving the middle of the hall open: on the tables are nothing but cups. Two groups of squires pass quickly across the stage to the back of the scene while the still moving knights sing in unison an invocation to the eucharistic meal of which they are about to partake; and as they seat themselves at the tables a choir — invisible in the mid-height of the dome — of boys' voices gives out the anguished No. 26 to the words:

> *A world sunk in sinning*
> *His pangs redeeméd,*
> *its innocence restoring;*
> *now to Him, our Saviour,*
> *my soul in gladness its offering*
> *of blood is pouring:*
> *upon the Cross He gave His breath, —*
> *now lives He in us by His death;*

followed by a call to drink the wine and eat the bread. During this chorus Amfortas has been carried in on a litter by the knights; before them go four squires bearing a shrine enveloped in a purple-red cover. The King is taken to the centre background and placed on a raised couch beneath a canopy; in front of the couch stands an oblong marble table, on which the squires deposit the shrine.

When all are seated, and the singing has ceased, there comes a long, impressive silence: then, from a vaulted niche in the extreme background, behind Amfortas's couch, we hear the blanched voice of the aged Titurel, coming as if from a tomb. Shall he look upon the Grail again and be quickened, he asks, or must he die? To the strains of No. 26 Amfortas begs his father to take over his office again from his own unworthy hands: "live thou, and let me perish". "Too old and feeble am I", Titurel replies, "to serve the Redeemer: do thou serve, and in serving atone for thy guilt. Uncover the Grail!" But before the squires can do so Amfortas rises on his couch, and in a long monologue pours out all the pain and bitterness of his unworthy soul — "Grievous the birthright to me descended; I, the only sinner among the brethren, to minister the holy relic and pray its blessing on these pure ones!"

No.28

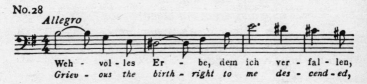

He bids them leave the Grail still uncovered. Once again he relives in imagination his fall from grace; he feels his own blood stir in rapture and pain in mystic communion with the blood in the Cup; once more he feels the torture of his wound, with its likeness to that of the Saviour on the Cross, for the same Spear had pierced them both; and it was he, the Grail's appointed, who had brought this disaster on himself and the brotherhood. With an impassioned cry for mercy and forgiveness and for purification by death he sinks back on his couch, as if unconscious. The orchestral texture throughout his monologue consists of the finest interweaving of many of the motives familiar to us by now; sometimes they are subtly modified, as when the serene Grail motive (No. 3) undergoes a harmonic and (in the accompaniment) a rhythmic change:

As the King falls back exhausted the boys' voices from the mid-height intone softly the mysterious motive of the Pure Fool (No. 10), which is followed by that of the Grail as Amfortas raises himself slowly and with difficulty from his couch. The squires unveil the golden shrine and take from it the Grail, which the stage directions describe as "an antique crystal cup"; this they uncover, and then place it in front of Amfortas. He bows devoutly before it in silent prayer as the altos and tenors, from the height of the cupola, sing quietly, to the melody of No. 1, the words with which Wagner began his analysis of the prelude for King Ludwig:

> *Take my body and eat,*
> *take and drink my blood;*
> *this be our love's remembrance;*

to which the boys' voices add:

> *Take and drink my blood,*
> *take my body and eat,*
> *the while of me ye think.*

As in the prelude, between the two enunciations of the theme, and again after the second of them, the trumpet, in soft, solemn tones, throws out the motive in high relief against a background of shimmering arpeggios.

28

During all this the hall has grown completely dark; but as the melody rises to its greatest height (as in No. 2) a dazzling shaft of light falls from above upon the Cup, making it glow with an ever-deepening purple that casts a gentle radiance on the scene. Amfortas, his face transfigured, raises the Grail aloft and waves it gently from side to side in consecration of the bread and wine:

the knights, who have sunk upon their knees as twilight descended upon the hall, raise their eyes in devotion to the Chalice. Titurel breaks into a cry of rapture. Amfortas sets the Grail down again, and the squires replace it in the shrine, which they cover with the cloth once more. As the purple glow fades, darkness gives way to twilight in the hall, and this in turn to full daylight.

Now comes the serving of the eucharist. The four squires who have borne the Grail, having closed the shrine, take from the altar table the two wine flagons and the baskets of bread that Amfortas has consecrated. The knights, including Gurnemanz, seat themselves at the tables; the old man, however, has kept a place empty next to his. He signs to Parsifal to come forward and take part in the meal; but the uncomprehending boy remains motionless, lost in amazement. The serving of the communion is accompanied by some higher boys' voices from above:

No.30

and then by lower boys' voices reinforced by a few high tenors. Finally the knights themselves take up the strain in a modified form, and the long episode ends with the Grail motive rising slowly from the depths to the supreme height of the dome and dying away as the knights rise from the tables, pace slowly towards each other, and embrace.

Amfortas has taken no part in the meal, of which he feels he is unworthy by reason of his sin against the Grail and his loss of the Spear. His momentary exaltation has ebbed from him: he bows his head in utter weariness, and as he passes his hand to his side and the squires tend him solicitously we realise that his wound has broken out afresh. They place him in the litter and bear him and the shrine out of the hall, followed by the knights in solemn procession. During all this the orchestra pours out motive after motive associated with the Grail and the brotherhood and the anguish of Amfortas. The last of the knights and squires having departed, Gurnemanz turns, half in ill-temper, half with a last faint stirring of hope, to Parsifal, whom he has been watching for some time. Only once has the spellbound boy made the smallest movement since he entered the hall: at the climax of the grievous cry of Amfortas when he confessed his sin and cried out for the mercy and pity of heaven:

> *Have mercy! Have mercy!*
> *Thou God of pity! Oh, have mercy!*
> *Take back my birthright,*
> *so Thou but heal me,*
> *that holy I die now,*
> *pure for thy presence!*

the boy had pressed his own hand convulsively to his heart and held it there for some time: he is at the beginning of the fulfilment of his destiny — through pity he will come to understand the sorrow of earth and grow slowly wise. But nothing yet is clear to him; all he knows is that the cry of the suffering King, of whose story he knows nothing, has unlocked something in his own breast that makes him one with suffering creatures everywhere.

Even when he and Gurnemanz are left alone in the empty hall he stands petrified, mute. The disappointed old man goes up to him in ill humour and shakes him roughly by the arm. "Why standest thou here still?" he asks him. "Know'st thou what thou saw'st?" Parsifal shakes his head and again clutches convulsively at his heart, but cannot speak. Gurnemanz's patience is now at an end, his last hope destroyed. "Thou art but a fool, then", he says irritably:

> *Hie thee hence, get thee gone from us!*
> *Take this from Gurnemanz:*
> *leave thou our swans for the future alone,*
> *and seek thyself, gander, a goose!*

He opens a small side door, pushes the boy out roughly, closes the door on him angrily, and follows the knights. But the last word is not with him. His furious gesture is followed by a suggestion to us of something he himself does not know: the orchestra hints stumblingly at the fact that this ignorant boy is after all the one chosen by the Grail:

No. 31

(See No. 10). A single alto voice, piercing the fateful stillness from the height of the dome, clinches the point by murmuring, "Made wise through pity, the Blameless Fool"; other voices rise on the air with a murmur of "Blessed in Faith" that dies away into the distance, the Grail bells give a last soft peal, and the curtain falls.

29

In the second act we see illumination coming slowly to Parsifal. The other characters whom we have so far met disappear from our sight, with the exception of Kundry; and though Klingsor makes two appearances, it is upon Kundry and Parsifal that the main burden of the act rests. For Kundry is, in a sense, the hinge of the drama, linked as she is on one side of her complex being with the sorcerer, on the other side with the company of the Grail. She stands between the two opposing worlds of good and evil, with something of each of them in her; and it is through her, though without her intending it, that Parsifal will learn the secret of the fall of Amfortas and the meaning of the pang that had shot through his own heart as he watched the agony of the King.

Before the curtain rises, a wild orchestral prelude, of the colour and the demonic power of which no piano arrangement can give any idea, sets before us Klingsor and all he stands for. First of all we hear the sinister motive of the magician himself (No. 18); then the Grail as the object of Klingsor's hatred:

(The upper part of this quotation shows a harmonic distortion of the Grail theme, the lower part the Klingsor motive). This runs into contrapuntal combinations of No. 18 and, first of all, the motive of Amfortas's agony, then that of Kundry as the instrument of the sorcerer (No. 12).

At the rising of the curtain we see the inner keep of a tower of Klingsor's castle, with steps at the side that lead down to the edge of the battlements. From the projecting wall the stage runs downwards towards the back. The tower is stocked with magical implements and necromantic apparatus. Through the darkness that envelops the scene we catch sight of Klingsor, seated on the projecting wall, gazing into a metal mirror that shows him all that is going on in his domain. He is brooding mischief: a hint of the Pure Fool motive in the orchestra, followed by that of Kundry (No. 12) and that of Magic (No. 15), gives point to his opening words:

> The time is come.
> My magic tower the Fool now lureth;
> with childish shouting lo! he draweth nigh.
> In deadly slumber fast the witch lies bound.
> The spell that binds her I will loose.
> Up then! To work!

He descends a little towards the centre and kindles incense, which fills part of the background with a bluish vapour. As No. 15 writhes its way through the orchestral texture he seats himself once more before his magical apparatus and calls with mysterious gestures into the depths below: "Arise! To me! Thy master summons thee, nameless one, first of witches, Rose of Hell! Herodias wert thou, and what besides? Gundryggia there, Kundry here! Come hither, Kundry!"

In the bluish light in the background we see the wild creature's figure gradually defining itself. She seems to be waking slowly out of a sleep in obedience to the magic summons:

No.33 *Lento*

The orchestra has sunk to a boding pianissimo: then suddenly there comes a startling fortissimo ejaculation of the discordant No. 12, and Kundry awakes with a blood-curdling shriek — awakes at the bidding of her master to another of the tasks she hates: then her wail subsides into a low moan of terror. Where has she been of late? he asks her: with the brotherhood on the other side of the mountain, where she is regarded as no better than a brute beast? Why has she fled from her master after she had accomplished his design upon their King? She struggles numbly to find speech again and to shake off her torpor and the sense of madness that comes with the torturing recall of the past. Yes, she replies, she has been occupied in service among the knights. He scoffs at her repentance: as for the Grail brotherhood, to them she need not look to win freedom, for he can seduce them all to him, as he had done Amfortas, by bidding the fitting price — they will succumb to Kundry, and in their weakness he will deal them a wound with the Spear he has ravished from their King.

But today, he says, there is one in the field against him whom he feels to be the most dangerous of all, "strong as fools alone are strong". She struggles impotently against the compulsion of his will. He reminds her that he, Klingsor, alone is proof against her female wiles: she breaks into mocking laughter over his enforced chastity, and he broods darkly and savagely upon it, for his self-mutilation has after all been unavailing — still the old fierce lusts rage within him, and he can neither gratify them nor quell them. Because of his failure he is consumed with hatred for the knights of the Grail; and he gloats over the destruction he had brought on their King, who of old had spurned him and driven him forth from the holy company. Soon, he is sure, the Grail itself will be his. But Kundry bemoans her servitude to him, and most of all her victory over the weak Amfortas. Could she but sleep for ever, she wails, and work no more evil! and we hear in the quiet strings the subtlest and saddest chromatic musing upon the theme of Amfortas's anguish:

No. 34

She protests passionately when Klingsor tells her of the new task he has for her, the seduction of the fair stripling who is drawing near; and she breaks into hysterical laughter, followed by a convulsive cry of woe, as the magician describes what he can see from his tower. He sounds his horn, and to the accompaniment of feverishly hurrying figures of the type of No. 11 he tells — not without a certain unholy glee, for he hates his own servitors as malignantly as he does the Grail brotherhood — of the havoc that is being wrought among them by this new assailant of theirs. The identity of the newcomer is established for us by some subtle transformations of the Pure Fool motive in the orchestra; and the theme of Parsifal himself (No. 20) comes out powerfully.

30

Klingsor makes it clear to us that the intruder is a mere boy, now surveying with a childlike wonder the garden the defenders of which he is routing. The magician has other ways of dealing with him, however, than by the sword. He knows that the stripling's strength is in his primal purity: if that should go, all will go, and accordingly he sends Kundry to work upon him in his and her accustomed fashion. Gradually the bluish light that had spread over the background is extinguished, and Kundry has vanished in the darkness. The tower disappears, and Klingsor with it; and instantly the magic garden comes into sight, occupying the whole stage. "Tropical vegetation, luxuriant flowers", say the stage directions. "At the back the scene is closed by the battlements of the ramparts, which are flanked by projecting portions of the castle (in a rich Arabian style) with terraces." Wagner thus follows the legends that place the Grail setting in Arabic Spain, with Monsalvat on one side of a mountain and the domain of Klingsor on the other.

On the ramparts stands Parsifal, gazing down in amazement at the garden beneath him. Beautiful maidens run in from all sides, clad in light soft-coloured veils that have been hastily gathered about them, as if they had been startled out of sleep. They have heard cries and the clash of arms, and have rushed in to see what was afoot. They are divided and subdivided musically into two groups, each with three leaders and a semi-chorus, a disposition which makes it possible for them to dialogue excitedly as they enter.[1] They have seen their lovers struck down by the comely boy who now stands on the ramparts, in his hand a sword, red with blood, which he had wrested from one of Klingsor's knights, Ferris. To the Maidens' question of why he had smitten their lovers the boy gives the naïve answer, "Need I had to smite them, for my passage to you they would fain have barred."

As he comes nearer they lose their first fear of him and entreat him to join them in their games. Some of them slip away behind the hedges and return entirely decked in flowers; and their example is soon followed by the rest. In childlike glee they group themselves round him and sing their subtly seductive melody (No. 19), accompanying it with caresses and promises of the delights of an earthly Paradise if he will be theirs. They even bicker among

---

[1] The Flower Maidens' choruses can never have been sung in any opera house as magnificently as they were at the first production of the work in Bayreuth in 1882, when, as Wagner wrote to King Ludwig, he had for the leading sopranos of his chorus distinguished artists who had sung parts like Elsa, Isolde, Eva, Brynhilde, Sieglinde and so on in the leading German theatres.

themselves for the possession of the charming boy. But he is too ignorant to understand: half-angrily he repulses them and is about to flee, when — one of the most arresting dramatic moments of the opera — the voice of Kundry strikes through the turmoil with his name:

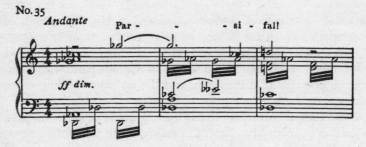

He pauses in perplexity: "Parsifal"? he says; "so named me in a dream once my mother." At the sound of Kundry's voice the Maidens have recoiled in terror, and at her bidding they disappear one by one from the scene, with a parting jibe at the unsophisticated boy — "Farewell, thou proud one, thou Fool!"

31

Parsifal stands as if in a dream. Looking round timidly to the quarter from which the voice had come he sees a young and entrancingly beautiful woman — Kundry completely and unrecognisably transformed: she is robed in a light, veil-like, fantastic garment of Arabian style, and reclines on a couch of flowers. "Parsifal!" she greets him again: "Fal-parsi, Pure Fool!" [1] By this name, she says, before ever he was born, his father Gamuret, dying in a foreign land, had greeted him; and to tell him this has Kundry waited here, and what, except the desire to know it, had drawn him thither? She is not a flower of the garden, as the wondering boy imagines, but one who has come from afar, after seeing and learning many things, to tell him what he should know. She begins in low sweet tones her long narration of his childhood:

[1] Wagner took over from Görres, a German writer of the early nineteenth century, the theory that the name "Parsifal" came from two Arabian words, "Fal" and "Parsi", meaning Pure Fool. The derivation has not found favour with modern scholars.

No.36

Molto moderato e tranquillo

Strings alone

Ich sah das Kind an
I saw the babe up-

sei- ner Mut- ter Brust,
-on its mo- ther's breast.

etc.

The orchestra develops symphonically this motive and that of Herzeleide (No. 23) with many metamorphoses of them as she tells the tender story made familiar to us by Wolfram — how the widowed Heart-in-sorrow had tended the babe of her sorrow, how, in fear of losing the boy as she had lost his father, she had brought him up in the forest in secret and in safety, "afar from arms, from man in madness slaying man", always racked with foreboding when he strayed from her care, raining kisses on him when he returned, till at last there came a day when he wandered away and did not return, and after long days and nights of anxious waiting

> *too full was her heart of pain;*
> *for death's release she prayed:*
> *her anguish broke her heart,*
> *and — Heart-in-sorrow died.*

Then, for the first time, the boy has an inkling of wrong done by him all unknowing, pain inflicted without understanding and without intent. As Kundry speaks of his mother's death he sinks at her feet, crushed with grief, cursing himself for his childish folly:

> *Mother! Sweetest, dearest Mother!*
> *Thy son, thy son must be thy murderer?*
> *Oh fool! Blind and credulous fool!*

> *Where wandered'st thou, her love forgetting, —*
> *Dearest, fondest of mothers!*

But had he never known this grief, Kundry insinuates, never could love have brought him its solace. But he is inconsolable:

> *My Mother, my Mother — I could forget her!*

he moans:

> *Ha! What more have I, blind one, forgot?*
> *What have I e'er remembered yet?*
> *'Tis only folly dwells in me!*

By knowledge, Kundry tells him, sense returns to the Fool. It is for him now to learn the rapture of love that once burned in Gamuret for Heart-in-sorrow:

> *For she, the woman loved who bore thee,*
> *can death and folly far remove:*
> *she sends thee now a mother's blessing,*
> *greets thy lips —*
> *with this first kiss of love!*

and she bows her head over him and joins her lips to his in a long kiss.

32

But there is evil, the root of the whole world's sad evil, in the kiss, as the slow ascent and fall of the dark motive of Magic (No. 15) in the orchestra warns us. We have arrived at the ethical crux of the drama, a crux that is Wagner's own, not that of any of his predecessors. It is not by surrender to the senses that the brave, simple Fool can become "slowly wise", but only through the lesson of suffering with and pity for others. A shaft of blinding light shoots through Parsifal. A great and terrible change has come over him; he presses his hand against his heart as if to still a rending pain, for now he senses the secret of the agony of Amfortas from his wound. The motive of Suffering (No. 26) goes through transformation after transformation in the orchestra as he pours out his wild lament, for now he is one by sympathetic intuition with the King and what he had once stood for. He understands everything: it is not merely that the guardian of the Grail, sworn to purity, had succumbed to the lure of the senses but that the sanctuary of the Saviour itself, and all it stands for in a world of evil, has been polluted and now calls to him for cleansing:

> *And I — the fool, the coward,*
> *to deeds of boyish wildness hither fled!*
> *Redeemer! Saviour! Lord of grace! —*
> *How for my sin can I atone?*

and he throws himself despairingly on his knees.

His outburst has filled Kundry with wonder and passion. Timidly she approaches the boy who has suddenly become a man, and bids him shake himself free of this madness and accept the grace that *she* can bring him. But now he sees her as in essence she is, sensual seduction incarnate, the plague and ruin of noble life; and the primal Kundry motive (No. 12) takes on a new and more insinuating form:

No. 37 Lento

as, still in her arms yet far withdrawn from her within himself, he transfers in his awakened imagination each in turn of her cajolements and caresses to Amfortas:

> *Ay! Thus she called him! This was the voice,*
> *and this her glance — truly I know it now —*
> *what torment its smiling menace brought him!*
> *The lips too — aye — so thrilled they him;*
> *so bent this neck above him —*
> *so boldly rose her head;*
> *so fluttered her locks as in laughter,*
> *so twined she this arm round his neck;*
> *so fawningly smiled she on him;*

in league with every direct torment,
his soul's salvation
with that one kiss he lost! —
Ha! — this same kiss!

and he thrusts her from him violently and rises to his feet.

And now the enigmatic woman feels, or imagines she does, a new kind of passion for him. Since he can thus experience compassion for another, let him now be *her* deliverer, for whom she has been waiting since the day, long ago, when she had reviled and mocked the Saviour of the world, and he gave her — one look! — the deliverer she has ever since been seeking, feeling his eye to be near her in her moments of deepest spiritual need, though always she had laughed her accursed laugh as yet another sinner sank to ruin on her bosom:

He I desired in death's deep anguish,
he whom I knew, so weak, derided,
let me upon his breast lie weeping,
be but one hour with thee united,
and though by God and man cast forth,
in thee be cleansed of sin and redeemed!

But Parsifal replies that were he to yield to her, he who has been destined for her salvation, he would be false to his mission. She must repent of her old desires; for the solace that can end her grief must flow from another source than those desires, and will not flow until that fountain of longing dries up within her. Not this fount of desire was it that his intuition had divined in the suffering hearts of the brotherhood:

But who with soul unclouded knows
the fount whence true salvation flows?
Oh mis'ry — that all hope destroys!
Oh, error's night appalling:
in quest to find salvation's joys
to lusts of hell a victim falling!

Then she exults that it is she who, by her kiss, has unlocked this wisdom in him, shewn him the world's own heart. In her arms let him learn what it is to be a god, the deliverer of the world; let her perish, unhealed, damned to all eternity, so she but hold him in her embrace. But once more he repulses her: redemption will be hers, he says, only by her showing him the way that will lead him back to Amfortas. At this she breaks out in fury against him. Never shall he find that way; as for the fallen King, the weak sinner whom she had tempted and derided, let him go to ruin, brought down as he had been by the loss of his own Spear. "Who dared then to wound him with the Holy Lance?" asks Parsifal. It was he, Kundry replies, who once had chastised her laughter, by the power of whose curse she now has strength to call up the Spear against Parsifal himself if he still bestows his compassion on the one who had lost it by his sin. And once more she tries to take him into her embrace.

When he again repulses her she recovers herself by a violent effort, and with a cry of rage breaks from him and calls towards the background, invoking the aid of Klingsor and his warders: "thou whom I know, take thou this boy for thine own". As for Amfortas, Parsifal shall never find him:

> *For fleddest thou from here, and found'st*
> *all the ways of the world,*
> *the one that thou seek'st,*
> that *path thy foot shall find never:*
> *each track, each pathway*
> *that leads thee from Kundry,*
> *thus — I curse beneath thy feet.*

By now Klingsor has appeared on the castle walls, to end the matter by means of the only weapon meet for this Fool — the holy Spear that had brought low the King the boy now would serve. He hurls the Spear at Parsifal, over whose head, however, it remains suspended in air. The boy seizes it and holds it aloft. "And with this sign", he cries, "I rout thy magic":

> *as the wound shall be closéd*
> *by the Spear that dealt it,*
> *in rack and ruin*
> *thy lying pomp shall it lay!*

With the Spear he makes the sign of the Cross: at once the castle collapses as if in an earthquake, the garden withers, the earth is strewn with faded flowers. Kundry sinks to the ground with a cry. Parsifal turns to her again as he is making his way across the ruined wall: "thou know'st", he says gravely, "where thou may'st find me when thou wilt". Kundry raises herself a little and gazes after him, and the curtain falls to a few bars in the orchestra that begin passionately and end with the conveyance, by their colour, of a sense of utter bleakness and desolation, material and spiritual:

No. 38

col 8va bassa

With the loss of the Spear and the transformation that has taken place in Kundry, Klingsor's power is at an end: but for Parsifal the long and dolorous quest for Amfortas and the Grail is now to begin.

33

The third act opens with a grave orchestral prelude the subtle chromaticisms of which are a foretaste of a harmony, throughout the act, the like of which had not been known in music until then, even in the work of such a master of chromatic nuance as Wagner: in some places it marks an advance upon *Tristan* in this field as great as that of *Tristan* — which is the great dividing line between the older harmony and the new — had been upon the *Rhinegold* and the *Valkyrie*.

The prelude covers, in its own purely musical way, the weary years that have elapsed between Parsifal's regaining of the Spear, the origin, the properties and the appointed function of which he now knows, and his arrival once more, all unaware of it, in the domain of the Grail, which Kundry had told him jeeringly he, the youthful Fool, would never find again. (According to the legend it is of the essence of the Grail that he who seeks for it can never find it: he must be led to it by the Grail itself at the Grail's own time). Parsifal has wandered far in these years, been engaged in many battles and beset by difficulties and racked by self-doubts of all kinds; but always with the one great purpose of pity burning within him, some day to light upon the castle of the Grail again and heal Amfortas with a touch of the Spear that had dealt him his wound.

When now we meet with him once more he is no longer the ignorant boy of the first act but a thoughtful man, sobered by suffering and made wise by compassion. We see him on the last stage of what has been a pilgrimage of endless frustration; in the opening bars of the prelude he, and the community of the Grail with him — for it too has suffered from his inability to find it again — are shown bowed down beneath a load of desolation:

No. 39

while a motive of Straying, as we may most conveniently call it:

No. 40

suggests his confused and stumbling course all these years through a world that has failed to grant him the one thing his heart desired — to find his way back again and heal Amfortas with the Spear. Then comes a subtle modification of the motive of the Pure Fool:

followed by others in which the original simple harmonies of that motive (see No. 10) are made still more poignant, as in this example:

Interwrought with these reminiscences of the Pure Fool of the first act is a figure (shown in No. 41 A) to be associated later with the tortured winter sleep and awakening of Kundry. Now and then we hear also (No. 1 C) the theme of the Spear that is at once the instrument and the symbol of the destiny that has been laid upon Parsifal.

The prelude, however, must not be regarded as a mere stringing together of motives in quasi-narrative or pictorial form. It is through-and-through psychological, spiritual: it has a meaning that is none the less definite because it cannot be expressed by us in words. Wagner himself, we learn from a jotting in Cosima's diary, said when he was writing it that his task — and it had been a difficult one — was to get down to the "fundamentals" of musical expression.

34

When the curtain rises at the conclusion of the prelude we see a pleasant open landscape in the domain of the Grail, with gently mounting flower-strewn meadows in the background. The foreground represents the edge of a forest which stretches out on the right to rising rocky ground. In the front, on the side of the wood, is a spring, and opposite this, a little further back, a humble hermit's hut, leaning against a mass of rock. It is the early morning of a beautiful spring day.

To the soft accompaniment of No. 39 Gurnemanz, now a very old man, garbed simply in the tunic of the knights of the Grail, comes out of the hut and listens in the direction from which he has heard groans that had struck him as too piteous for those of any beast, especially on this holiest of mornings. As he speaks these latter words we heard the first foreshadowing of a motive which later, in various forms, plays a large part in this scene; it is that of Atonement:

No. 15 (Klingsor's Magic) and No. 18 (the sorcerer himself) in the orchestra tell us that Kundry, still subject to him, is somewhere near: her groaning is that of one tortured by evil dreams in profound sleep. Gurnemanz discovers her when he strides towards a thorn thicket at the side of the stage and draws aside the

dense underwood. "Up, Kundry! Up!" he calls to her; "awake, for winter is fled and spring is here!"

The wailing No. 41 A is dwelt upon in the orchestra as Gurnemanz chafes the hands and temples of Kundry, whom he has drawn, stiff and numb, from the thicket and borne to a grassy mound near by. At last she opens her eyes, and greets her return to a life she does not desire with a frenzied cry as the orchestra crashes in with the wild dissonance that had accompanied her first entry in act one (No. 12). She is clothed, as when we saw her first, in the rough garment of a penitent; but she is paler now, and the old animal wildness of look has left her. She stares long and uncomprehendingly at Gurnemanz, and as consciousness slowly returns to her she rises, arranges her clothing and her hair, and at once betakes herself humbly to the duties of a serving-maid: the only word she can utter in reply to Gurnemanz's questionings is a hoarse "Service! Service!"

The old man shakes his head sadly: light will be her toil, he tells her, for it is long since the knights of the Grail have sent any message to other lands. The brotherhood has fallen from its ancient high estate: each man lives now on herbs and roots which he has learned from the beasts of the forest to find for himself, the nourishment of the Grail being denied them. But Gurnemanz is struck by the change in Kundry, which, as the orchestra gives out some of the music associated with the Grail and the Spear, he puts down to the benign influence of the Holy Morn: it is not alone her body but her soul also, he feels, that has been awakened from sleep; and the strings breathe softly the tranquil melody of the Flowery Meadow:

No. 44 Tranquillo

which will later come fully into its own in the Good Friday music.

Kundry, who has gone into the hut, returns with a pitcher, which she goes to fill at the spring. While waiting for it to fill she sees someone approaching from the wood, and turns to point him out to Gurnemanz. The Parsifal motive (No. 10) is intoned in the solemn colours of horns, trumpets and trombones:

No. 45 *Tranquillo*

It is heavy now with the load of Parsifal's long and fruitless quest.

35

He enters from the wood, a sombre figure in black armour with closed helm, holding the Spear in his hand. He strides forward slowly and wearily, with bowed head, as if in a dream, and seats himself on the little grassy mound. Gurnemanz hails him as a guest, to whom he offers his services; but Parsifal only shakes his head without speaking. The old man gently chides him: the new-comer's vow, he says, may constrain him to silence, but he must be told that now he is in a hallowed place, in which no man must go with shield, spear, and closed visor, and least of all on this day. Does he not know what holy day it is?. Parsifal shakes his head. Then from what heathen land has he come, Gurnemanz asks, that he does not know that this is Good Friday? He bids the knight lay down his weapons, that are an offence in the sight of the Lord who shed His holy blood for the atonement of sin.

To the accompaniment of solemn music Parsifal humbly obeys. Still without speaking, he thrusts the Spear into the ground before him, lays sword and shield beside it, opens his helm, removes it from his head and places it with the weapons: then he kneels before the upright Spear in silent prayer. Gurnemanz gazes at him in wonderment and beckons to Kundry; and as the orchestra gives out the full motive of the Spear (No. 6), followed by that of the Love Feast (No. 1) he says to her, "Surely this is the Fool whom in my anger I drove away?" Looking fixedly at Parsifal she inclines her head but does not speak. Gurnemanz has now recognized the Spear also, and in deep emotion he praises the Holy Day for what it has brought him.

His prayer ended, Parsifal rises slowly to his feet, looks tranquilly around him, recognises Gurnemanz, and gently holds out his hand to him: "'tis well", he says, "that again I have found thee!" Whence and how has he come, the old man asks. "Through error and through suffering lay my pathway", Parsifal replies, to the accompaniment of No. 40; "from their illusion free I sure may deem me, now that this woodland's murmur I have heard once more and give the kind old man a second greeting. Or am I in error still? For all about me seems changed." One alone has he been seeking all this weary while, "him whose dire lament in foolish wonder once I heard, and for whose healing, I deem, I bring now what may serve. But ah! a curse lay on me ne'er to find him. In blindest error through trackless wilds have I come hither: woes without number, battles and conflicts, drove me from the pathway, even when, methought, I knew it. Then dark despair descended on me to keep the treasure unsullied. The sacred relic ever guarding, from every weapon wounds did I win; for it I might not bear with me in battle. Unprofaned at my side I bore it, and now I bring it to its home: lo, there it gleameth bright and pure, — the Grail's own hallowed Spear!"

"Oh bounteous grace! Oh wonder! Holiest, highest wonder!" cries Gurnemanz in transport, as the wood wind breaks into the motives associated in the first act with the agony of Amfortas (No. 17), followed by that of the Spear and that of Faith (in the form the latter takes in No. 16). Parsifal is back again in the Grail's domain, he assures him. Long have they waited for him. They have been in sore need of him, for since the day when he had come among them and left them again the anguish of the King had increased: from the torment of his wound he had craved release in death, and to achieve that end he had refused, despite the entreaties of the brotherhood, to perform his holy office: the Grail had lain hidden in its shrine, the King hoping that deprived of the sight of it he might die. No longer do they eat the divine bread: common food supports them now, and their strength has departed. No longer come messages calling them to holy war in the world outside; weak and sad and leaderless they drag out their painful existence. Gurnemanz himself has come to this forest to await death in solitude and silence, while Titurel, denied too long the renewal that the Grail was wont to bring him, "is dead, a man, like all men"; and the quiet strings clinch the sad story with a solemn enunciation of the desolate No. 39.

36

Parsifal breaks out into passionate self-reproach. And 'tis he, he cries, who has wrought all this woe! What curse has been laid on him from birth, what load of sin must he carry, that no repentance, no atonement could lighten his blinded eyes, since he, the appointed deliverer, arriving here at last after having been caught in so many toils, finds himself in the end defeated! He seems about to fall, powerless: Gurnemanz supports him and lowers him to a sitting posture on the mound, while Kundry hastens to him with a cruse of water with which she sprinkles him. At this point the motive of Devotion is breathed softly by the wood wind:

It had first been heard in the second act, at the point where Kundry, at the commencement of her Narration, had told Parsifal that she had waited there for him to tell him of the death of his father and his mother; and it had reappeared later in that scene when, after being repulsed by him, she had cried, "Cruel one! If e'er thy heart could feel another's sorrow, then let it suffer with mine now! Art thou Redeemer, what bars thee now, harsh one, from making me one with thee in salvation?" Still later it had accompanied her despairing appeal to him — "He whom I longed for in death's deep anguish, he whom I knew and laughed at as a Fool, let me upon his breast fall weeping, be but one hour with thee united, and though by God and man cast forth, in thee be cleansed of sin and redeemed." His reply then had been, "Eternally would'st thou with me be damned if but one hour, unmindful of my mission, into thine arms I gave me." For first of all she must repent: [1] it is not through the flesh but only through the wisdom that comes slowly by understanding and pity that he can bring her salvation. The Devotion motive had been hinted at again, almost imperceptibly, at the moment when, in the third act, Gurnemanz had found Kundry in the thorn thicket. And now, at the point we have just reached, it becomes of prime significance. It is always enigmatic, both in itself and in its various comings upon the scene; but then Kundry herself is all enigma. Yet, as so often happens in Wagner, the music, if we surrender ourselves to that, has a logic of its own that cannot be rendered into words. It is clear, however, at the point at which we have now arrived, that the redemption for which she had longed at Parsifal's hands is nigh, but on his own spiritual terms and those of the Grail and the Spear.

Gurnemanz is wiser than she. He gently repulses her when she would sprinkle Parsifal; for that lustration, he tells her, only the water of the holy spring itself will serve. A new motive, that of Benediction:

[1] Wagner's stage directions for her entry in the third act are "Kundry is in the rough garments of a penitent, as in the first act". He must have forgotten that on her appearance in the first act she had on "a wild garment, looped-up high", with "a snake-skin girdle with long ends": "her hair is black and hangs in loose locks: her complexion is a deep reddish-brown: her eyes are black and piercing, sometimes flashing wildly, more often fixed and staring like the eyes of the dead": all which agrees with the description of her in the Prose Sketch. The Kundry of the third act is another being altogether, both in temperament and in appearance. I suspect a last-minute change in Wagner's plan at this point, which he failed to bring into full relation with his general scheme. For in the opera Gurnemanz, after the rising of the curtain, finds her in the thicket, where she has been lying all unknown to him until he heard her groaning, whereas in the Sketch he had found her long before the action of the third act opened, and she had "given him meek and constant service"; until one day, while the old man was praying in front of his hut and she was fetching water for him from the spring, they see Parsifal approaching from the wood.

No. 47

to which are linked further developments of No. 43:

No. 48

No. 49

is given out softly by the orchestra as Gurnemanz tells her that this day a wondrous work shall be done among them by the knight: "for holy office is he chosen; if he be pure of stain, then the dust of his long wanderings the sacred stream will wash away."

They lead Parsifal gently to the edge of the spring, where Kundry undoes the greaves of his armour and Gurnemanz removes his breastplate. They will go to the castle, he says, where the funeral rites of Titurel are to be celebrated and the Grail once more unveiled. At the mention of the dead Titurel we hear in the orchestra a suggestion:

No. 50

of the solemn theme of the Funeral Procession, which will later dominate the episode of Parsifal's re-entry into the castle.

37

But first he must be prepared for the new high office that is to be his, in succession to the fallen Amfortas. Gurnemanz takes in his hand some water from the spring and sprinkles Parsifal's head: let it wash away all guilt and grief from him! Kundry humbly and silently bathes his feet, then draws a golden phial from her bosom and pours part of its contents over his feet, which she dries with her hastily unbound hair. But he takes the phial from her and hands it to the old man: "let the friend of Titurel anoint me", he says, "for today he shall greet me as King". Gurnemanz empties the phial over his head, upon which he lays his hand in blessing, passing it through Parsifal's hair. "All-pitying sufferer!" he says, to a new and sweet mutation of the Pure Fool motive (No. 10), "all-wise deliverer! As the redeemed one's sufferings thou hast suffered, now lift thou the last load from his head!" and the motive of Parsifal himself (No. 20) rings out majestically in the solemn tones of trumpets and trombones.

Parsifal takes, unobserved, some water from the spring and sprinkles the head of the kneeling Kundry, saying gently, to the accompaniment of No. 47, "My first office I perform: baptised be thou, and believe in the Redeemer." The penitent lowers her head and seems to weep passionately.

He turns his ecstatic gaze on the forest and meadow, which are now glowing in the morning light. The oboe gives out the tranquil theme of the Flowery Meadow in its full form:

No. 51

and the great musical picture begins to unfold itself that is known in the concert room as the Good Friday music. Never, says Parsifal, has the meadow seemed to him so fair as today, never has he seen it put forth such beauty of flower or breathe such fragrance: all is sweetness and loving-kindness. That, Gurnemanz tells him, is Good Friday's magic, the grateful earth not weeping for the Saviour's suffering but rejoicing at its own rebirth through it:

> *His wasted body on the Cross it sees not:*
> *and so aloft it looks to man redeemed,*
> *set free from sin and all its load of terror,*
> *by God's love-sacrifice made clean and pure:*
> *today each blade, each flower that blooms in meadow*
> *knows well no foot of man will tread it down,*
> *but e'en as God unmurm'ring died for him,*
> *in love and pity the Cross endured, —*
> *so man in tender, holy mood*
> *treads soft the earth today.*
> *Thus grateful all creation sings,*
> *all that doth bloom and fade again,*
> *well knowing nature's pardon won,*
> *stainless and pure earth's heart today.*

Still lost in the quiet ecstasy that is in nature's heart and in his own, Parsifal gently kisses the forehead of Kundry, who has slowly raised her head again and is gazing at him with a look of calm and earnest entreaty. This music of a dream-world of

> *"summers of the snakeless meadow, unlaborious earth and oarless sea"*

spins itself out tranquilly, unhurriedly, loath, as it were, to lose the savour of a single drop of its own sweetness.

At last there steals upon the now almost silent air a peal of distant bells. It is midday, Gurnemanz reminds Parsifal: the hour has come for the new King of the Grail to take possession of his heritage. The motive of Parsifal (No. 20) is significantly combined with that of the obsequies of Titurel (No. 50) as Gurnemanz brings his own Grail-knight's mantle out of the hut and throws it over the shoulders of Parsifal, who takes up the Spear, and, with Kundry, follows the old man towards the castle.

38

The situation and the stage mechanism of the Transformation Scene in the first act are now reversed; the scenery changes gradually in character, as it had done then, but this time from right to left, and the three figures disappear from our view as the woodland changes to rock. The transitional music here is mainly woven out of the motive (No. 50) of the funeral procession:

Wagner distils the last essence of chromatic subtilisation out of this dominating figure [1] and a successor:

through the texture of which pierces the clang of the castle bells, coming nearer and nearer.

At last the walls of rock open, revealing the hall of the Grail, as in the first act, but now, significantly, without the communion tables, for the brotherhood of the Grail has been brought to the last pass of frustration and dejection. The hall is only faintly lit. From opposite sides come two processions of knights, one bearing the coffin of Titurel, the other Amfortas in his litter, preceded by the covered shrine of the Grail. To music through which the figure shown in the lower part of No. 52 runs like a basso ostinato the two files of knights dialogue as they pass each other:

[1] On the probable origin of this theme see the final section of the present chapter.

"I. We bring the Grail in its shrine: whom bear ye in yon coffin?

II. A hero, Titurel, and with him the holy power that of old God gave into his keeping.

 I. What hand laid him low whom God protected?

II. He sank beneath the load of age when the Grail he could look upon no more.

 I. Who stayed him from the sight of the Grail?

II. He whom ye carry there, the relic's sinful guardian.

 I. We bear him here today once more that — for the last time, alas! — he may perform his high office."

"The last time! the last time!" both groups repeat in anguish; "be mindful once more of thy office, but once more!":

No. 54

Amfortas raises himself wearily on his couch, and, to the accompaniment of the motive of Desolation (No. 39), breaks into a lament for the suffering he has brought on them all through his sin. A general cry of woe goes up as Titurel's coffin is opened. A new theme:

No. 55

wells up in grave brass colouring as Amfortas turns to the body, to bid a last farewell to the father of whose death he has been the instrument. No. 16, in the soft wood wind, recalls the modified version of the Faith motive first heard in the opening scene of the opera, when Gurnemanz told the squires how the Saviour's messengers had appeared to Titurel, bringing him the sacred Chalice. Now it is a bitter memory for Amfortas as, to the accompaniment of this No. 16, he implores his father to intercede for him before God's throne: may the life-blood of the brethren be quickened again, but for himself the greatest boon will be death:

No. 56

"This were the last mercy! That the poison, the wound, the horror may die in me, that my corroded heart may cease to beat! My father, take this my cry to Him on high — 'Redeemer, give my son release!'"

39

They press in upon him with a wild cry of "Uncover the Grail! Serve thou thy office!". But he springs up in despair and rushes at the knights, who recoil from him. Mad must they be, he tells them, if they would have him live. As the old motive of his sickness and weariness (No. 9) piles up in a new form in the orchestra he tears open his wound and bids them draw their swords and plunge them into it: "slay ye the sinner and put an end to his woe!"

They fall back again in horror before his delirium. While the confusion has been thus mounting to its climax Parsifal, accompanied by Gurnemanz and Kundry, has entered unobserved. Now he advances, stretches forth the Spear, and touches Amfortas's side with the point of it. "One weapon only serves", he says quietly; "thy wound must be healed by the Spear that dealt it." The face of Amfortas is illumined with ecstasy: he staggers and is upheld by Gurnemanz as No. 9 now winds its way through the orchestral texture in soft colours and transfigured forms. "Be whole, absolved and atoned", says Parsifal, "for I now take on me thy holy office. Blessed be thy suffering, for pity's highest might and wisdom's purest power it taught the tim'rous Fool!" His characteristic motive (No. 20) rises to a new majesty in the orchestra as he steps towards the centre of the stage, holding the Spear high before him. "The holy Spear I bring to you again", he tells the knights, who gaze at the restored symbol in rapture. Motives connected with the Grail and its mysteries of Faith and Love and Hope succeed each other as he bids the squires open the shrine. They do so. Parsifal ascends the altar steps, takes the Grail from the shrine, and breathes a silent prayer before it. The Chalice gradually becomes suffused with a soft glow, while darkness slowly descends upon the hall, which in the end is lit only by an illumination that filters down from the heights. The main motives of the prelude to the work are subtly interwoven with each other, a peculiarly mystical effect being obtained by the crossing and re-crossing of the Faith motive (No. 5) in strings, wood wind and harps:

No. 57

"Wondrous high salvation! Redeemed the Redeemer!" sing the squires and knights in the lines and harmonies of the Pure Fool motive and that of the Love Feast (No. 1), with mystic voices (sopranos and altos) floating down from the middle height and the dome. A ray of light falls upon the Grail, which now glows ardently, and a white dove descends from the dome and hovers over Parsifal's head.[1] Kundry, her enigmatic course through the world completed, her part played to the end in the enlightenment of Parsifal through pity, sinks to the ground lifeless, her last look being turned on him. Amfortas and Gurnemanz kneel in homage before Parsifal, the new King, as he stands aloft among the worshipping brotherhood, waving the Grail from side to side in blessing of them. The harmonic and contrapuntal interweavings shewn in No. 57 become more and more etherealised and mysticised in the orchestra, and the curtain falls to No. 1 rising softly through the texture with a final gentle insistence in the rich tones of trumpet and trombone.

40

In 1871 Wagner thought of writing a symphony of mourning (*Trauersymphonie*) for the German dead in the war of 1870/1. But from official quarters in Berlin he learned that the idea of thus dwelling on the more painful aspects of the conflict was not viewed with favour; so he wrote his *Kaisermarsch* instead. The plan for a *Trauersymphonie* was not given up, however, as is evident from a passage in Cosima's diary in October 1876. (They were in Italy at the time). Cosima had urged him to try to rid his mind of the cares of Bayreuth by writing a new work; "and curiously enough", says her biographer Du Moulin Eckart, "his thoughts were once more turning to the *Trauersymphonie* for those who had fallen in the war; it was to be based on the theme conceived for *Romeo and Juliet*." "He said", Cosima noted in her diary that day, "that he saw the biers being borne into the hall, more and ever more of them, so that the individual grief was always being merged in the suffering of all. Not until after that would come the song of triumph."

Some three and a half years before then he had promised to write for Cosima, Du Moulin informs us, "a composition of a quite peculiar kind, that should in a certain sense constitute a sombre pendant to the *Siegfried Idyll*, a foreshadowing of future destiny — a funeral march from *Romeo and Juliet*."

[1] The spectator should guard against the too common error of identifying Parsifal vaguely with Christ. Any suggestion of that sort angered Wagner. "The idea of making Christ a tenor!" he said: "phew!"

Evidently this "funeral march from *Romeo and Juliet*" and the projected *Trauersymphonie* of 1871 and 1876 were at bottom much the same. Virtually nothing is known as yet about the plan for a musical work on the Shakespeare subject. In 1943, however, Dr. Otto Strobel, the Wahnfried archivist, published a facsimile of a short sketch found in Wagner's "Brown Book". It consists of thirteen bars of music in the key of A flat minor, originally jotted down in pencil and then inked over at some later date; it is headed "Romeo und Julia", and bears the end-date, in Wagner's hand, "7 May, evening". Dr. Strobel gives the year as 1868.

Not only did this theme, we may conjecture, recur to Wagner in 1873 when he thought of writing "a sombre pendant to the *Idyll*", and again in 1876, in connection with the idea of a *Trauersymphonie;* it apparently became the basis of the funeral music that accompanies the bringing of Titurel's body into the hall of the Grail in the third act of *Parsifal*. The two situations were fundamentally similar — in the one case a succession of biers being carried into a hall amid universal mourning, in the other case a procession of knights bearing the coffin of Titurel. And basically the music is much the same. The sketch of 1868 begins thus:

No. 58

The dominant figure seen twice in the first bar of this recurs seven times more in the course of the short sketch, and it correlates with the ostinato bass figure that accompanies the greater part of the Titurel procession. (See No. 52). We meet with it again in the opera in the following passage, which is the continuation of our No. No. 53:

No. 59

while there is a family likeness between a figure that appears three times in the sketch:

No. 60

and passages of this type:

No. 61

etc.

in the Titurel music. In the opera, of course, the elaborate tone-picture develops in its own musical way that is also the psychological way of the drama, for Wagner's unique blend of imagination and craftsmanship enabled him to combine the basic elements of the *Romeo and Juliet* sketch with some of the leading motives relevant to the Titurel scene; but there cannot be much doubt that the *Romeo and Juliet* music, the *Trauersymphonie* and the Titurel processional music all stemmed from the same mood within him.

Note to section 2, paragraph 1, of the *Parsifal* analysis.

My quotation from the Sketch was taken from the imprint of the latter in Vol. XI of Wagner's *Sämtliche Schriften und Dichtungen*. But after the proofs of this chapter had come through I received from Dr. Otto Strobel a complete facsimile of Wagner's manuscript of the Sketch made for King Ludwig; and in this the parenthesis signs to which I have referred do not appear. If, therefore, they are not Wagner's own my argument is to that extent weakened. But the variants between the manuscript and the imprint are so many and so pronounced that it appears probable that the latter was made from a *draft* of Wagner's for the Ludwig Sketch: the parenthesis signs may therefore have really been in this draft. No hint is anywhere given by the anonymous editor of Vol. XI of the *Sämtliche Schriften* as to the provenance of the documents he is dealing with; and there are many indications that the editorial work has been done in a very slapdash way.

Index